D0842370

Eating Landscape

Mesoamerican Worlds: From the Olmecs to the Danzantes
Life and Death in the Templo Mayor, Eduardo Matos Moctezuma
Mesoamerica's Classic Heritage: Teotihuacán to the Aztecs, Davíd
Carrasco, Lindsay Jones, and Scott Sessions
The Offerings of the Templo Mayor, Leonardo López Luján
Tamoanchan, Tlalocan: Places of Mist, Alfredo López Austin
Twin City Tales: A Hermenueutical Reassessment of Tula and Chichén Itzá,
Lindsay Jones
*Utopia and History in Mexico: The First Chronicles of Mexican Civiliza-
tion, 1250–1569,* Georges Baudot

Series Editors:
Davíd Carrasco
Eduardo Matos Moctezuma

Editorial Board:
Michio Araki
Alfredo López Austin
Anthony Aveni
Elizabeth Boone
Doris Heyden
Charles H. Long
Henry B. Nicholson

Eating Landscape

Aztec and European Occupation of Tlalocan

Philip P. Arnold

University Press of Colorado 1999

Copyright © 1999 by the University Press of Colorado

International Standard Book Number 0-87081-518-0

Published by the University Press of Colorado
P.O. Box 849
Niwot, Colorado 80544

The University Press of Colorado is a cooperative publishing enterprise supported, in part, by Adams State College, Colorado State University, Fort Lewis College, Mesa State College, Metropolitan State College of Denver, University of Colorado, University of Northern Colorado, University of Southern Colorado, and Western State College of Colorado.

The paper used in this publication meets the minimum requirements of the American National Standard for Information Sciences—Permanence of Paper for Printed Library Materials. ANSI Z39.48-1984

Library of Congress Cataloging-in-Publication Data

Arnold, Philip P., 1957–
    Aztec and European occupation of Tlalocan, the eating landscape /
Philip P. Arnold.
        p.   cm.
    Includes bibliographical references and index.
    ISBN 0-87081-518-0 (hardcover : alk. paper)
    1. Aztecs—Rites and ceremonies. 2. Aztecs—Land tenure.
3. Aztec cosmology. 4. Tlaloc (Aztec diety) 5. Geographical
perception—Mexico—Mexico, Valley of—History. I. Title.
F1219.76.R57A75   1999
972'.49—dc21   99-10880
                                                                       CIP

08 07 06 05 04 03 02 01 00 99   10 9 8 7 6 5 4 3 2 1

For Sandy

Contents

Contents

Illustrations

Foreword

Our series, Mesoamerican Worlds, is significantly enriched by Philip P. Arnold's highly innovative *Eating Landscape: Aztec and European Occupation of Tlalocan*. Arnold, a historian of religions argues that the best way to think about Mesoamerican religion is in terms of the question, "how do people meaningfully occupy the land?" and he shows that the Spaniards and Aztecs occupied the same land in radically different ways. Using his own version of creative hermeneutics to decipher the Aztec and Spanish imagination of matter and the material environment of the Valley of Mexico, Arnold presents us with a new way to understand Tlaloc, child sacrifices, and the rites of reciprocity that animated the Aztec urban world. He also presents us with a fresh reading of Sahagún's intellectual and spiritual cravings in carrying out his research and writing. One could say that he shows us that for the Aztecs, the earth was an eating landscape while for the Spaniards, the earth and its indigenous people, myths, and gods were only to be eaten—a colonial meal. We are pleased that Arnold's work now occupies a part of our series.

—Davíd Carrasco and Eduardo Matos Moctezuma

Acknowledgments

This project was initiated fifteen years ago, and since that time a long list has accumulated of people without whose help it could not have been completed. Many of these influences are impossible to trace, but I want to mention some of them that are. At the Mesoamerican Archive and Research Project in Boulder, Colorado, Davíd Carrasco introduced me to Mesoamerican studies and the significance of the Tlaloc cult. Since that time, my growing intensity of interaction with an international group of scholars can be directly traced to Davíd's continued interest in my work. I thank Lawrence Desmond and Irene Vasquez, also from Boulder, for helpful conversations. Warwick Bray was very helpful in orienting me to archaeology and grounding my interest in religion through site data. Other colleagues and teachers at the University of London include Elizabeth Baquedano, Robert Novella, and Johanna Overing. While working on my Ph.D. in Chicago, I found myself under the formative direction of Lawrence E. Sullivan, whose gentle influence pushed me far outside of Mesoamerican studies. Classes with Frank Reynolds, Wendy Doniger, Nancy Munn, and Jonathan Z. Smith stretched my interests inalterably to other methods, religious geographies, and epochs. Others to whom I am indebted at Chicago include William Hanks, Norman McQuown, Jane Rosenthal, Kay Read, Karen Pechilis, Fran Chou, Clair Carty, David Tracy, Scott O'Mack, Bernard McGinn, Thomas Kasulis, W. Clark Gilpin, Jon Walters, and Ioan Culianu, whom I miss very much.

Acknowledgments

This work has been strengthened by conversations with many different people over the course of several years. In addition to those mentioned above, deep-felt thanks go to Charles Long, Michio Araki, Alfredo López Austin, Elizabeth Boone, Peter van der Loo, Eduardo Matos Moctezuma, Jeffrey Parsons, Doris Heyden, Jorge Klor de Alva, Louise Burkhart, H. B. Nicholson, Eloise Quiñones Keber, and Edward Calnek. There are also a few who have overseen the details of this project from near its beginning. A very special thanks to Johanna Broda, Anthony Aveni, and Davíd Carrasco for reading over versions of this manuscript. Their fine-grained comments have helped it invaluably. Thanks also goes to Jeffrey Bittner, a computer graphics wizard, who generated the illustrations for this book.

Thanks also goes to Sigma Xi for funding two short field trips to Mexico in January 1988 and January 1989. Also, thanks go to my colleagues in the Department of Religious Studies at the University of Missouri at Columbia from 1990 to 1996, and to current colleagues in the Department of Religion at Syracuse University.

Finally, I thank Sandy Bigtree, without whose inspiration and shared commitment to the material this project would never have been possible. As an artist and mother to our twin sons, Clay and Kroy, she has grounded this work by her keen awareness of the challenges and possibilities of an ever-emerging American landscape that has been created by a turbulent past.

Preface

Through the myriad changes in perspective that this project has undergone over the last fifteen years, one original inspiration has remained constant: developing an understanding and appreciation of indigenous religions in relationship to a living landscape. I chose to focus on Tlaloc (a pan-Mesoamerican deity of rain, fertility, and, for some, the embodiment of the land) because he has held my fascination and consistently challenged my cultural presuppositions. Understanding Tlaloc through colonial documents, however, meant teasing out the remains of a pre-Hispanic worldview through the lenses of those bent on its destruction. As a result, attaining access to the internal dimensions of Tlaloc's ritual cosmology was not only a frustrating process but a nearly impossible one. I discovered that an understanding of the meaning of Tlaloc from the inside was not available to me. In the end, the disjunction between Aztec and colonial understandings (assuming the scholar's understandings are closer to the colonists' than Aztec's) was used as an opportunity for reflection rather than as an obstacle to overcome.

I have found methods of the history of religions particularly relevant in explicating this relationship, and I have utilized (and at times abandoned) these methods to more accurately reflect hermeneutical troubles germane to Mesoamerican studies. And yet, seminal thinkers such as Rudolph Otto, Gerardus van der Leeuw, and Mircea Eliade, among others—while generously giving us a powerful language with which to describe traditions widely divergent from our modern views—are at the same moment woefully inadequate, even disinterested, in the postmodern conundrum of how we can more responsibly understand other religions. In Native American studies (and Mesoamerican studies), these interpretive issues loom large because it has been a long history of genocidal practices, directed by an Old World cosmology, which have generated our texts and oriented the American experience toward the colonist's point of view.

For these reasons, which will soon be more fully examined, I have initially accepted the tenuousness of my interpretations of Tlaloc. Unlike some of my predecessors, I don't claim to have revealed a religious system from the inside out. Given the distance of five hundred years and texts generated by those intent on their destruction, the Aztec deities must remain an enigma. That is not to say, however, that they must remain uninterpreted, or that an enigma is not significant. To tentatively solve this interpretive crisis I want to rely on my own wits, so to speak, by focusing our attention on a seemingly particular aspect of Aztec tradition: how rituals to Tlaloc, performed at specific times and places, articulated their occupation of the Valley of Mexico. This is not to simply reveal an internal dynamic of Aztec religion but, more significantly, to critically assess our (colonial, modern, or postmodern) occupation of the Americas. At this herm-eneutically creative moment, I will suggest an interpretation of Aztec ceremony as an orientation to land that engages our legacy of dis-orientation inherited from colonialism.

This cannot be all, however, because the Aztecs require more substance than simply my own creative efforts. By utilizing a phenomenological category of landscape (complete with watery cycles, mountains, plants, and animals), I will suggest that land is not just meaningful to particular cultural orientations, but rather something which (unlike texts) more reliably arbitrates between cosmologies. If land organizes religious worlds, then the process of orientation to *American* religion (in an indigenous sense) can begin with an assessment of the disjunctive and antagonistic meanings of land in indigenous and colonial contexts. My intention here is twofold. First, I want to push toward the materiality of religion; and second, I want to more fully develop a methodology of orientation that necessitates commitments to land. "Commitments to land" does not simply express a sentimental confidence in having revealed the interior of Aztec devotions, nor in having predetermined its relative value (as with real estate, for example), but to the superabundance of land as a substantive (i.e., necessary) yet meaningful object for reflection. While at formative stages these methodological remarks may seem part of a fanciful strategy of imaginative recall, focusing on specific material referents of religious action calls into question definitions of religion as ideology (or internal to bodily and mental processes). A renewed understanding of land, through an Aztec ritual process, likewise redoubles commitments to an integrity of the landscape in which are housed a diversity of cultural expressions. In other words, once land is seriously engaged as a religious structure (for the Aztec or modern alike), another sort of significance for material life takes hold that is more fully located in a living landscape. In addition, this evaluation of religion as tied to the meaningful occupation of land shifts our focus to those processes by which the colonial imagination occupied the Valley of Mexico (namely, establishing the millennial "kingdom of God"), a utopian cosmology that organizes much of our contemporary existence as well.

Much has been made of the brutality of Aztec religion. What is often not mentioned, however, is that throughout the Americas Europeans killed, or were directly involved in the deaths of, millions more human beings than the Aztecs. Ironically, while the Aztecs fully understood the violent nature of human existence and articulated it in their rituals, Europeans, while professing a peaceful yet millenarian-utopian dream, were unable to reconcile those dreams with the brutality of colonialism. Books, in their capacity to authorize the colonial enterprise, camouflaged the violence of New Spain by reproducing an American identity as utopian.

Utopia, derived from the Greek, means "no place," and contrasts with the Aztec "locative" religious emphasis. Does the "conquest of the New World" signify a cultural turn toward "placelessness"? Does an erosion of the meaningfulness of place participate in what David Stannard calls the "American holocaust"? Does the meaning of land also signify the meaning of people? These questions, engaged here, make the study of sixteenth-century Mexico urgently relevant to our contemporary world.

Eating Landscape

1 Introduction

Orienting Questions and Methods

The central question of this book is: How do people meaningfully occupy the land? While there are features of a landscape that are intrinsic to it (for example, fertility, minerals, bodies of water, animals, native plants, human beings, etc.), the meaning of land, and by that I mean a series of understandings that determine the character of a human relationship with land (and its other inhabitants), is widely variable. Using distinctive meanings of land as a central focus highlights religious consequences of occupying land. First, distinctive inhabitants necessarily develop a "hermeneutics of occupation," or an understanding of an appropriate human relationship to the material world. Second, an interpretation of particular lands substantiates and challenges assumed understandings held by people who inhabit meaningful places. Third, particular kinds of interpretations of other beings (humans or others) are generated from different hermeneutical perspectives with respect to land. How a human community understands its appropriate relationship with the material world will reflect how it understands its relationship with other beings.

My case for examining these issues is contained in rituals to Tlaloc, a pan-Mesoamerican deity of rain and fertility, who is often described as a coherent bodily reality in the pre-Columbian landscape of the

Valley of Mexico. Ritual activities pertaining to Tlaloc were oriented to specific features of the local landscape and were seen as significant locations to interact with Tlaloc and his realm—Tlalocan. Some of these features included mountains, earth, water, trees, crops, birds, and animals. Through ritual practices, pre-Columbian people articulated an engagement with material elements necessary for the continuance of life in the valley. The Aztecs focused their interaction with Tlaloc around material attributes of their environment that were directly associated with human survival. In this study, these rituals will be examined as organizing the Aztec occupation of the valley.

What scholars have traditionally called a "fertility cult" is characterized here as a hermeneutics of occupation. Rather than just a way of magically conjuring arbitrary unseen forces solely for *human* welfare, the Tlaloc cult was a series of prescribed actions that oriented pre-Columbian people to the meaning of the material world. Rituals to Tlaloc explored correspondences between Tlalocan and Aztec (i.e., hidden and human) landscapes to keep Tlaloc's body, and therefore the cosmos, alive. In this study, these cultic activities are reconceived as practices that oriented the Aztecs to material conditions in the valley environment. These rituals also provide an opportunity to become self-critically aware of what constituted appropriate human activity with respect to a living landscape. In an effort to compare Aztec and European hermeneutics of occupation, this study is concerned with the human process of meaningfully occupying land, which may or may not be associated with fertility cults.

It would be a mistake, however, to make a direct connection between the physical geography of the Valley of Mexico and Tlalocan. Tlalocan was one of several hidden and significant places where deities resided. For contemporary Nahua people, Tlalocan is associated with the underworld.[1] Though Tlaloc and the worlds he oversaw were evidently of extreme importance, neither Tlaloc nor Tlalocan should be considered the most important deity or otherworldly realm of the Aztecs. Although Tlalocan was very important, there were also other deity complexes that had powerful expressions as places.[2] It is not my argument that Tlaloc's was the most significant group of gods for the Aztecs, but that, more than other god complexes, devotions to these deities articulated an Aztec understanding of their landscape. Moreover, Europeans, from the colonial period to the present, have made strenuous efforts to justify their occupation of the Americas by attempting to interpret the Aztecs. By invoking Tlaloc, and his realm, Tlalocan, I am primarily interested in how human performances (i.e., rituals) were modes by which the Aztecs meaningfully oriented themselves to the material world in such a way as to critically reflect on European and European-American understandings of land. Therefore, I am referring to the *processes* of orientation, in both Aztec and European contexts, rather than only to the physical landscape of the valley.

It should also be stated at the outset that placing emphasis on Tlalocan as a way of understanding the totality of Aztec religious life could lead one to some confusion. My decision to emphasize Tlalocan merely reflects what is closest to answering my initial question of how people meaningfully occupy land. Tlalocan, while not expressing a total pre-Columbian meaning of land in itself, nonetheless was the most significant articulation of material life. In Part 1 ("Explorations of Tlalocan"), four key rituals to Tlaloc will be examined from the vantage point of the Mesoamerican preoccupation with the violence of consumption. As expressed by rituals regarding Tlalocan, the Aztec inhabited an *eating landscape*.

The primary intention of Part 2 ("Tlalocan and New Spain: Hermeneutics of Occupation in the Valley of Mexico") is to develop a method by which to discuss the significance of the pre-Columbian Tlaloc cult. The methodology of the history of religion is used here to generate critical reflections on Aztec hermeneutics of occupation through an analysis of the disjunctions between Spanish and Aztec modes of occupying the Valley of Mexico. What is currently known of pre-Columbian devotions to Tlaloc comes largely from the work of the sixteenth-century missionary Fray Bernardino de Sahagún. It is necessary, therefore, to address the issues of cultural contact embedded within the very documents used to gain access to Aztec ritual life. Due to difficulties encountered in using Mesoamerican materials, the implications of my analysis must extend wider than the Tlaloc case itself. An examination of data regarding Tlaloc requires an acknowledgment of the processes by which occupation of land was a meaningful activity in both colonial as well as indigenous contexts.

THE MATTER OF UNDERSTANDING

The guiding perspective of this work comes from the discipline of the history of religion. While it boasts a checkered history of its own (as discussed below), which is associated with essentialism and near missionary zeal, the history of religion offers insights and challenges to assumed understandings of the human occupation of what is now known as the Americas.

The emphasis of this study holds ritual activity as meaningfully oriented to tangible features of a given landscape. A practice of occupation, particularly as expressed in the Tlaloc cult, was a mode of actively forging a human place within substantive features of material existence. Therefore, ritual can be seen as a type of human activity that presents a broad field of commonplace subsistence practices that are used for self-conscious inspection. It is an active moment of self-reflection that renders meaningful many of the processes that are assumed to be practical by a community. Following from this understanding of ritual, religion is a culmination of the activity of ritual reflection with reference to tangible material realities. This definition of religion follows Charles Long's, in which religion is seen as a human orientation to a world upon which life is ultimately contingent. Religion, therefore, is primarily not an ideological creation of the human imagination, but rather is intimately involved with material realities.[3] Underlying the inevitable human need for continuing material existence, rituals exhibit a drive toward understanding. Long has expressed this understanding of religion as *materiality;* or religion as an understanding of and orientation to the *meaning of matter*.

Expanding the defining characteristics of ritual and religion as strategies of orientation, however, requires that this study also self-consciously reflect on the orientations of the production of Mesoamerican ethnographies; particularly on the work of Sahagún's *Florentine Codex* and on the state of current scholarship. Given the limits of Tlaloc data, understandings of the pre-Columbian world gener-

[4]

ated in this study are achieved by an analysis of the disjunctions between colonial and indigenous practices of interacting with material life within their respective landscapes, in the same place. Contact between human groups, as well as contact with the material world, is informed by the various ways in which matter is situated within a given cosmology. Interaction with the material world, therefore, is expressed primarily through religious data (rather than anthropological, economic, or social). This underlies the character of other types of interaction; including the infamous human encounter between Aztec and European people. By shifting attention from a strictly human interaction to one of how Native and colonial people were oriented to the Valley of Mexico through the context of interhuman contact, new understandings of their respective religions emerge.

Jonathan Z. Smith's distinction between locative and utopian (i.e., placeless) religions offers a critical point of entry into sixteenth-century Mexico.[4] While his cases are largely taken from ancient Mediterranean urban centers, pre-Columbian cities of the New World present both similar and distinctive hermeneutical challenges. They are similar in the sense that they too underwent a shift from locative to utopian worldviews imposed by outside forces, and distinctive because of the veracity of European occupation of the New World and the near total otherness of a utopian world that emerged in the Old World. Following Smith, the gradual development of utopia by diasporic European groups that grew from the destruction of locative worlds is directly attributable to what has been called the "invention of America."[5] At the risk of reducing the historical dynamics of utopian religions to psychological categories, perhaps a religious perspective of "nowhere" and in "no place" leads to a totalizing, world-conquering spirit. Or to put it another way, the pain of the diaspora (in its cultural expressions) exhibits an impulse for extending that pain to other people and places.

Traditionally, Mesoamerican studies have featured a weaving together of various types of data into a synthetic whole. Principally, the data has been of two sorts: archaeological and textual. Likewise, this study utilizes both of these types of evidence. Other studies of pre-Columbian civilization, however, locate the difficulty of their task in stripping away the layers of analysis that lay between their authors and the Aztec world. For example, in the case of the Tlaloc cult, primary sources such as pre-Columbian documents and archaeological evidence are carefully aligned with secondary sources, including sixteenth-century and contemporary ethnographies. More self-conscious authors would also include in their studies a close scrutiny of their own biases, which shape their studies. In all, achieving an authoritative rendering of Aztec culture has been seen as overcoming a series of interpretive blockages (including the author, secondary sources [and their authors], and the various readings of primary sources) to finally arrive, at least in theory, at the authentic Aztec. Undoubtedly this is a highly imaginative and subtle enterprise that enlists a host of creative interpretations.[6]

There are, however, several problems with this methodology as I have characterized it. First, it assumes that authentic Aztec realities are relegated to a prehistorical, preliterary past and therefore out of our immediate reach. At first this sounds like a reasonable assertion. If this is the case, however, then no amount of creativity could be mustered to overcome this historical distance, and therefore *any* study would be preordained to fall short of accurately representing Aztec reality. Second, and following from the first, scholarly methods are generally textually centered approaches. A textually oriented model is temporally arranged chronologically in that its task is seen as the undoing of historical moments. As will be examined in the chapters to come, a textually centered methodology skews our entrance into the performative, "preliterate," Aztec worldview. Therefore, modern assumptions overdetermine an understanding of Mesoamerican cults. Third, an approach that assumes that cultural distances can be overcome generally disallows an investigation of the consequences of contemporary renderings of Aztec religion. How can one account for creative scholarly activities in our current cultural context? What do they have to say to current cultural fashions and conditions? Finally, there is no "materiality" for grounding a text-centered method that attempts to connect the scholar with the pre-Columbian Aztec. The only field of interaction between Aztec and researcher is an abstract temporal/textual space that is determined solely by the creative endeavors of colonial and more immediate predecessors.

To overcome some of these difficulties, my methodology will take a practice-centered approach to the Tlaloc cult. There are various foci for this approach already generated from the phenomenal attributes of material life. In many ways this is not a new approach. For example, beginning with the work of Robertson Smith and Durkheim, the focus of the study of religion has shifted from sacred texts to a practice.[7] Both of these early scholars were interested in how rituals at once expressed a community's interaction with their material world while also integrating the community. An understanding of ritual as work, however, should be seen as involved in the interpretive labors of both the Aztec and the scholar.

Relationships between distinctive attributes of the cosmos are also implied in ritual processes of occupation. This was expressed by the Aztecs as a constant commitment to reciprocity. Gift exchanges maintained formal relationships between various cosmic beings, which included human beings. Connections between human and other sacred beings were fostered through offerings that linked a community to the deity. The medium of reciprocity was material and intimately tied to the human body.[8] Emphasizing ritual processes as an interpretive method involved with occupying land, however, expands the notion of "gift" in different directions. For example, the performative aspects of scholastic labors as well as the Tlaloc cult must be adequately accounted for in the gift model. While there are important intersections, in this study ritual practice is seen as a hermeneutical strategy of occupying a meaningful landscape with reference to particular material realities, rather than adapting the theoretical model of the gift.[9] Likewise, the practice of interpreting these cultic devotions (i.e., the writing of this book) requires its own relationships to the occupation of the Pan-American landscape.

In order to further develop and clarify the methodological issues of this study, what follows is a brief outline of the importance of materialist debates regarding Mesoamerican cultural phenomena in the fields of anthropology, archaeology, history of religion, and linguistics.

In Mesoamerican archaeology, a materialist examination of culture has developed over the last forty years. It has been tied to a new wave of archaeological investigation based on studies of common house-mound excavations in relationship to the environmental attributes of their local habitats. Cultural ecology, in some of its expressions, claims to reveal causal mechanisms underlying the rise and fall of ancient cultures.[10] By examining the ability of physical characteristics of a given environment to support human populations (for example, with respect to a landscape's "carrying capacity"), cultural ecologists claim to have discovered a direct link between regional subsistence potential and social "superstructure." Initially, in this "new archaeology" attention swerved away from the monumental buildings of state cults and spectacular works of art to center on more pedestrian aspects of human life.

The present analysis of the Tlaloc cult has benefited from data generated out of the new archaeology. The methodological assumptions of cultural ecology, however, present a number of interpretive problems. In Mexico, this conceptual model was employed for the monumental task of surveying the entire Valley of Mexico.[11] Underlying assumptions that guided this survey emphasize a direct relationship between carrying capacity, demography, variable access to arable land, and social differentiation.[12] The hope of cultural ecology was that the valley's ecology could be seen as directly contributing to the rise of its civilizations.[13] In this view, the epiphenomenal elements of cultural life (including state formation, warfare, religion, etc.) could be traced directly back to ecological "realities." Ecology was thus seen as the overarching unifying factor for apprehending the structure of cultural formation, circumventing the need for a methodology that accounted for the cultural diversity within Mesoamerica. Ethnohistorical sources such as the *Florentine Codex* were used in this work only insofar as they could substantiate the Native people's response to their environment. At first, cultural ecology seemed to offer a unifying, if not essentializing, method of analysis that was independent of textual sources.

Some of the findings of cultural ecology, however, turned out to undermine the very assumptions that drove their research. For example, during the period immediately before Teotihuacan's rise to power in the valley (200 C.E.–700 C.E.), a large population center, Cuicuilco, emerged in the southern valley region, the setting for *chinampa* agriculture and ecological bounty. Various hamlets and farms in this area were organized around this city. As Teotihuacan gained prominence in the valley, Cuicuilco and its environs became virtually depopulated as people moved north. According to Sander's team, Teotihuacan's prominence was attributable to their control of the obsidian industry and therefore over the capacity to make tools of war. Ironically, the Teotihuacan sub-valley region had a very low carrying capacity as compared with the Cuicuilco region. It had a lucrative item of trade, but not the ecological carrying capacity to sustain large numbers of people. Ecological determinism, as outlined in the survey team's model, is therefore not able to adequately account for Teotihuacan's prestige in the valley.[14] If, for example, Teotihuacan was a greater military power than Cuicuilco and overran this city, then according to cultural ecology the sensible thing to do would have been to move back to the southern valley. Why, then, did the people of Teotihuacan decide to stay where they were? What could account for their desire to remain in this more ecologically difficult landscape? Unless we think that Teotihuacanos were simply more enamored with warfare than other cities in the valley, then systems of value other than the immediacy of food must have been dictating the use and significance of material goods in the Mesoamerican landscape.

Many other scholars have taken issue with the assumptions of cultural ecologists. Calnek examined food networks in Tenochtitlan using ethnohistorical documents.[15] He found that urban food systems were primarily arranged through tribute networks and were therefore tied to state control, warfare, and trade. Material existence in these urban settings was determined by political rather than ecological criteria. For the Aztecs, political realities were informed by ritual and divinatory activities. Therefore material life was in the service of a Mesoamerican cosmology. Although material goods were the focal point of the community existence, their value was associated with their circulation within a framework of cosmological relationships.[16] Matos Moctezuma has tied a political strategy of organizing human resources to the construction and activation of the Templo Mayor, the central temple complex of the Aztecs.[17] The link between political domination and religious cosmology powerfully tied their empire together by devotions to the gods. Tlaloc, associated with rain and fertility, expressed the agricultural support of Aztec power while Huitzilopochtli, associated with warfare, was tied to tribute.

Carrasco has pushed the political "solution" to cultural ecology by interrogating the attributes of the prestige of Tenochtitlan from the perspective of the history of religion. In a series of articles on the Templo Mayor and Tenochtitlan, he has negotiated issues of materiality and the prestige of the ceremonial center away from a determinist line.[18] Utilizing the work of Wheatley and Eliade on the primary areas of urban generation, Carrasco has shown how the Aztecs orchestrated places of prestige.[19] The Templo Mayor was an articulation, in stone, of access to dimensions of being that oriented Aztec political and material realities. The symbolism of the center, particularly as it was expressed ritually, organized a dynamic relationship with the periphery. The force of its presence in a Mesoamerican landscape was its ability to organize space within a larger cosmological order.

Sahlins has highlighted some distressing consequences of ecological determinism.[20] In his discussion of a book that ties Aztec human sacrifice to protein deficiency in the Americas, he links cultural ecology to Sartre's notion of "intellectual violence." According to Sahlins, by giving up the "phenomenon" of the varieties of human existence for its "causes," cultural ecologists deprive Native Americans of their own logic and world, which center on alternative systems of value. For Sahlins, cultural ecologists do violence against the humanity of indigenous people by ruling out the interpretations of causes embedded in their worldviews. He suggests that all discussions of causes are culture-specific, including those of cultural ecology. Examinations of material existence must account for a variety of interpretations. At the same time, explanations of matter in which what is considered "real" has already been rigidly predetermined do violence to the scholar by limiting an understanding of alternative modes of existence. Interpretive violence is suffered in both directions. Contemporary renderings of pre-Columbian Aztec social forms have direct consequences for contemporary Nahua and non-Nahua people. In the case of the Tlaloc cult, which is still practiced among many Nahua people, typologizing the significance of matter in a way that excludes Aztec interpretive strategies establishes an artificial social context by which to judge Mexican Indians. While the stated intention of cultural ecology is to learn about other cultures and civilizations, it often ends up limiting understandings of the diversity of human expression. It does this by overdetermining material "realities," thereby neglecting them as being cultural artifacts themselves. An overconfidence in the *factuality* of a contemporary scientific understanding of matter disallows a self-conscious appraisal of the *significance* of matter from the perspective of alternative worldviews.

According to Sahlins, cultural ecology's overconfidence in its own interpretive stance limits the scholar's ability to self-consciously reflect on the consequences of its own cultural interpretive limits. Ecological determinism becomes cumbersome because the function, and therefore the meaning, of matter has already been determined. A determinist stance expresses a commitment to an interpretation of the material world as a reality distinct from, and not fully interactive with, human existence. Material reality for cultural ecology is already completely known; its meaning is transparent to the investigator prior to any interaction. Merleau-Ponty describes this as an essential prejudice that is a necessary part of living in the world. In his method, van der Leeuw advocates *epoché*, or interpretive restraint, as a way of overcoming an investigator's preknowledge of existence. By bracketing one's own categories, one can effectively enter into meaningful relationships with those who have rendered the world in other ways. While cultural ecology shares the same commitment to material existence as does phenomenology and the Tlaloc cult, it is unable to exercise *epoché*. What is required is a materialist stance that takes as its subject and object of study the performative aspects of meaningful existence.

The critics of cultural ecology insist on inserting a system of value into the scholarly evaluations of various cultural interactions with the environment. Neither modern scholars nor preliterate Aztecs are able to resist imparting material life with cultural values. For these critics, the fight has been to place the reins of cultural formation back in the hands of human beings. Cultural ecology has seemingly tried to place it in external material realities. While aware of the deficiencies of cultural ecology, however, this study also seeks to locate an analysis of the Tlaloc cult in material life rather than strictly in the human imagination. Moreover, data collected by the valley survey in the 1960s and 1970s has formed a large part of the present work because it traces relationships between human beings and the valley landscape in great detail.[21] Cultural ecology privileges the place of matter in its determination of what constitutes human societies. The Tlaloc cult was involved with a similar view of human-environmental relationships. As a result, an anthropocentric view of ritual as a human process of invention gives way to an ecological perspective based on ritual as a process of interaction between material beings used to promote life. Through their ritual interaction with, and articulation of, material existence, the Aztec came to know an appropriate human place in the cosmos. Even with its overdetermined stance in its own relationship with matter, cultural ecology and the Tlaloc cult share a common involvement with, and confidence in, material life. Their distinctive deliberations serve as a context to think about distinctive cultural formations. Matter, as it was articulated through fertility cultic practices, was an encounter with another reality upon which human life was contingent. It was both the otherness and necessariness of matter that elicited a human response.

The centrality of "Otherness" has been a traditional feature of the history of religion and phenomenology.[22] For van der Leeuw, for instance, human meaning is initiated through a confrontation with absolute, incomprehensible power that is manifest in the material world. This is what he calls the "object" of religion.[23] For Merleau-Ponty, phenomenology proceeds from a conviction of a world prior to reflection; it expresses a confidence in material existence even though it must remain unknown.[24] A method in which ritual is understood as an articulation of a human embeddedness in material life must, at once, acknowledge the social construction of meaning as well as grapple with the essential Otherness of matter. In some readings, Eliade's work in the history of religion has focused on the phenomena of material life. Elements of sky, trees, mountains, water, etc., are the nodes of his discernment of patterns in human religious existence. Unlike the phenomenologists, he emphasizes these material attributes less as material facts than as sites of religious reflection, which often take the form of performance.[25] For example, his work on alchemy uses the smelting of metal as the central feature of a widely comparative study. As one traverses the worlds of ancient China, India, Babylonia, and medieval and modern Europe, metal takes on a cumulative significance. Particularly in traditional societies, emphasis is placed on metal as an interactive and transformational substance. The metal worker, through his ability of accelerating the transformation of ores born in the womb of the earth into tools (themselves having transformative effects in the world), also has the ability to "know things." The philosopher's stone and forger's fire are interactive sites for interpreting a human place in the cosmos due to their positions as transforming agents. Alchemy is the rigorous development of knowledge through a human engagement with matter.[26]

Linguistic approaches to culture have fruitfully utilized areas of performance and ritual as interpretive models. For example, Malinowski extended his study of fertility rituals into areas of magical speech.[27] In his analysis of Trobriand agricultural incantations, he asserted that language stands in a definite and practical relationship to the life of a community.[28] His aim was to separate theories of language from historically bounded philological (i.e., text-centered) approaches in order to investigate verbal acts as having a substantive and corporeal force on the world. Language defines one's relationship with the world and therefore meaningfully connects people to material realities.[29] Malinowski, rejecting Saussure, conceived of language as an activity; as a mode of human behavior directly interrelated with bodily activities. Against the dualism of ideas and words, and the context and medium theories of his time, Malinowski insisted on an examination of context, on the nonverbal matrix of the *speech-event*. He had a consistent concern for what he called "actual concrete facts" over and against the "ideal."[30] Analogously, garden magicians performed incantations over agricultural fields to produce an effect on their fertility. Although their words and actions often appear untranslatable and esoteric, their effect is nonetheless profound on the community. Malinowski, while maintaining that language events have a material effect on the fertility of gardens, understood this accomplishment by noting its effect on the human community.[31] The real "magical" effect on the fertility of the land is that these formulas brought people together at important times of the season to work. Malinowski at once shifted his emphasis on ritual uses of language to their material and dynamic effects within a human community. Significantly, formal categories of cultural thought, in this case, were expressed through ritual, but coalesced around material referents.

Bourdieu's use of *habitus* and critique of objectivism in the social sciences is also conceived around a theory of practice.[32] Hanks has recently formulated a theory of language as "lived space" among contemporary Maya people. Rejecting an objectivist view of language that follows from Saussure, as well as a subjectivist language theory, he develops a third option that he calls "native practice"—"Unlike objectivism, a practice approach locates language in the situated processes of verbal communication and foregrounds the articulation of speech with other aspects of the social world."[33] For Hanks, the grammarian's "rules" are replaced with "strategies" of verbal action and the "embodiment" of language, which then translates into fields for cultural production. The body is the point that grounds meaningful processes of interaction. Meaning is socially constructed, according to Hanks, through a negotiation of indexical referents to the world relative to the body (I, he, she, it, etc.).[34] Similarly, Basso has utilized a linguistic model associated with places among the Apache.[35] Apache history and identity are directly associated with their landscape. Place names evoke stories of Apache ancestral actions. Being located, or oriented, in Apache land is a state of being that fosters wisdom. Basso's case is a powerful illustration of language as a practice of orientation to material attributes of the landscape that embody deep cultural meanings.

Recent studies present the activity of language as a reciprocal one in which meaning (i.e., orientation) takes shape by referring to the world. The articulation of meaning in words, as in ritual, is embedded in bodily articulation; the movement of bone and muscle. Ritual, seen as a "referential practice," is an embodied articulation of a meaningful condition of occupying land. Human communities variously construct their articulations of residence through a confidence in material realities. In the end, however, bodily referents (and their articulations) become meaningful only in interactive lived space. The practice of language as embodiment is not limited to an isolated acting subject. Rather, language is played out in a "corporeal field" of reference in which meaningful orientation is negotiated between beings.[36]

The methodology of hermeneutics situates itself between culturally constructed meanings and otherness of various sorts.[37] Ritual is a performative process by which meaningful orientation to the landscape is promoted and sustained. The cult of Tlaloc, in this sense, constitutes an indigenous (i.e., locative) hermeneutic in which reciprocal relationships between beings develop an understanding of occupying the Valley of Mexico. This study will focus on both anthropological (social constructive) and material moments. The otherness of the material conditions of human existence were articulated ritually.[38] Reciprocity between human beings and the *tlaloque,* the deities responsible for various climatological manifestations of Tlaloc, became meaningful through the manipulation of materials. Ritual established and maintained a set of homologies, or correspondences, tying the material and social worlds together into a single cosmos.[39]

Recently, archaeologists have been reevaluating methods for studying human relationships with material artifacts. Arnold has employed a cybernetic model in his analysis of ceramic production.[40] Ceramics are cultural creations and, as with Hanks's native practice model of language, each shard can be seen as a phoneme that ties cultural systems of meaning to ecological realities, and which together channel a flow of information within a community.[41] On the side of adjudicating the investigator's perceptions of material objects, Hodder has examined the plurality of theoretical readings that result from various interpretations of artifacts. By enumerating systems— structuralist, Marxist, historical, and contextual archaeologies[42]—he suggests that the interaction of material and human culture is a dialectical relationship between past and present with reference to the presence of the artifact.[43] The dynamic of interpreting material culture is embedded in contemporary power relations necessitating a plurality of approaches rather than too tightly circumscribing them by determinist and intolerant rhetoric. Similarly, Tilley moves archeological investiga-

tion of prehistorical Celtic ruins in the United Kingdom from the excavation site to consider their situatedness in the land.[44] He utilizes an
approach that creatively promotes an understanding of the interaction
of human beings with their environment by appealing to the insights of
phenomenology.

Methodologically, the approach of this study can now be characterized as a phenomenology of ritual practice that is less involved in
ascertaining essences (as with van der Leeuw or Merleau-Ponty) and
instead more involved with bringing an interpretation of an Aztec
understanding of land to bear on colonial and contemporary understandings of land. An assumption in this task is that many contemporary interpretations of the meaning of land have been inherited
from the colonial era. In other words, Aztec history does not stand at
a distance from one's relationships with an object of study, but influences and pressures a given interpretive location. I hope that through
an examination of the diverse consequences of interpretive practices
in pre-Columbian, colonial, and modern contexts a methodology self-
conscious of its own limits and realities can be fostered.

The focal point of this study is the process by which the otherness of the material world pressures interpretive activity. First, the
rituals to Tlaloc operated with reference to material attributes of the
Valley of Mexico. Second, the work of Sahagún, our most authoritative documentation of these events and the colonial world that influenced him and his work, inevitably reconfigured the meanings of
material life in Mexico. Third, as with others involved in the history
of religion, I am self-consciously acknowledging my place in a
performative hermeneutic by situating elements of material life at
the center of the study. It is assumed that in an interaction with matter, all three players (the Aztec, the scholar, and the material artifact)
in these discrete performative moments converge.

Some terminology clarifications are in order. First, this book will
argue for a necessary distinction between "land" and "landscape."
Some, primarily from cultural ecology, have argued that by examining the material environment in which a culture flourishes, a scholar
can gain an uncompromised, objective vantage point. Others more

versed in the ambiguous methodologies of the humanities, claim that all of material life is interpreted and is, therefore, not available to human perception as a "natural" or "objective" reality. Still others have suggested that the world is another species of text demanding the same techniques of interpretation as other, human-created, objects.

From the history of religion perspective, cultural ecology is itself overdetermined (and therefore substantially similar to a hermeneutical perspective), and I will concur by maintaining that "land" is a necessary Other with an integrity previous to human interpretation. This expresses a tightly referenced phenomenological position distinct from the universalistic and/or essentialist phenomenology sometimes expressed by historians of religion and theologians.[45] The Otherness (with a capital O) of land is critical for a consideration of "landscape," or, in the context of this work, how people meaningfully occupy land. My position is that land is necessarily independent from human creativity and that any articulation of an Other (through various practices and media) "scapes" or reorders it; and necessarily formulates the conditions by which human-land relationships are forged. While I am sympathetic to a hermeneutical stance, in its most extreme expressions it tends to obscure a powerful imperative that was central to Aztec tradition—land as an autonomous living being—or in more contemporary parlance, the Otherness of land. I am likewise sympathetic to a neo-Marxist perspective regarding the solidity of the material environment, not because that position makes it more knowable, but because it expresses the autonomy of land. By working somewhere between these positions, this study hopes to indicate that there is a "land" previous to human labor and upon which human life is predicated. From a "native practice" perspective, human survival hinges on one's ability to interpret a relationship with land in such a way as to ensure one's continued existence. "Landscape," therefore, is an articulation of the land-human interactions required for occupation and that encompass the hermeneutical work necessary for human survival. In sixteenth-century Mexico, the degree to which the Otherness of land was acknowledged determined the distinctive characteristics of Aztec and European occupation of the Valley of Mexico.[46] As Bateson has said, "[n]o man, after all, has ever seen or experienced formless and unsorted matter; just as no man has ever seen or experienced a 'random' event."[47]

Second, a delineation will be made between "space" and "place," which extends the previous discussion. This follows a distinction made by several others.[48] "Space" is conceived as being constructed from the imagination with or, more often, without reference to a particular geography. Space, to use Ricoeur's terminology, is a "second order reflection"[49] of the human imagination without reference to a landscape, but with reference only to the self. European "space" was initially fashioned with attention to worlds housed in books.[50] Aztec "place," on the other hand, was articulated in ritual practice and therefore less self-referential than European "space." Yet both groups occupied the same place at the same time, during and after the Conquest. Therefore, the distinctive work of human imagination in Aztec and European contexts will be examined with respect to material referents. "Place," in contrast, refers to direct negotiation of material life. Hanks's phrase "referential practice" expresses well the dynamics of place as the ongoing creative effort of its inhabitants.

Third, and also following from the first, "occupation" is not only the mechanics of how a land is settled by human beings, but refers to the all-encompassing, ongoing interpretive labors required to live in a place. Dual meanings of "occupation" in current usage, as both residence (also having the connotation of invasion) and line of work, fit with this use of the term. Special emphasis, however, is on the performative and ritual labors involved in the process of occupying land. Performative rather than ideological constructions involved in the occupation of land are more reflective of Aztec understandings, and of indigenous conceptions in general. This is attributable to the centrality of the book and of writing in the development of European culture. Moreover, when applied to European occupation of the Americas, we will see other aspects of religion come to light.

Fourth, "religion" will be used in this work with a different emphasis. Like other terms applied to indigenous people, a definition of religion takes on a distinctive character that is often at odds with its assumed definition. Even a cursory examination of Native American traditions reveals that what orients these cultures is not a sacred text but a series of practices that extend an oral tradition into human activity. The textual orientation of what have been regarded as the "great" (i.e., global) religious traditions, however, has tended to over-emphasize an interpretation of indigenous religions as ideological constructs more reflective of religions of the book.[51] To overcome this deficiency, I will define "religion" as an articulation of what Long has called "materiality." Materiality is not just an ideology of matter (i.e., materialism) but, like my use of "landscape," the result of tightly referenced interaction between matter and the human imagination.[52] Likewise, this interpretive shift has consequences for the academic study of religion. In colonial Mexico, what constituted religion was involved with obtaining legal title to land, book production, and mining, for example, as well as developing utopian models for New World communities, evangelizing, and building churches. Emphasis here is on an understanding of religion as formed by the human interaction with an exterior material world rather than on religion as formed by reflections interior to the human beings previous to interaction with the material world. "Religion" defined thusly reveals both an indigenous, or locative, religious understanding, and highlights significant yet unprobed dimensions of the Pan-American experience.

Fifth, I will generally use the term "Aztec" rather than "Mexica" or "Nahua." This term is a sixteenth-century derivation of those Nahua-speaking people of Tenochtitlan who probably referred to themselves as *Mexica*. "Aztec" refers to the mythical sojourn of the Mexica from an unknown region in the north, called Aztlan, to central Mexico. My intention is not to suggest that the mythical origins were more significant to their self-definition, but only to appeal to a more popular rendering, particularly in North America. There are particular histories to our categories that cannot be overcome by renaming. In order to heighten self-consciousness about the fashioning of the world (i.e., the Americas), my strategy has been to utilize more pedestrian concepts (landscape, occupation, religion, and Aztec) to orient us to the oftentimes elusive meanings embedded in existence. A peculiar attribute of modern[53] existence is that the *meaning* of material life necessarily remains insignificant.[54] Exploring the significance of occupying the Americas becomes more powerfully expressed using language closer to home.

Part 1, "Explorations of Tlalocan," is a careful reconstruction of devotions to Tlaloc using ritual descriptions from the *Florentine Codex*. Although it is a creative enterprise, the interpretation of Tlalocan that follows is worked out with reference to a variety of material conditions of existence emphasized by the Aztecs. In order to highlight implications of a pre-Columbian "hermeneutic of occupation," stress is placed on the landscape of Tlalocan, rather than on the landscape of the New World, in order to bring the full weight of Aztec religious practices to bear on the colonial and modern understandings of land. A discussion of the consequences of the present interpretation of Tlalocan are explored in Part 2, "Tlalocan and New Spain: Hermeneutics of Occupation in the Valley of Mexico." The intention will be to utilize the processes of a secondary creation of Tlalocan to pressure our current dominant understandings of occupying land. Thus, disjunctions between Tlalocan and the New World will be emphasized in chapter 7.

Sahagún can be said to have been straining to occupy a utopian, or placeless, world. Contrary to indigenous understandings, a dominant colonial emphasis was placed on transcendence, salvation, heaven, etc. The defining features of colonial religion initiated an emphasis on carving out that utopian vision, which in turn transformed the materiality of the Americas into an abstract ideology. As such, Mesoamerican ritual practices still present us with a world that challenges, even threatens, our modern (or postmodern) modes of occupying the world. For many reasons, interpretations of Tlalocan, and indigenous landscapes like it, are urgently needed to pressure the overdetermined status of the meaning of the Americas.

NOTES

1. See Tim Knab, "Geografía del inframundo," *Estudios de cultura Nahuatl* 21 (1991): 31–57.

2. Afredo López Austin's work, in particular, seems to strain for an articulation of a complete vision of the Mexica cosmos. Moreover, these various manifestations of deities are tied to landscapes that are no less complex or important than Tlalocan. See *Tamoanchan y Tlalocan* (Mexico City: Fondo de Cultura Económica, 1994).

3. This follows from Long's working definition of religion as orientation—"orientation in the ultimate sense, that is, how one comes to terms with the ultimate significance of one's place in the world." See Charles H. Long, *Significations: Signs, Symbols, and Images in the Interpretation of Religion* (Philadelphia: Fortress Press, 1986), p. 7.

4. "For the native religionist, homeplace, the place to which one belongs, was the central religious category. One's self-definition, one's reality was the place into which one had been born—understood as both geographical and social place. To the new immigrant in the diaspora, nostalgia for homeplace and cultic substitutes for the old, sacred center were central religious values. For the thoroughly diasporic member, who may not have belonged to the deity's original ethnic group, freedom from place became *the* central religious category. Projecting the group's diasporic existence into the cosmos, he discovered himself to be in exile from his true home (a world beyond this world), he found his fulfillment in serving the god beyond the god of this world and true freedom in stripping off his body which belonged to this world and in awakening that aspect of himself which was from the Beyond. Diasporic religion, in contrast to native, locative religion, was utopian in the strictest sense of the word, a religion of 'nowhere,' of transcendence." Jonathan Z. Smith, *Map Is Not Territory, Studies in the History of Religions* (Leiden, Netherlands: E.J. Brill, 1978), "Preface," p. xiv.

5. Edmundo O'Gorman, *The Invention of America: An Inquiry into the Historical Nature of the New World and the Meaning of Its History* (Bloomington: Indiana University Press, 1961).

6. A recent effort that successfully demonstrates this kind of work is Alfredo López Austin's *Tamoanchan y Tlalocan,* which will be discussed in more detail below. In particular, see his "Unas palabras sobre el método," pp. 10–17.

7. Robertson Smith examined the place of sacrifice as an act of negotiation between a community and their deity. The currency for this reciprocity was blood. The common blood of the community embedded in kin relations was expressed through sacrificial bloodletting. Offerings of blood were at once a reification of community identity and necessary for the acquisition of food and water. See W. Robertson Smith, *Lectures on the Religion of the Semites* (New York: Meridian Books, 1957), p. 173. Durkheim effectively extended the relationship between ritual and identity by focusing on their symbolic attributes. Ritual, for Durkheim, is the *work* of a society in the process of creating itself. See Emile Durkheim, *The Elementary Forms of the Religious Life,* translated by Joseph W. Swain (New York: The Free Press, 1965), p. 257.

8. Animistic beings, in his view, consumed offerings, thereby traversing realms of being. More than a sympathetic or symbolic relationship, the gift is a material offering given for the purpose of actively engaging in contact with the deity. See Sir Edward Burnett Tylor, *Primitive Culture,* volume 2, *Religion in Primitive Culture* (New York: Harper Torchbooks, 1958), p. 462, where he makes a materialist argument for the genesis of religion:

> Beginning with cases in which this transmission is performed bodily, it appears that when the deity is the personal Water, Earth, Fire, Air, or a fetish-spirit animating or inhabiting such element, he can receive and sometimes actually consume the offerings given over to this material medium.

Also see Marcel Mauss's study, *The Gift: Forms and Functions of Exchange in Archaic Societies*, translated by Ian Cunnison (New York: W.W. Norton & Co., 1967), of how a theory of gift exchange extends throughout social relationships. His view refines a functionalist interpretation connecting a social structure to ritual.

9. Catherine Bell's theoretical work on ritual is helpful in appreciating the work of ritual as strategy. See her *Ritual Theory, Ritual Practice* (New York: Oxford University Press, 1992).

10. See Julian H. Steward, "Introduction," *Theory of Culture Change* (Urbana: University of Illinois Press, 1955).

11. Elements of this work come from several small publications from Ann Arbor and Pennsylvania. Jeffrey R. Parsons, *Prehistoric Settlement Patterns in the Texcoco Region, Mexico*, Memoirs of the Museum of Anthropology, no. 3 (Ann Arbor: University of Michigan, 1971); Jeffrey R. Parsons, Keith Kintigh, and Susan Gregg, *Archaeological Settlement Pattern Data from the Chalco, Xochimilco, Ixtapalapa, Texcoco, and Zumpango Regions, Mexico*, Museum of Anthropology Technical Reports, no. 14, Research Reprints in Archaeology Contributions 9 (Ann Arbor: University of Michigan, 1983); Jeffrey R. Parsons, Elizabeth Brumfiel, Mary Parsons, and David Wilson, *Prehistoric Settlement Patterns in the Southern Valley of Mexico, the Chalco-Xochimilco Region*, Memoirs of the Museum of Anthropology, no. 14 (Ann Arbor: University of Michigan, 1982); Richard R. Blanton, *Prehistoric Settlement Patterns of the Ixtapalapa Peninsula Region*, Occasional Papers in Anthropology, no. 6 (University Park: Department of Anthropology, Pennsylvania State University, 1972). A cumulative volume was also produced on the findings: William T. Sanders, Jeffrey R. Parsons, and Robert S. Santley, *The Basin of Mexico: Biological Processes in the Evolution of a Civilization*, book and maps (New York: Academic Press, 1979).

12. For example, see William T. Sanders and Michael H. Logan, "The Model," in *The Valley of Mexico: Studies in Pre-Hispanic Ecology and Society*, edited by Eric R. Wolf, School of American Research (Albuquerque: University of New Mexico Press, 1976), pp. 31–58.

13. The survey project was the composition of various ground surveys of valley occupation. Teams of four or five archaeologists would walk over an area collecting pot shards, noting their frequency and distribution. Over time, a relationship between shard frequency and their association with mounds would suggest population density during each phase of occupation. Their survey was a total survey (not statistical) covering all reasonably accessible areas. Sanders, Parsons, and Santley, *The Basin of Mexico*.

14. Bray suggests that examples like this one point out the weakness of the survey team's assumptions. Teotihuacan is archaeologically the best-documented *political* restructuring in the Valley of Mexico and does not obey Sanderian rules at all. A test of its scientific value would be its ability to predict the rise of Teotihuacan after having collected all pertinent ecological data (personal communication). See also his theoretical model in: Warwick Bray, "Landscape with Figures: Settlement Patterns, Locational Models, and Politics in Mesoamerica," in *Prehistoric Settlement Patterns: Essays in Honor of Gordon R. Wiley*, edited by Evan L. Vogt and Robert M. Leventhal (Cambridge, MA: Harvard University Press, 1983), pp. 167–193.

15. Calnek has been a vocal opponent to the cultural ecology school in Mesoamerican research. Instead he proposes a historical-cultural approach to the material. Edward Calnek, "Settlement Pattern and Chinampa Agriculture at Tenochtitlan," *American Antiquity* 37, no. 1 (1972): 104–115; and "Organización de los sistemas de abastecimiento urban de alimentos: el caso de Tenochtitlan," in *Las ciudades de América Latina y sus áreas de influencia a través de la historia*, edited by Jorge E. Hardoy and Richard P. Schaedel (Buenos Aires: Ediciones SIAP, 1975), pp. 41–60.

16. Also see Nancy D. Munn, *The Fame of Gawa: A Symbolic Study of Value Transformation in a Massim (Papua New Guinea) Society* (Cambridge: Cambridge University Press, 1986). *Kula*, a shell ring, as a currency of exchange among New Guinea islanders takes on value through its circulation. While it is a material object that comes to symbolize the worth of foodstuffs and other needed items, its value takes on greater weight through its association with ownership by other people in other places. The history of its circulation is integrated into its symbolic worth.

17. Eduardo Matos Moctezuma, "The Great Temple of Tenochtitlan," *Scientific American* 251, no. 2 (1984a): 80–89, and "The Templo Mayor of Tenochtitlan: Economics and Ideology," in *Ritual Human Sacrifice in Mesoamerica*, edited by Elizabeth Boone (Washington, DC: Dumbarton Oaks, 1984b), pp. 133–164.

18. See Davíd Carrasco, "Templo Mayor: The Aztec Vision of Place," *Religion* 11 (1981): 257–297; "Myth, Cosmic Terror, and the Templo Mayor," in *The Great Temple of Tenochtitlan: Center and Periphery in the Aztec World*, edited by Johanna Broda, Davíd Carrasco, and Eduardo Matos Moctezuma (Berkeley: University of California Press, 1987), pp. 124–162; and "Toward the Splendid City: The Study of Mesoamerican Religions," *Religious Studies Review* 14, no. 4 (1988): 289–302.

19. See Mircea Eliade, "Celestial Archetypes of Territories, Temples, and Cities," and "The Symbolism of the Center," in *Myth of the Eternal Return, or, Cosmos and History*, translated by Willard R. Trask (Princeton, NJ: Bollingen Series, Princeton University Press, 1954), pp. 6–17; and Mircea Eliade, "Sacred Places: Temple, Palace, 'Centre of the World,' " in *Patterns in Comparative Religion*, translated by Rosemary Sheed (New York: Meridian Books, 1958), pp. 367–387.

20. Marshall Sahlins, "Culture as Protein and Profit: Review of *Cannibals and Kings*, by Marvin Harris," *The New York Review of Books* (November 23, 1978): 45–52.

21. Background for the present analysis of cultural ecology is found in my M.A. thesis in archaeology. Philip P. Arnold, "The Aztec Ceremonial Landscape in the Valley of Mexico: Implications of Examining Religion and Environment," submitted to the Institute of Latin American Studies, University of London, 5 September 1986.

22. In Otto, the "Wholly Other" is characterized as a transcendent reality that invades human consciousness. However, an exploration of the Other can only be advanced through an examination of experience. While otherness, for him, seems to be a general feature of existence, its physical expressions are understood as degradations of the "Holy." See Rudolph Otto, *The Idea of the Holy: An Inquiry into the Non-Rational Factor in the Idea of the Divine and Its Relation to the Rational*, translated by John W. Harvey (Oxford: Oxford University Press, 1923), pp. 25–30.

23. See Gerardus van der Leeuw, *Religion in Essence and Manifestation*, translated by J. E. Turner, edited by Hans H. Penner (Princeton, NJ: Princeton University Press, 1986), p. 23.

24. See M. Merleau-Ponty, *Phenomenology of Perception* (London: Routledge and Kegan Paul, 1962), p. vii.

25. See Mircea Eliade, *Patterns in Comparative Religion*, translated by Rosemary Sheed (New York: Meridian Books, 1958). I would differentiate Eliade from the phenomenologists precisely around his use of material forms. While he grounds his work in and around objects, his project always attempts to comprehend the *significance* of these forms in the context of human imagination. Thus matter is less of a brute fact of existence, or Otherness, than for van der Leeuw, and more a site of hermeneutical activity. His emphasis on a discussion of religion as a historical enterprise, where meaning is negotiated between the Otherness of the world and human creativity, suggests that meaning is embedded in the historical and experiential attribute of material forms. On the other hand, like the phenomenologists, in the end Eliade seems to express confidence in his being able to illuminate the essence of religion through his historical method.

26. See Mircea Eliade, *The Forge and the Crucible*, 2nd ed., translated by Stephen Corrin (Chicago: University of Chicago Press, 1978). Bruce Lincoln has also utilized transformative aspects of ritual in his examination of female initiation rites in *Emerging from the Chrysalis: Rituals of Women's Initiation*, 2nd ed. (New York: Oxford University Press, 1991). Lincoln, however, does not center his study on the central image of a caterpillar becoming a butterfly. While Eliade grounds the studies mentioned above around material referents to spin out their historical particularities, Lincoln's objects of study are various human communities. Through this strategy, in the end, he maintains that this image is in the service of maintaining control over women.

27. Sir James George Frazer also tied cultic devotions to a theoretical notion of magic. See his "Sympathetic Magic," in *The Golden Bough: A Study in Magic and Religion*, vol. 1, abridged edition (New York: Collier Books, 1950), pp. 12–43. Frazer posited that there was a system of laws of sympathy that dominated primitive rituals of devotion. Homeopathic magic assumes that things that resemble each other are the same, and contagious magic assumes that things that at one time were in contact always remain so. Likewise, in fertility cults, the magician will coax various sorts of desirable weather or children to appear in a woman's womb through the manipulation of objects that obeyed these laws of sympathy. Fertility cults have traditionally been seen as human attempts to overcome physical difficulties through a creative ability to integrate the cosmos. They work to establish and/or reinforce physical connections by sympathetic means.

28. Bronislaw Malinowski, *Coral Gardens and Their Magic*, vol. 2, *The Language of Magic and Gardening* (Bloomington: Indiana University Press, 1965), pp. 3–74.

29. His overenthusiasm for this approach, however, tended to alienate him from anthropologists of his day. Generally, he came to believe that cultural expressions could be completely known through a fine-grained investigation of a physical environment in a manner similar to the cultural-ecology school of archaeology. He thereby expressed his own confidence in his own culturally constructed understanding of matter.

30. See Jack Berry's "Introduction," in Malinowski, *Coral Gardens and Their Magic*, vol. 2, pp. x–xi. He illustrates the process of speech-events with a hypothesis of child development. Children learn quickly that through verbal acts (and we may include actions as well) they can have an effect in the world, through adults, to satisfy their needs. "Thus a small child acts on its surroundings by the emission of sound which is the expression of its bodily needs and is, at the same time, significant to the surrounding adults." Ibid., p. 63.

31. Although he would not admit it, in this sense he is close to Durkheim's understanding of the evolution of religion in which the predominate a priori category is society. While Durkheim is more interested in cognitive models than Malinowski, both nonetheless see the efficacy of religious devotions as a cultural reality. See Durkheim (note 7 above), pp. 28–29, for his reaction to those who promote religion as an a priori category. It is ironic, however, that while Malinowski insisted on the materiality of language to a determinist extreme, he counted its only real effect as a social one. Others since him have moved into a more cognitively oriented side of human interaction with the world.

32. Pierre Bourdieu, *Outline of a Theory of Practice*, translated by Richard Nice (Cambridge: Cambridge University Press, 1977), p. 22.

33. William F. Hanks, *Referential Practice: Language and Lived Space Among the Maya* (Chicago: University of Chicago Press, 1990), p. 9.

34. See his "Deixis and Its Double," ibid., pp. 5–9.

35. Keith H. Basso, *Wisdom Sits in Places: Landscape and Language Among the Western Apache* (Albuquerque: University of New Mexico Press, 1996).

36. Mythic thought too, according to Lévi-Strauss, shares similar characteristics. For him there is more than an interest in food acquisition for the "savage mind" when dealing with material realities. As for the scientist, there is also a fervent interest in the acquisition of knowledge. As he says, "[a]nimals and plants are not known as a result of their usefulness; they are deemed useful or interesting because they are first of all known." In Claude Lévi-Strauss, *The Savage Mind* (Chicago: University of Chicago Press, 1966), p. 9. The materiality of mythic language is valuable for Lévi-Strauss in that it creates opportunities for cognitive structures to emerge. Reciprocity, as expressed in myths, negotiates the distance between physical binary oppositions. While categories of raw/cooked, fresh/decayed, moistened/burned, etc., have more propositional than ontological importance for Lévi-Strauss, mythic thought initiates its constructive activity with reference to empirical realities. It is his conclusion that his structural method follows the natural sciences (in his view, as does all social science). Myths tell us nothing about world order as it is, but instead give us a language by which we metaphorically express human anxieties basic to our material existence. See Claude Lévi-Strauss, "Finale," in *The Naked Man: Introduction to the Science of Mythology*, vol. 4, translated by J. and D. Weightman (London: Jonathan Cape, 1981), p. 629. Unlike Lévi-Strauss's mythic thought, however, ritual, as he indicates, is an activity more closely grounded in an embedded reality. In a discussion of Victor Turner's work, Lévi-Strauss acknowledges the link between myth and ritual while asserting their distinctions in performing this function. While myth moves from the continuous to the discontinuous, ritual moves in the opposite direction. Ibid., p. 665.

This position should not be taken lightly, for Lévi-Strauss's project is to develop a "grammar" of mythic thought following the work of Saussure, thereby undercutting a referential analysis. See Claude Lévi-Strauss, "Overture," in *The Raw and the Cooked: Introduction to the Science of Mythology*, vol. 1, translated by J. and D. Weightman (London: Jonathan Cape, 1970). For example, Mary Douglas, in "Deciphering a Meal," *Daedalus* 101, no. 1 (1972): 61–81, criticizes Lévi-Strauss's codification of food because he gives no emphasis to the constructive activities at work in a community of eaters, other than the activity of the "savage" intellectual. As with the reciprocity of the gift, the meal is meaningfully codified as edible or inedible in a particular social context. Nevertheless, he establishes his line of inquiry by an analysis of the reciprocity of kinship alliances and marriage practices, the exchange of physical bodies, as a structural means by which to overcome social Otherness. See Claude Lévi-Strauss, "Structural Analysis in Linguistics and in Anthropology," in *Structural Anthropology*, translated by Claire Jacobson and Brooke Grundfest Schoepf (New York: Basic Books, 1963), pp. 31–66.

In the history of religion, some theoretical stances could be characterized as structuralist. Jonathan Z. Smith's, *To Take Place: Toward Theory in Ritual* (Chicago: University of Chicago Press, 1987), applies a grammatical interpretation to the historical reformulation of the Temple of Jerusalem during the early Christian period. As he says, "There is nothing inherent in the location of the Temple in Jerusalem. Its location was simply where it happened to be built . . . the Temple in Jerusalem was the focus of a complex, self-referential system." (pp. 83–84) He goes on to say that the rituals in this central temple cannot be decoded because they are contentless. It is not the terms that mattered but their relations. Perhaps Smith would say the same of the temple rebuilding period during Josiah's reforms. In Smith's analysis of bear-hunting rituals among paleo-Siberian people ("The Bare Facts of Ritual," in *Imagining Religion: From Babylon to Jonestown* [Chicago: University of Chicago Press, 1982], pp. 53–65), he concludes that ceremonially killing the bear, in the closely managed space of a village context, overcomes a conceptual incongruity of an actual hunt. In reality hunters kill a bear in the bush any way they can. The essential incongruity is a conceptual one between how a wild bear is killed and how one ought to be killed. Taken to this extreme, ritual has no referential status outside itself. Smith's theories conform more closely to Saussure's linguistic analysis where performance is relegated to an ideological construct and not a material one. See also Catherine Bell, "Discourse and Dichotomies: The Structure of Ritual Theory," *Religion* 17 (1987): 95–118, and *Ritual Theory, Ritual Practice* (New York: Oxford University Press, 1992), in which she applies the conventions of Smith's historical work more self-consciously to the work of theory building in the academy.

37. In Gadamer's treatment of history, for example, the Otherness of temporal periods removed from our experience is subjected to the investigator's prejudices to arrive at a meaningful resolution. For him, understanding begins when something confronts us and has the logical structure of a question. See Hans-Georg Gadamer, *Truth and Method*, 2nd ed., translated and revised by Joel Weinsheimer and Donald G. Marshall (New York: Continuum, 1989), pp. 265–307. Likewise, Ricoeur sees the interpretive process as dialogical in which the reader and "text" are engaged in an "ontological condition of reference." See Paul Ricoeur, *Interpretation Theory: Discourse and the Surplus of Meaning* (Fort Worth: Texas Christian University Press, 1976).

38. This distinction is analogous to Eliade's delineation between interpretive moments of *homo faber* and *homo religiosus*. See Mircea Eliade *"Homo Faber* and *Homo Religiosus,"* in *The History of Religions: Retrospect and Prospect,* edited by Joseph M. Kitagawa (New York: Macmillan Publishing Co., 1985), pp. 1–12.

39. See various treatments of homologies in Bruce Lincoln, "Cosmogony, Anthropogony, Homology," in *Myth, Cosmos, and Society: Indo-European Themes of Creation and Destruction* (Cambridge, MA: Harvard University Press, 1986), pp. 1–40; Brian K. Smith, "Gods and Men in Vedic Ritualism: Toward a Hierarchy of Resemblance," *History of Religions* 24, no. 4 (1985): 291–307; and Brian K. Smith, *Reflections on Resemblance, Ritual, and Religion* (New York: Oxford University Press, 1989). For both of these Indo-Europeanists, contrary to Eliade, the construction of resemblance, or homology, with a cosmological archetype, is always a human project. Religion is created to serve human goals. While Eliade tends to emphasize *homo religiosus*, Lincoln and Smith emphasize *homo faber*. See also Lincoln's analyses of female initiation ceremonies, "On the Nature of Women's Initiations" and "Afterword: Rethinking Rituals of Women's Initiation," in *Emerging from the Chrysalis,* pp. 91–119.

40. Dean E. Arnold, *Ceramic Theory and Cultural Process* (Cambridge: Cambridge University Press, 1985). He is following the cybernetic model used by Kent Flannery, "Archaeological Systems Theory and Early Mesoamerica," in *Anthropological Archaeology in the Americas,* edited by Betty J. Meggers (Washington, DC: The Anthropological Society of Washington, 1968), pp. 67–87.

41. "Culture and the environment constitute the 'system' discussed in this book . . .[t]he interrelationships of ceramics to environment and culture can be described as a channel for the flow of information between parts of the ecosystem—in this case between the environment and human beings . . . Besides water, energy and nutrients, ceramics can also provide a channel for ideological and/or social structural information between members of the society when ceramics reflect mythical themes and/or are used in ritual or in burial." (Arnold, *Ceramic Theory and Cultural Process,* pp. 16–17.)

42. He also suggests that there is a real need to include other kinds of archaeological readings of artifacts, including, for example, feminist and indigenous archaeologies. See Ian Hodder, *Reading the Past: Current Approaches to Interpretation in Archaeology* (Cambridge: Cambridge University Press, 1986), p. 157.

43. "In relation to the real, structured system of data, archaeologists critically evaluate their theories." (Hodder, ibid., p. 154.)

44. Christopher Tilley, *A Phenomenology of Landscape; Places, Paths and Monuments* (Oxford: Berg Publishers, 1994), p. 25.

45. Debates on the nature of the Other have a long history in the history of religion. Representing an essentialist phenomenological view are Otto, *The Idea of the Holy,* and van der Leeuw, *Religion in Essence and Manifestation.*

46. As Christopher Tilley says, "I reject a notion of landscape as inhering solely in the form of mental representation and cognition. By 'landscape' I want instead to refer to the physical and visual form of the earth as an environment and as a setting in which locales occur and in dialectical relation to which meanings are created, reproduced

and transformed. The *appearance* of a landscape is something that is substantial and capable of being described." *A Phenomenology of Landscape*, p. 25.

47. Gregory Bateson, "Introduction: The Science of Mind and Order," *Steps to an Ecology of Mind* (New York: Balantine Books, 1972), p. xxv.

48. The phenomenological school of geography, and its adoption by archaeology, has been developing since the 1970s. According to Tilley,

> the usefulness of a "scientific" conception of space abstracted from human affairs has systematically been called into question. . . . New geography and new archaeology considered space as a abstract dimension or container in which human activities and events took place. The implication of this perspective was that activity and event and space were conceptually and physically separate from each other and only contingently related. Such a view of space decentred it from agency and meaning.

Instead Tilley suggests another model drawn from phenomenology:

> These spaces, as social productions, are always centred in relation to human agency and are amenable to reproduction or change because their constitution takes place as part of the day-to-day praxis or practical activity of individuals and groups in the world . . . Socially produced space combines the cognitive, the physical and the emotional into something that may be reproduced but is always open to transformation and change . . . The specificity of place is an essential element in understanding its significance . . . Space has no substantial essence in itself, but only has a relational significance, created through relations between peoples and places. Space becomes detotalized by virtue of its relational construction and because, being differentially understood and produced by different individuals, collectives and societies, it can have no universal essence. (Tilley, *A Phenomenology of Landscape*, pp. 1–11.)

49. Ricoeur, *Interpretation Theory*.

50. Jonathan Z. Smith expresses this position in several contexts. See his *Map Is Not Territory* and *To Take Place: Toward Theory in Ritual*. Also see Anthony Grafton for a fine-grained analysis of the transformations to the culture of books during the Age of Discovery (*New Worlds, Ancient Texts: The Power of Tradition and the Shock of Discovery* [Cambridge and London: Harvard University Press and The Belknap Press, 1992]).

51. For example, see my "Paper Ties to Land: Indigenous and Colonial Material Orientations to the Valley of Mexico," *History of Religions* 35, no. 1 (August 1995): 27–60.

52. See David Carrasco, editor, *The Imagination of Matter: Religion and Ecology in Mesoamerican Traditions* (Oxford: B.A.R. International Series no. 515, 1989).

53. I prefer to use the term "modern" rather than "postmodern" when referring to our current material context. The reason is that material life today seems to me to be perfectly consonant with the colonial period in that the modes for understanding and settling land have remained in place since the Age of Discovery. If anything, our current world has the flavor of being ultramodern rather than postmodern. From the indig-

enous perspective I hope to suggest that modernity has not ended but, on the contrary, has become more voracious.

54. In recent lectures by Lawrence E. Sullivan, his comparative work dealing with the Mall of America reveals that, for many, regarding a mall as expressing some religious perspective was a painful prospect that most informants would avoid discussing. Likewise, Ira Zepp's work, *The New Religious Image of Urban America: The Shopping Mall as Ceremonial Center,* 2nd ed. (Niwot: University Press of Colorado, 1997), points out the irony of malls being the most potent material force for the survival of modern people but completely antithetical to religious life. While our consumer apparatus demands tremendous energies, commitments, and resources, it must remain insignificant.

Part One

Exporations of Tlalocan

2 Introduction to a Mesoamerican Landscape

This chapter deals with various interpretations of Tlaloc. As a deity of rain and fertility, he oversaw the sustenance of bodies (human as well as others). The substantive interactions between various beings in ancient Mexico was the world he controlled. Behind these material interactions was knowledge. The practice of interacting with Tlaloc through rituals, as an expression of physical life in the Valley of Mexico, was a hermeneutical practice of occupying the land. In the end, a general picture will emerge of Tlaloc as an embodiment of the Valley of Mexico rather than as a discrete anthropomorphic projection.

To appreciate this dimension of Aztec existence, discussions of philological, iconographical, and ethnohistorical evidence will follow. Then there will be an initial examination of the Tlaloc cult, followed by a more detailed analysis of particular rituals in chapters 3 and 4.

TLALOC AND THE SOURCES

Tlaloc was a Mesoamerican deity of rain and fertility with an ubiquitous presence throughout central Mexico. His first appearance in

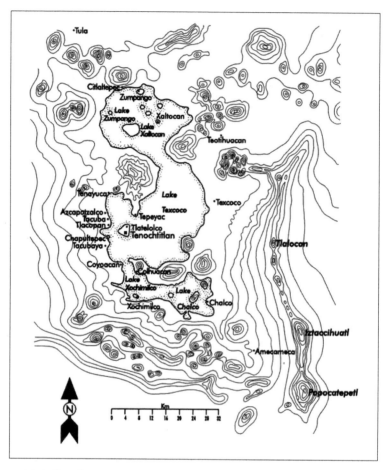

2.1. Valley of Mexico circa 1519.

Teotihuacan was followed by numerous other manifestations throughout Mesoamerica. His presence in pre-Columbian Mexico, from 200 C.E.
(and perhaps earlier) to 1521 C.E., has defined him as a pan-
Mesoamerican deity. From the glory days of Teotihuacan until today,
shrines dedicated to Tlaloc continue to be sites of devotion for the Nahua
people. Contemporary Nahua continue to refer to "Tlalo," as he is sometimes called, as their deity of rain and fertility.[1] Because of Tlaloc's
continuing presence, he is well represented in both primary and secondary source material and in the archeological record.

ETYMOLOGIES OF TLALOC

Linguistically, the name Tlaloc is difficult to unravel. There are a variety of interpretations of this name from different Nahuatl scholars. Mapping the intricacies of the etymology of Tlaloc reveals the rich contextual nuances that surround this deity. The most authoritative voice for Nahuatl linguistics is the work of Fray Alonso de Molina, whose *Vocabulario en lengua castellana y mexicana* of 1571 was the closest to expressing "classical" Nahuatl of the sixteenth century. Unfortunately Molina does not include any deity names in his dictionary. Like his pupil Sahagún, Molina's express purpose for composing the word list was to eradicate the indigenous religion. None of the linguists working in Mexico at the time would have included what they regarded as pagan material. This is an unfortunate loss for us today. It is possible that from Molina's temporal proximity to Aztec life in the valley, and given his linguistic skill, he could have more thoroughly traced the roots of Tlaloc. It is also possible, however, that Tlaloc, due to its problematic grammatical structure, also combines a number of central-Mexican languages.[2]

Karttunen defines Tlaloc (plural Tlaoh-queh) as the god of water and rain; host of the rain gods (plural).[3] Siméon and Andrews agree that while Tlaloc refers to the god of rain and water, the word itself is connected with earth (*tlal-li*). Both of these linguists translate Tlaloc as "one who lies or rests on earth."[4]

There are also descriptive definitions of Tlaloc from the sixteenth century that give insights into this deity. Sahagún states that the name Tlaloc Tlamacazqui (the provider) means he gave things that were necessary for life and was called the divine provider.[5] This seems to apply particularly to the plurality of the gods of the rain who oversaw the earthly paradise of Tlalocan, or the place of Tlaloc. According to the Dominican Fray Diego Durán, Tlaloc means "Path Under the Earth," or "Long Cave,"[6] presumably derived from *tlalli*, earth, and *ohtli*, road.[7]

Fray Juan de Torquemada wrote about Aztec religion during the early seventeenth century, but used sources from the sixteenth century. The title to chapter 23 of his sixth book of *Monarquía Indiana* is

"Where the God Tlaloca Tecuhtli is treated, called Neptune, by the Ancients, God of the waters; and of other Gods, his companions; and of the errors of these Indians about these Gods."[8] In it he says, "These Indians had another god they called Tlalocatecuhtli,[9] which means Lord of Paradise (Tlalocan) or of the place of supreme delight which was consecrated to the god of water and rain." According to Torquemada, the Aztec paradise was an earthly one ruled by a Tlaloc who resembled Neptune, even down to the use of the trident. Tlalocan was a place of great fertility. As he says, "The Indians called Tlaloc burgeoner of the earth and patron of the good rains."[10]

Seler claimed, in 1890, that "[t]he name, according to the rules [of Nahuatl grammar] should be translated 'pulque of the earth.' "[11] This would seem to be derived from *tlalli*, earth and *octli*, pulque.[12] However, this would result in *Tlaloctli* and not Tlaloc. Later, Seler discarded this translation for a verbally derived noun from *tlaloa*, "to run, flee, or sprout." In his commentary to the *Borgia Codex*, Seler goes into more detail, stating that when used reflexively *tlaloa* can only be translated as "to sprout."[13] His analysis is based on the occurrence of the phrase *motlalotehua*[14] in Sahagún's *Primeros Memoriales*. Seler translates this as "he gets up" (*se levanta*) equating the action of rising up with sprouting. The difficulty, according to Sullivan, is that *ehua*, in compounded form, has two possible meanings, neither of which means "to rise." It means either "to depart" while performing the action of the primary verb, or to perform the action of the primary verb quickly. Sullivan translates *motlalotehua* as "he quickens into life."[15] If *tlaloa* were the basis for Tlaloc, as Seler claims, it would have to appear with the reflexive pronoun as *Motlaloc* or *Netlaloc*. Moreover, Seler's translation of the name Tlaloc[16] as "he who makes sprout," has a transitive meaning, which he claims to be derived from *tlaloa*, "to sprout," which has an intransitive meaning. Sullivan claims that many have followed Seler's translation including Spence, Caso, and Soustelle.

Another etymological avenue of approach has been attempted by Garibay and León-Portilla. They translate Tlaloc as "he who is upon the earth" (el que está en la tierra). This connects *tlalli*, earth, and the verb *onoc*, "to be lying stretched out." The difficulty is that the verb *onoc* can only be compounded with another verb; never a noun. It also requires the ligature -*ti*-, which is not present in the god's name and, according to Sullivan, there is no exception to this rule.

Sullivan's solution is that "[s]trictly and grammatically speaking the name Tlaloc must be related to the adjective *tlallo* which means 'full of earth,' 'covered with earth,' or, 'made of earth,' the plural of which is *tlaloque*, which also happens to be the plural of Tlaloc and the name for the multiple gods of rain." The singular, Tlaloc, must have originally been *tlalloqui*, which follows the rules of similar verb-derived nouns. *Tlalloqui* went through a process of "suffix-erosion," thereby reducing the word to *tlalloc*. Sullivan goes on to cite several cases from Olmos's grammar of 1875—*tepuzzo, mecapallo, tlallo, zoquitl, teyo, cuauhyo*—that are translated as "he who has the quality of an ax, of a tumpline, of earth, of clay, of stone, or wood."[17]

> That is, he does the work of these objects, *he is the embodiment of these things*. The slave *is* the ax that hews the wood, the tumpline that carries the burdens, the earth that is cultivated and productive, and so forth. Therefore the name Tlaloc, which correctly should be spelled Tlalloc means, "he who has the quality of earth," "he who is made of earth," *"he who is the embodiment of the earth."* Since the names of Nahuatl gods are literally or figuratively a description of their nature, it would appear that Tlaloc was essentially an earth god.[18]

Sullivan bolsters her etymological analysis with a story of creation in the *Histoire du Mexique*[19] in which the eighth heaven was inhabited by *Tlalocanteuctli*, or Tlaloc, the "god of the earth."

> In the same source is the myth of the creation of the earth by Quetzalcoatl and Tezcatlipoca from the goddess Tlaltecutli, a kind of monster whose joints were entirely made up of eyes and predacious mouths, the two gods transformed themselves into great serpents, one of whom took the goddess' right hand and left foot and the other, her left hand and right foot and they twisted her with such force that they split her in two. From one half they created earth and from the other, the heavens. To compensate her for the damage she had suffered, all the gods ordained that the sustenances

of life issue from her. From her hair they made the trees; from her numerous eyes, the springs and fountains and caves; from her mouths, the rivers and great caverns; from her nose, the valleys and mountains.[20]

According to Clendinnen's interpretation of this cosmogony, this goddess "wailed in the darkness and refused to yield her fruits until she was soaked in human blood and fed hearts of human victims."[21]

Three principal iconographic characteristics of Tlaloc are emphasized in this story. First, the two intertwined serpents correspond to representations of Tlaloc in which serpents in a similar position go over his eyes, forming eyebrows, and intertwine to form his nose. Second is Tlaloc's large, gogglelike eyes from which were formed fountains, springs, and caves. Third is the predacious and devouring mouth, accentuated in Tlaloc iconography by large fangs, from which were formed rivers and caverns. For Sullivan, a strong association between Tlaloc and the earth is revealed through the cultic practices of ancient and contemporary Nahuatl.

Caves, and their consistent relationship with springs running through the interior of the earth, are a recurrent element of Nahua ritual life. A metaphor for a spring, in Nahuatl, is *in texcalli, in oztotl*, "crag and cave," and according to one source refers to each of the two springs that joined at the place where the Mexicans founded Tenochtitlan, the ceremonial center. The metaphoric relationship between water, particularly sweet water, and earth directly corresponded to agricultural activity. The creation of plant life to sustain human beings required the correct and proper combination of these elements, both of which Tlaloc articulated. In the *Leyenda de los Soles*, when the god Quetzalcoatl fails to carry the Mountain of Sustenance to the people, Nanahuatl is ordered to shake out the kernels of corn.[22] When this happens, the text states, *niman ye netlalhuilo in tlaloque*, "then the Tlalocs were covered with earth," or "were transformed into earth": *netlalhuilo* can have either meaning.[23] Utilizing both definitions of Tlaloc connected to sprouting or embodiment, the gift of corn to people can be seen as facilitated by the Tlalocs due to their transformative capabilities as seed or earth.

Before leaving the etymological analysis, certain larger implications should be highlighted. The story of *Tlalteuctli*, "earth lord," and the associated deity Tlaloc, dramatizes how the creation of the earth was formed from a coherent bodily structure. Creation required that a sacrifice take place. Violence became the necessary ingredient for the propagation of life through the reciprocity and transformation of living beings into individual material elements. So while the landscape was conceived as a corporeal entity—a living being—it was the destruction or reformation of that being that was required to promote a wider spectrum of life. Life, in the Aztec cosmogony, was not composed of a unified body but rather as a result of the violent actions of destruction; of tearing a body apart to create new combinations of matter sustaining a plurality of beings.

There is clearly no easy interpretation of Tlaloc. It should be noticed that water, earth, plants, and animals are all intimately connected with Tlaloc. Yet based on recent attempts to understand this deity's name, he articulates a living force that is simultaneously bound up with the processes of the ongoing creation of agricultural life and the embodiment of those processes. Tlaloc's appearance is not as a distinct being but rather as an appearance embedded in various aspects of material life. Enlarging the implications of these various etymologies situates Tlaloc at the center of a consumptive cosmos, or at the center of a reciprocity between life and death that was tied to the daily activity of destroying life so that various other forms of life could be sustained.

TLALOC ICONOGRAPHY AT TEOTIHUACAN

According to Covarrubias, Tlaloc iconography begins in the Olmec period (1500 B.C.E. to 300 B.C.E.) with the "baby jaguar" motif that Furst has more recently tied to the "toad mother" fertility symbol.[24] Particularly, the overexaggerated mouth and teeth in humanoid form suggested to Covarrubias that Tlaloc had his inception during this early period. Tlaloc appears as a combination of human and predatory animal during the Olmec period, or as an eating human closely linked to carnivores of the forest.[25]

Tlaloc's most dramatic appearance, however, is at the Classical site of Teotihuacan (100 C.E. to 700 C.E.), which translates from Nahuatl as the "place where the gods are sent." During this period, Tlaloc images also appeared on stelae in the Maya area at Tikal.[26] Many have taken this as evidence of the large political and cultural impact of Teotihuacan throughout the Mesoamerican area. Some believe that Teotihuacan imposed itself more and more on the Maya, particularly in Yucatan, during the post-Classic era. An insightful recent analysis by Jones of architectural similarities between central Mexico and Yucatan, however, has tied the use of these forms to a ritual history in their individual contexts. While there may be iconographic similarities between

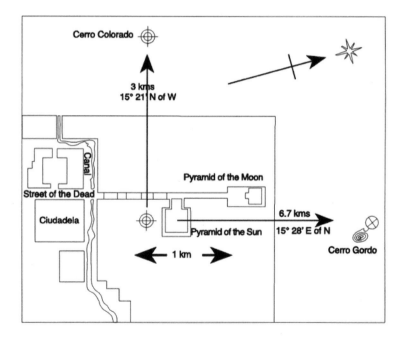

2.2 . Urban planning at Teotihuacan related to hills and water, redrawn from Aveni (1980).

these cultural areas, they seem to have functioned performatively and ritually in distinctly different ways.[27]

Teotihuacan was an enormous ceremonial complex and at its height had a population bigger than that of Rome.[28] While it is known primarily for its large pyramids of the Sun and the Moon, water was the central element of the bureaucratic structure of Teotihuacan. The city planners took the natural water course called the Río San Juan, which flowed down the valley, and realigned it to correspond to a grid pattern predominantly based on the near-cardinal directional orientation of the city. According to Millon and his co-workers on the Teotihuacan mapping project, this city was aligned to two directions: a north-south direction of 15° 28′ east of north and an east-west direction of 16° 30′ south of east.[29] While these two directions are only one degree off perpendicular to each other, this deviation was probably a deliberate part of the city planning. The structures in the city are aligned to both the first and second orientations.

Aveni has examined some of the alignments at Teotihuacan. Of particular interest to him have been the first (15° 28′ east of north) of the two dominant orientational schemes found by Millon and his team. The well-known Street of the Dead (which is not actually a street at all but a series of ascending ceremonial plazas) is the most significant north-south axis of the city. At its northern end sits the Pyramid of the Moon, which is framed to the north by the largest mountain in the area, Cerro Gordo, and at its southern end by the Ciudadela. Between these two points is the Pyramid of the Sun, the largest structure of the city. The Street of the Dead is oriented 15° 28′ east of north.[30] Halfway down the Street of the Dead on its eastern side is a plaster floor into which is fashioned what Aveni calls a "pecked circle."[31] This consists of a set of two concentric circles that are bisected in four parts by two perpendicular lines. The circles and lines were made in either plaster or rock by boring small indentations into the surface. According to Aveni, these have calendrical and cosmological associations and were probably used to orient systematic observations of the sky, thereby orienting building projects within the city. Another pecked circle is located at the summit of a small rise three kilometers west of the ceremonial precinct on Cerro Colorado. The orientation of an imaginary line from the pecked circle near the Street of the Dead to the one on the slope of Cerro Colorado is

15° 21' north of west, or only seven minutes of arc off the perpendicular alignment of the Street of the Dead (see figure 2.2).

Aveni's hypothesis is that the pecked circles created a baseline for orienting the building of Teotihuacan. Most significant, however, is that this alignment corresponds to the setting of the Pleiades, an important star constellation throughout Mesoamerica. The "heliacal rising" of the Pleiades corresponds with the first of two annual passages of the sun across the zenith, when the sun casts no shadow at noon, and an important day in demarcating the seasons.[32] The appearance of the Pleiades on the western horizon, on approximately 18 May 150 C.E., would herald the summer season, the rainy season, and hence agricultural production.

It is significant that in this first city of Tlaloc the orientation for urban planning was with reference to water and agriculture. The east-west alignment conforms to celestial events with reference to particular landscape features. As with the etymological analysis, the orientation of Teotihuacan was organized around an architectural interaction between the land and sky *at the horizon* (i.e., at the point of contact). This interaction produced the necessary requirements for the sustenance of a human population and the basis of ceremonial planning. Water from the Río San Juan was reconfigured to fit this stellar alignment, which corresponded to the interaction of a larger cosmology of rain and earth.

Pasztory worked with the Tlaloc iconography at Teotihuacan, in particular with the murals of Tepantitla. These murals depict the Tlalocan cosmos as a paradise comprised of lush foliage, abundant water, and idle hours of relaxed play.[33] This world was overseen by various deities associated with water and fertility (the *tlaloque*) who were the source of continuous rain, and therefore wealth. These murals explored a cosmology of wealth based on water. Their rich colors and elaborate detail celebrated an unseen, yet corporeal reality upon which the physical existence of the people of Teotihuacan was predicated.

Iconographic features of Tlaloc at Teotihuacan are clearly outlined by Pasztory. She states that

Tlaloc is the Nahuatl name of the Aztec rain god, who is represented in art by eyes surrounded by rings and by a moustache-like upper lip with long fangs. Among the thousands of figurines found at Teotihuacan in the excavations at the close of the nineteenth and the beginning of the twentieth centuries, a large number represented the same goggle-eye personage.[34]

Pasztory's early associations of Tlaloc at Teotihuacan were with the crocodile. As she states, "[i]n Mesoamerican mythology, the crocodile is the symbol of the earth, par excellence; the world is visualized as a large crocodile floating in a lake covered with water lilies."[35] This manifestation of Tlaloc was connected with the post-Classic (or Aztec) "crocodilian Earth Monster," or "earth lord."[36] She claims that, unlike at Tenochtitlan, there is no Earth Monster depicted at Teotihuacan because that position was filled by the Crocodile-Tlaloc. Tlaloc and the Earth Monster were both closely associated with earth, water, and the annual solar and ritual cycles. The Crocodile-Tlaloc at Teotihuacan carries vessels filled with water and lightning staffs. The rains would originate from Tlalocan either from the *tlaloque* striking these vessels with lightning or from their pouring water out from these vessels.[37]

Pasztory's study of the Teotihuacan Tlaloc, linking it with the post-Classic deity Tlalteuctli (the earth lord) and the crocodile, underscores Tlaloc's ecological attributes. Tlaloc iconographically articulated interactions between humans and the landscape; between the earth and sky; between soil and water. His ecological attributes were the basis of human life, yet Tlalocan, the place of Tlaloc, was hidden from immediate sensory apprehension. Tlalocan ecology, in this sense, encompassed a needed yet magical interaction of elements that he himself embodied.

Recent excavations led by Eduardo Matos Moctezuma at Teotihuacan have unearthed important new insights into the Classical period's associations of land and water. At the Quetzalcoatl Temple, excavations have unearthed a *cipactli* genus of animals (toad, crocodile, alligator, and sawfish) that all have large mouths and exaggerated upper teeth. These animals are also associated with water.

[43]

Excavations by Cabrera, Sugiyama, and Cowgill have also found around two hundred sacrificed warriors distributed numerically in their tombs, reminiscent of a calendrical order.[38] Many of these warriors had shell collars with pendants fashioned to imitate human jaws made from shell teeth set in stucco. A few of the burials had real jaws. Other objects included greenstone beads, earspools, nose pendants, figurines, conical objects, obsidian blades, figurines, shells, and remnants of wood and textiles.[39]

In the archaeological description of these remains, there emerges a symmetry between warrior sacrifice and the shell jaws. The Teotihuacanos placed particular emphasis on the upper jaw, or maxilla, which was connected with the voracious mouths of the iconography of the temple. That they are made of shell is also suggestive of a connection between fertility and warfare. Perhaps this is also indicated by the east-west axis of the burials. Doris Heyden's important article on the cave underneath the Pyramid of the Sun contains a number of examples that depict caves as open mouths with teeth.[40] The fact that these warriors were buried, or entombed in the earth, may also symbolize fertility. This could indicate that sacrificial burials were an extension of cave symbolism within a consumptive cosmology. Military activity may have been seen as part of the reciprocity of life and death. Warriors at Teotihuacan may have been understood to be the human extensions of the voracious jaws of an "eating landscape" and therefore integral to the production of food.[41]

The *cipactli* also had direct associations with time. According to López Austin, López Luján, and Sugiyama, the Quetzalcoatl Temple is dedicated to time.[42] The *cipactli* was the first cosmogonic force of creation and, in combination with the symbolism of Quetzalcoatl, represented the *divine-temporal-destiny-force* that was borne by the deity and by human beings. The forces that animated life carried with them a temporal burden, which was articulated in the Mesoamerican calendar systems. Quetzalcoatl is depicted with a *cipactli* headdress that at once symbolized the authority of Teotihuacan and its burden (or duty) of occupying a consumptive cosmogony. This temporal burden is encoded in stone on the Quetzalcoatl Temple.

Sugiyama has extended this temporal building plan into the urban design of Teotihuacan.[43] Combining the unit of 83 centimeters with other numbers of astronomical significance (52 [x 10], 73, 260, 584, and 819), the urban planners of Teotihuacan created a city of time. Like the "yard" of ancient Europe, 83 centimeters is a bodily measurement from heart to fingers, or from shoulder-blade to fingers. Moreover the north-south axis of the city was symbolically seen as traversing the upper- and underworlds. Time was thus materially articulated and located in the ceremonial space of Teotihuacan.

What kind of time does Teotihuacan exhibit? Surely not the abstract chronological succession of moments from one to the next that seems to dominate our modern notions, but instead an *embodied* time located in a particular place. Similar to the integration of celestial movements into the urban design, as noted by Aveni, time had a locative character. Likewise, the Nahuatl term for time, *cahu(i)-tl*, is also used in terms that describe a place. Molina, for example, translates the "space of time" as *cahuitl* and the "space of place" as *tlacauhtli, cauhtica,* and *tlacauilli*.[44]

Sugiyama's suggestion of a bodily unit of measure in this ceremonial space brings other located temporal structures to mind. There are other locations for time that more directly adhere to the human body. Music, rhythm, and dance are also temporal units. Unlike the nearly mute condition of the site today, the Teotihuacan of 1,500 years ago was a vital place full of rich sights, smells, and sounds. Ritual performances, sacrifices, etc., all have a bodily temporal dimension. These performances meaningfully articulated a living connection with the world. The city itself, as a monument to time, may have been seen as a coherent bodily structure enlivened by the ceremonial activity of its inhabitants. As the earth is a body, can the city also be interpreted as a body whose view of life is uniquely Mesoamerican?

With the discovery of a canal around its base, Matos Moctezuma and Manzanilla have presented a new interpretation of the Pyramid of the Sun as a manifestation of "water mountain" (*altepetl*) and "mountain of sustenance" (*tonacatepetl*).[45] The coincidence of water, caves, and mountain raises new possibilities for appreciating the prestige of this pyramid as a consumptive center of the world. These phenomena were deliberately pushed into alignment with other celestial and topographical phenomena. From a history of religion perspective, the prestige of Teotihuacan was articulated as the central axis for accessing the upper and lower worlds. Moreover, the regenerative elements of earth and water were organized by, and emanated from, a sacred reality upon which human life was materially contingent.

Tlaloc Archaeology, Ethnology, and Ecology

Recently Broda has laid out the contours of ritual action with reference to the Aztec gods of rain.[46] After extensive analysis of various sources, she has described general characteristics of indigenous, agrarian-based cults. Aztec culture had two primary strata: first, an ancient locative culture based on agriculture, and, second, immigrant tribal deities of the Chichimecs,[47] or "barbarians," whose orientation was astral with an emphasis on solar and Venus cults.[48] The second group of migrating gods, however, necessarily took on characteristics of the indigenous agricultural deities. They became localized to the environment through the appropriation of an indigenous cultic expression. This process of indigenization, in large measure, legitimated the Aztec occupation of central Mexico. With the Tlaloc cult, the Aztec simultaneously shifted their worldview from a nomadic to a sedentary one and thereby legitimized their claims to occupation of the valley.

Tlaloc was linked to a wide spectrum of Mesoamerican deities associated with rain and fertility. Some other manifestations include *Chac* among the Maya, *Cocijo* among the Zapotecs, *Tzahui* among the Mixtecs, and *Tajin* among the Totonacs. Broda thus sees Tlaloc as a pan-Mesoamerican deity whose central-Mexican presence predates all the above-mentioned manifestations.

His most important ties to the Mesoamerican landscape were mountains, high mountains of the sierra covered with evergreen plants and snow that symbolized fertility. According to Soustelle,[49] the Aztec expressions *xiuhcalco*, "green house," and *acxoyacalco*, "house of fir branches,"[50] were synonymous with Tlalocan. The tendency of clouds to form on mountain peaks before rain was taken as a sign of his presence. The *tlaloque*, known as rain dwarfs and the assistants to Tlaloc, were associated with various climatological phenomena such as lightning, thunder, hail, snow, and wind.[51] Tlaloc's familiar iconographic features of goggle-eyes and a serpent nose were ancient symbols of water (particularly mountain lakes) and lightning. Ritual adornments associated with the *tlaloque* were heron feathers placed in the hair, which signified clouds on the mountain peaks; they also symbolized the maize flower. The *tlaloque* were innumerable deities located at specific places serving as intermediaries between humans and Tlaloc. They were also responsible for sending various diseases associated with rain brought by cold winds from the mountains. These included dropsy, leprosy, and drowning. Ritual bathing during the festival Tepeilhuitl, "Feast of the Mountains," helped cure these ailments. Diseases were seen as manifestations of reciprocal relations between particular human beings and the deity.

The *tlaloque* were the original owners of maize. In the *Leyenda de los Soles*,[52] Nanahuatl, "the buboes one" (a diseased state associated with Tlaloc),[53] stole white, purple, yellow, and red maize (colors associated with the four cardinal directions), beans, chia, and amaranth from the *tlaloque* to give to humans. Among some Nahua people today, maize is believed to have been stolen from "los muchachos de la lluvia" ("the boys of the rain") from their numerous abodes inside of mountains. Sustenance has been understood to be a give-and-take arrangement between human beings—the consumers of food—and the *tlaloque*—the suppliers of food. This relationship was mediated through the sacrifice of children during annual festivals.

This arrangement was inherited from the Toltec empire and therefore was integral to Aztec political power.[54] Sustenance was their basis of authority and food was understood to arise from the bottom of water. Indeed, the earth was seen as being full of water, as Sahagún explains:

> And they [the Aztecs] said that the mountains were only magic places, with earth, with rock on the surface; that they were only like *ollas* (or vessels) or like houses; that they were filled with the water which was there. If sometime it were necessary, the mountains would dissolve; the whole world would flood. And hence the

> people called their settlements *altepetl*. They said, "This mountain of
> water, this river, springs from there, the womb of the mountain."[55]

Altepetl, "water mountain," referred to both town and temple. Water, understood as interior to the earth, was the basis of wealth for these communities. Various places on mountains associated with the *tlaloque* and water were the sites of offerings and ritual observances. From as early as Teotihuacan, *altepetl* expressed an indigenous understanding of occupying a particular place with reference to mountains and water.

Tlaloc was the locus for a complex of deities.[56] Gods connected with water and agricultural wealth were the focus of various festivals days. Most important of these deities was Chalchihuitlicue, "she with skirt of precious greenstone." Depending upon the mythic tradition, she was considered either the first or second wife of Tlaloc or the older sister of the *tlaloque*. She was the goddess of springs, rivers, and lakes—particularly the lake of Mexico—and was an ancient goddess of this region.[57] While Chalchihuitlicue was directly connected with sweet water, she was also related to the goddess Uixtocihuatl: "salt woman." During the festival of Etzalcualiztli, priests dedicated to her service made offerings to images of three principal goddesses: Chalchihuitlicue, Uixtocihuatl, and Chicomecoatl ("she of seven serpents"), a goddess of maize. According to Sahagún, "Thus they remembered the three. For they become indeed the livelihood of the people; through them the people are satisfied; through them they can live."[58] Other goddesses intimately associated with maize and the *tlaloque* include Xilonen, "doll or image of tender ear of green maize,"[59] Cinteotl, "maize goddess," and Ilamateuctli, "noble old woman." These last three goddess names probably symbolized maize at three stages in its maturation process.

Gods of pulque were also associated with the *tlaloque*. Pulque was and still is made from the maguey plant whose "heart," the shoot sent up from the middle of the maguey, was extracted so that a sugary sap (called *agua miel*) produced by the plant could be collected.[60] Mayahuel was the goddess of maguey, with her four hundred breasts signifying absolute fertility. The gods of maguey and pulque were numerous and corresponded to different regions of central Mexico. Deities of maize, maguey, and pulque constituted the nucleus of the fertility cult.

Templo Mayor

With the discovery of the now famous Coyolxauhqui stone and the subsequent excavation of the Templo Mayor from 1978 to 1982, interest in Tlaloc rituals has been reactivated due, in large part, to the ubiquity of objects found that directly relate to this group of deities.[61] With this new evidence, it is possible to conceive of an Aztec map of the universe through artifacts provided by the Templo Mayor excavation. The Templo Mayor was the center of the world (axis mundi) and therefore the center material power.[62] Aztec strategies of acquiring and maintaining power were based primarily upon agriculture and warfare. The Templo Mayor was a performative space at the center of the cosmos. Its architectural features and artifacts were consciously arranged to interact with and duplicate the cosmos. Most unexpected among the findings from the Templo Mayor excavation was the large quantity of offerings to Tlaloc.[63] "The pervasiveness of water symbolism in the excavation of the Templo Mayor can thus be related to a complex intertwining of concepts—for Broda a 'philosophy of nature.' "[64]

López Luján carried out the most intensive analysis of offerings at the Templo Mayor to date. His "reading" of archaeological contexts is informed by a syntactic approach to nonverbal, or performative, language that rests on horizontal, vertical, and tridimensional space internal to the organization of the offerings.[65] Several deities, as well as the tombs of significant individuals, were associated with rituals at the Templo Mayor.[66] Due to its position at the center of the cosmos, the function of these offerings seems to have served diverse functions, among which was the articulation of the cosmos.

A complex of offerings of blue jars, known as Complex N, provides insights into the Tlaloc cult. The hearts of human sacrifices during Etzalcualiztli (discussed in chapter 3), who personified the *tlaloque*, were placed in blue painted jars. In the *Historia de los mexicanos*

2.3. Tlaloc at the Templo Mayor.

por sus pinturas, there is a description of how various climatological phenomena are released from jars by the *tlaloque*.[67] Jars at the Templo Mayor were found on their sides with mouths facing north and west. *Cajetes*, small ceramic disks, were placed beneath the jar opening and represented the earth. According to López Luján, "[t]hese objects were probably placed there as an act of propitiation that gave the new building the attributes for a residence of Tlaloc—a room from which to generate rains and thus fertilize the earth."[68]

Offering 48 contained forty-two child skeletons and Tlaloc statues and was dated to the great drought of 1454. Due to the unusual contents and context of this offering site, López Luján concludes that it reveals a desperate ritual propitiation of the rain deities by a starving Tenochtitlan population.[69] The Templo Mayor was seen as a point of access to Tlalocan (the unseen world of Tlaloc that supported all life), upon which human survival was predicated. Drought was seen as evidence of some cosmological misalignment that could have been corrected only with drastic measures taken by the Aztec people.

A principal feature of the Templo Mayor as an *altepetl* (i.e., a "water mountain" like the Pyramid of the Sun at Teotihuacan) was that it embodied a cosmos of water. Many activities at an *altepetl* were linked to the sustenance of human and sacred worlds. In addition to Aztec art objects such as fish, frogs, shells, and serpents, many of the offering caches contained remains of aquatic flora and fauna. These included fish, swordfish, shark teeth, sea urchin, tortoise, crocodiles, conch shells, snails, corals (including brain coral). These objects were intimately connected with fertility, and as such also mapped an Aztec conception of meaningful space. Although Tenochtitlan was a significant distance from the coastal regions, from which many of these objects originated, fertility symbolism was often an attempt to conjure the presence of the sea in the center of the Aztec world.

> The earth was called Cemanahuac, "the place surrounded by water," and was conceived of as a disk or a huge alligator (cipactli) floating on the waters. These waters proceeded from Tlalocan, the paradise of the rain god, and came forth through springs to form the rivers, the lakes, and the sea. Tlalocan was, in a way, the

conceptualization of space underneath the earth full of water which connected the mountains with the sea.[70]

Saltwater came from celestial water and sweet water, fit for human consumption, was the result of seawater purified in its journey through the earth. These three waters (celestial, salty, and sweet) were not discrete types but denoted separate moments in a cosmic hydrological cycle. In Sahagún's description of the sea, we find the following:

> [I]s called *teuatl* (sea),[71] not that it is a god; it only means wonderful, a great marvel. And its name is *ilhuicaatl*.[72] The people of old, the people here of New Spain, thought and took as truth that the heavens were just like a house; it stood resting in every direction, and it extended reaching to the water. It was as if the water walls were joined to it. And hence they called it "water which reaches the heavens," because it stretched extending to the heavens. But now, because of the true Faith, it is only called *uei atl* (great water).[73]

The landscape upon which people lived was surrounded by water. Tlalocan was the place of an interactive system of waters whose occurrence on the earth at various times and places revealed the nature of Tlaloc's existence and his involvement in the world.

Broda concludes that "[t]he iconography of Cihuatl-Coatlicue-Coyolxauhqui, as well as the Tlalteuctli representations on relief stones, indicates that on the mythological level Templo Mayor, the sacred mountain, was the earth itself, the earth as a voracious monster devouring human victims and blood." Offerings entombed at the Templo Mayor should be seen in the wider context of "cosmovision." "Rather than being restricted to the god Tlaloc, they were brought to the earth itself. In a way, Tlaloc was also simply another male aspect of the earth."[74] These basic indigenous concepts had ancient roots in Mesoamerican culture and were distinct from the great public spectacles that took place at Tenochtitlan. The Templo Mayor excavation revealed a level of religious devotion that was rooted in a ritual devotion to the earth. It was upon this indigenous perspective that the Aztecs based their claims to meaningfully occupy the Valley of Mexico. López Luján pushes this interpretation further by emphasizing the presence of many other deities. The offerings reveal a ritual commitment to a consumptive cosmos of which the earth is a single aspect. The integration of the sky, earth, and underworld was centered by ritual activity at the Templo Mayor and was articulated by the exchange of types of foods necessary for the sustenance of various living beings (including gods and human beings). Tlaloc should be understood as articulating an Aztec orientation toward an "eating landscape" rather than as a discrete deity. Tlaloc seen as a personification of a consumptive process, and not as a distinct deity, highlights the ubiquity of his presence at the Templo Mayor and his ongoing presence in day-to-day subsistence activities.

The Templo Mayor was the site of an enormous earth opening. In particular, it was the mouth of the earth lord, Tlalteuctli, who would receive nourishment through blood sacrifices. Central to an exchange of food at this center was an Aztec understanding of bodily processes.

THE BODY IN MESOAMERICAN TIME AND SPACE

Bodily existence requires that human beings interpret and organize their world in order to function appropriately and successfully. As has been noted in chapter 1, an understanding of the relationship between a human ability to conceptualize and the material world people occupy varies dramatically from culture to culture; community to community. A diversity of understanding does not indicate, however, that this relationship is an "arbitrary" one. On the contrary, hermeneutical labor to promote physical survival is based on an ability to overcome the Otherness of the material world, and therefore suggests that understanding life, however it is construed, is a *necessary* feature of bodily existence. A plurality of interpretations of material existence (how humans meaningfully occupy land being but one dimension) among human groups does not mean that a particular interpretation of material life is an abstraction. Rather, as some phenomenologists maintain, understanding is only achieved through an engagement with an a priori materiality, or rather, a world that precedes a human presence and upon which human life is predicated.[75]

Occupation of land is situated, at once, in the necessary relationship between bodily existence and material life, and is not pre-determined, or over-determined, by a single cultural viewpoint. For example the Aztec and Spanish of the sixteenth-century necessarily occupied the same lands but also occupied nearly total distinctive landscapes.

Of primary methodological importance for this investigation is that the body can offer a shared referent of understanding. As with land, the body is a reality that closes the conceptual gap between pre-Columbian, colonial, and contemporary worlds. The possibility of the body arbitrating between worldviews has made it the subject of a number of recent projects in comparative studies.[76] While bodily existence is shared, however, the contexts of each cultural understanding of the body must be explored to more fully map its various realities. A generous disposition has traditionally been lacking in the scholarly investigations exploring alternative bodily understandings, particularly with reference to indigenous cosmologies.

The task of this section is to investigate an Aztec body cosmology as a reality that occupies both space and time, and as the vehicle for Aztec interaction with the hidden conditions of sustenance. Discussions of Tlaloc require an exploration of the *significance* of bodily existence among the Aztec. Dimensions of this are presented in the formation of the body, as well as how it was constituted, sustained, and animated.

According to López Austin, the structure of the Mesoamerican world was based on the opposition of male and female (also expressed as hot and cold) tendencies, each having its own attributes and expressions in the cosmos. The preeminent view was one of a dual structure of opposing elements that divided the universe so as to account for its diversity, order, and movement. The cosmos was divided into four quarters in the four primary directions, which was expressed at the Templo Mayor as *cemanahuac*. At each corner of this universe were sacred trees as well as four great *tlaloque* who held up the sky. These four great *tlaloque* would send the rains from outside the confines of the earth, being ruled by Tlaloc Teuctli: great lord Tlaloc. Along the central axis of the cosmos ran paths that were traversed by various other gods and their forces. From these four trees, influences of the gods of the upper and lower worlds would radiate toward the central point, also know as the navel.

The forces between the gods and the world were seen as two pairs of helical bands that were in constant motion making energies of the underworld ascend and those of the sky descend.[77] There was a dynamic interplay between center and periphery; hidden and material. Although López Austin emphasizes the communicative effect of these transmitted energies, their ultimate effect was one that constituted the very structure of existence. "These passageways provided communication between the turquoise place (the sky) and the obsidian place (the underworld) to create the center, the place of the precious green stone (the surface of the earth), as well as time, change, and conflict between the two opposing currents."[78] The world and its inhabitants were the result of an intersection of dynamic irradiations from the gods. These energies were simultaneously communicative and substantive.

The human body was wholly contingent on the proper mixing of emanations from the cosmos. The seven caves of Aztlan, from which the Aztecs emerged out of the earth, corresponded to seven orifices of the human body: two eye sockets, two nasal passages, the mouth, the anus, and the navel.[79] Part of a person's vital forces resided in the bones. Various spiritual entities penetrated the body through the joints, which were considered weak spots and thus a potential site for the entrance of disease, as well as benign cosmological emanations.

The circulation of blood through the body was through tubes. Stagnation of this movement, for whatever reason, was considered dangerous and one of the sources of disease. Blood strengthened people, making them live and grow by keeping muscles moist. Life and blood were equated.[80] This vital force could be passed on by contact, such as smearing blood on various parts of the body. With air, blood flowed inside the body. According to López Austin, "Nahua concepts about the inside of the body is that it was imagined to be a system of intercommunication through multiple canals which allowed fluids to flow with relative ease from one viscera to another."[81] The reproductive center of the body was within the kidneys, and conception of a child was achieved by mixing male and female fluids within the womb. Semen, for example, was sometimes called *omicetl*, or "coagulated bone substance," linking the male reproductive fluid with vital energies within the medulla, or bone marrow.

Animistic centers were those parts of the human organism in which there was a concentration of animistic forces or vital substances to give an organism healthy mobility and permit it to fulfill its psychic functions. The primary center was the heart, called the *yol*, or *yollo* group. This center included attributes of vitality, knowledge, inclination, and feeling. References to memory, habit, affection, will, direction of action, and emotion belonged exclusively to this center. In addition, the heart took part in each of the animistic states or processes used to classify material, with the exception of perception, which belonged to the *ix* ("face, surface, eye") group. Although the ego was subsumed within the heart, it was largely understood as consciousness that was dispersed throughout the body, as with the circulation of blood. The heart was the locus of bodily functioning in which humans would carry out the most important acts of existence and, as such, was seen as an autonomous internal center. "The heart can be reached, captured, read, seen; one can talk to it; it can be directed toward things. It is not identical, then, with that ego of which it makes up the most important part."[82]

The second animistic center of greatest importance was the *ix* group. Many have translated this to mean "the face," but the more correct translation, in the context of animistic centers of the human body, is "the eyes."[83] This center is the organ of perception while also an organ that performs the basic and simultaneous function of sensation. Both the heart and eyes "unite in order to integrate a complete consciousness that is found in communication with the outside world."[84]

The third most important animistic center was *el* or *elli*; "the liver." This is the organ of vitality and feelings and is associated with the energy needed to make someone strong and brave. The liver in its normal state produced happiness and tranquillity. This was largely due to the unification of feelings and passions and to the elimination of inner struggles among different affective forces. Disunity among the organs was expressed in the liver and would eventually produce emotional conflicts and mental anguish. Conversely,

[d]irecting the forces of the *elli* toward persons or objects provoked desire, which was sometimes manifested in the form of love, sometimes as desire or cupidity. In a parallel fashion, anger and hate were produced in the *elli*, feelings associated with a swollen state. To possess an abundance of this, to have the liver harden, gave vigor and sprightliness to a person. A decrease in its functioning, to the contrary, made its possessor a lazy person.[85]

While this was not an organ with attributes of knowledge, it granted a person vigor necessary to work carefully, intelligently, and diligently. Because it generated passions, its malfunction would result in evil or insanity. On the other hand, its cleanliness would permit a person to have normal feelings including being charitable and sincere.

Corresponding to these animistic centers were entities that gave life to the body. The most important of these was the *tonalli*, a noun derived from the verb *tona*, "to irradiate," and linked to the sun.[86] According to López Austin, *tonalli* has the following contexts in the sources: (a) irradiation; (b) solar heat; (c) summer; (d) day; (e) day sign; (f) the destiny of a person according to the day of their birth; (g) "the soul and spirit"; or (h) something meant for, or the property of, a certain person. The relationship between cosmic forces and the human body was a temporal-solar one. There was a tie between the actions of deities and humans expressed in the regular appearance of the sun.

It was believed that the forces manifested themselves as light-heat and that they were diffused over all the earth's surface, bathing and infiltrating all beings in this intermediate sector. Time and transformation—that is, earthly existence itself—were produced by the interplay of heat-light energy spread over the earth and by the past forces still remaining there. Each day a new force, more vigorous than the ones fading from the present, erupted from the sacred trees, interlacing ties between mythical and human time.[87]

As mentioned earlier, the gods would make their forces reach earth by means of a whirling movement represented by two intertwining bands called *malinalli*, from the verb *malin(a)*: "to twist or wind."[88] The unborn child would receive these irradiations as a divine gift in the form of the breath (*ihiyotl*) of the gods. The whirling movement of these forces was represented as a fiery drill and their circling movement signified descent. During intrauterine life, an infant was provided with its initial irradiation from the lowest of the heavenly levels. Immediately after birth, the child could not be exposed directly to solar rays but, depending on its sex, was dedicated with elements of fire and water.

The portent of a child's birthdate was divined by one who had knowledge of the *tonalpohualli*—the 260-day divinatory calendar. While there is wide speculation about why this 260-day interval was used, the most credible seems to be that it is approximately the time required for the gestation of human children.[89] After birth a child was protected by fire, offered to water, and then given its *tonalli* through naming. Through the water-bathing ceremony, the child became fully human and naming the child was seen as taking *tonalli* from the sun by means of the temporal dedication of their birth day.

One's shadow was specifically linked with a person's *tonalli*. Loss of one's shadow, which was naturally weak in the child and strong in the old, was linked with sickness. The diviner would carefully watch a patient's reflection in water while observing their pulse at the joints.[90] Indeed most diseases were associated with some sort of loss of *tonalli*.[91] This was, however, the natural result of growth. Nail clippings possessed *tonalli* and it was the custom of the Aztecs to offer nail clippings to the *ahuitzotl*, an animal belonging to Tlaloc who was a small dangerous beast, greedy for eyes, teeth, and nails of humans and who lived in the lake in charge of killing those who Tlaloc desired. Hair also possessed *tonalli*, as it was the recipient of energies emanating from the sun while also protecting the loss of *tonalli* from the head. During sex the *tonalli* was interactive between bodies. Sexual excesses, however, were harmful to the *tonalli* and could result in its loss. Specifically, startling people during sex or waking someone suddenly from dreaming could result in excessive loss of *tonalli* and lead to sickness.[92]

While loss of *tonalli* was a natural condition of living, excessive loss of it would result in a diminished vitality of the body. Just as vital energies were given to create earthly existence, these forces would naturally extend from their place of residence (i.e., the body) to the world it inhabits. For example this principle of extension of vital forces from the human body to the world and back was at work in the actions of the farmer and his family as they worked their fields, and when the life of a sacrificial victim was taken by their captor.[93] Extensions of *tonalli*, however, were reciprocal. While human bodies were the result of cosmic emanations, they were not the only ones. Successful life required that there be a balanced and appropriate reciprocity between various beings that inhabited the world.

While human life may be seen, in the Aztec context, as arising from the intersection of vital forces that spread over the earth in helical bands, this was a random event only from the human point of view. Knowing this, the Aztecs would enlist divinatory specialists to discern both the relative strength of *tonalli* forces, and the meaning of these emanations. Bodily sustenance was communicative because it was substantive.

The vessel of *tonalli* was the head and it contained the animating entity of the mind. It would enter the body either through the hair or the fontanel. A second animistic entity was the *teyolia*, which was identified with that part of a person that went to the world of the dead and, since very early colonial times, was identified by indigenous people as *ánima* ("soul" in Spanish). *Teyolia* had its seat in the heart and was the recipient of a divine force.[94] The third animistic entity was the *ihiyotl*, located in the liver. For the ancient as well as contemporary Mesoamericans, however, this entity is more difficult to locate in that it only finds autonomous expression as "night air," or "death air," or when otherwise external to its bodily origin. It is identified by the bad smell of a discharge and associated with the odor of cadavers.[95] *Ihiyotl*, however, was a animistic entity or a person's force tied to the breath of the gods. The breathing-in took place when a child was offered to water. This action would expel bad influences from a newborn's body and cleanse the animistic centers through water before finally inviting in those entities required for human vitality. When breath became deadly, it was primarily an attribute of the liver's condition. When polluted, through the filling and discharging of the gall bladder and the actions of bile in the blood, it could harm other beings. At other levels, the liver was addressed as an important component of other modes of existence. For example *elimiqui(n)* refers to farming the earth but literally means "to injure, or kill, the liver." Although a subsistence activity, farming was also understood as an act of violence on earthly and human organs. Violence expressed the reciprocal nature of sustenance activities.

The correspondence between the head and *tonalli*; the heart and *teyolia*; and the liver and *ihiyotl* also correspond, as discussed earlier, to specific psychic functions. Health required a proper balanced interaction between entities and their animating centers as well as entities and their cosmos. There are several examples of this relationship. *Aompayotl* refers to misfortune but can be translated as a "condition of something outside its place."[96] Prayers to various qualities of the landscape would address their animistic centers and resident entities of the body and cosmos simultaneously. In particular the heart of the earth, mountain, or lake received petitions from the ancient Nahua.

A dramatic symbolic elaboration of the reciprocity of body and cosmos is seen on page one of the *Codex Fejérváry-Mayer*, a fifteenth-century Mixtec codex. This single image dramatizes the unseen forces that animated existence.[97] In the center of this image stands Xiuhteuctli[98] armed with spears and an *atlatl* (spear thrower). Toward him flow four streams of blood from the corners of the cosmos, which animate his life and reciprocate the gift of blood through warfare and sacrifice. In the cardinal directions are pairs of deities who, including Xiuhteuctli, make up the Nine Lords of the Night. Each of these directions is associated with a tree. The top of the image is associated with east because the disk at the base of this tree is the sun in the act of rising over a templelike structure. In the west crouches Tlalteuctli, the earth lord, who swallows the sun at the close of each day. During the course of a single day, the life-and-death drama of the sun is played out in concert with the interaction of cosmic deities whose emanations animate worldly existence.

Aveni examined the calendrical significance of this frontispiece.[99] Along the border of this image are a series of twenty dots in thirteen intervals. These are day signs that add up to the 260 days of the *tonalpohualli* ($20 \times 13 = 260$). Each segment commences with the glyph

2.4. Aztec cosmology, redrawn from the *Codex Fejérváry-Mayer*.

that symbolizes these thirteen-day "weeks." Starting with *cipactli* (alligator), these glyphs proceed alternately through the intercardinal and cardinal directions. The intercardinal points symbolize the extremes of the sun that migrate throughout the year on the horizon north and south through four houses of the sun. "Thus, we have summer solstice sunrise at the upper left, winter solstice sunrise at the upper right, summer solstice sunset at the lower left, and winter solstice sunset at the lower right."[100] Time is thus expressed spatially in this image as embodied in the interaction of cosmic realities. Also depicted at these intercardinal points are body parts shown irradiating vital energies, by means of blood, into the central space: in the east is the hand, in the north the foot, in the west the throat, and in the south the head. Aveni links spatial and temporal realities through ritual actions that also

[61]

incorporate the two yearly calendars (the 260-day divinatory calendar and the 365-day solar year). In effect, the frontispiece of the *Codex Fejérváry-Mayer* symbolized the hidden conditions of existence that animated Aztec existence. Ritual activity, at centers such as the Templo Mayor, unified human qualities of space and time through the engagement and incorporation of these vitalizing actions of the deities. An economy of energetic and physical relationships was arbitrated by means of blood, which acted as the medium of reciprocity. The workings of the cosmos depended on appropriate exchange relationships between beings.

As we have seen, the *tonalli* was connected with specific attributes of time and divination. The *tonalli* was the integrative element that regulated body temperature and general animistic functions, while also being the agent of determining a given human being's fate. Because *tonalli* was acquired, and not the inherent property of living bodies per se, it granted the Aztecs an ability to travel to other areas of the cosmos in dreams. These trips were supplemented by various drugs, which also housed gods. "A drug produced a double effect: it gave shelter to the god contained in the drug within the body of the person ingesting it, and it projected the *tonalli* toward the god's dwelling."[101] Some people possessed a larger degree of *tonalli* than others, indicating their being chosen by a god. These attributes manifested themselves in their bodies. Particular physical "defects" identified certain people as individuals with supernatural powers. The shape of the head denoted valor, for example, and cowlicks were a sign of having been picked by the rain gods.

Interestingly, this cosmic drama was reenacted in the structure of Tenochtitlan, the Aztec city. Physically, it duplicated the cosmic structure. It was an island surrounded by water that was built up, like the *chinampa* fields, from mucking the lake bottom and placing it on a bed of reeds. The ceremonial complex, composed of various temples, was situated in the center of the city. In its center was the Templo Mayor. Four causeways emanated from the center into the four directions, upon which traveled porters and merchants bringing and exchanging goods to and from the periphery. Rituals in the center served to not only invigorate the Aztec city but also to invigorate the periphery by the constant flow of material goods.[102] The physical organization of Tenochtitlan corresponded with an a priori cosmic reality that promoted life and sustained human beings.

Bodily life was an event, or performance, and not an immutable fact of being. Humans were created from the fortunate intersection of vital forces that crisscrossed the earth, having originated with the creative activity of the deities. Indeed, the whole material world was propagated by the activities of unseen beings. Appropriately, the Aztec addressed their conditions of substantive existence through ritual activity. Life could not be sustained by treating beings as discrete entities, but as dynamic forces in time and space. As it was with the body, so it was with the Tlalocan landscape. In the *Codex Fejérváry Mayer* and in the urban layout of Tenochtitlan, emphasis was placed on movement, or *olin*, the fifth age of the Aztecs. Space (or place) and time created the locus and occasion for bodily existence, which was substantiated by cosmic emanations. To extend and revitalize earthly existence, ritual activity was required at particular places and times.[103]

To characterize Aztec religion as primarily an ideology would be misleading. For example, the activity of understanding cosmic forces through divination was a principal feature of many ritual events, yet the primary focus for this activity was not a mental activity but a physical reality. The human body, as a center for engagement with the world, was not just an ideology but an understanding of life based in a material context.

This is not to say, however, that there were not other understandings of bodily existence. As we have seen and will explore further in chapter 7, there were dramatic differences between Aztec and colonial European interpretations of land and body. But to characterize Aztec religion (or religion in general) as ideological (i.e., an attribute of belief) exclusively is to minimize the weight of Mesoamerican religion. This characterization minimizes the pressure that could be exerted by the Aztecs on contemporary religious understandings that tend to be devoid of material necessity. In the interest of promoting a view of Aztec religion that will exert some pressure on our modern understandings, I want, instead, to utilize a methodology of interpretive restraint (*epoché*) from phenomenology rather than to move too quickly to judgment. Framing the body as an ideological construct, rather than as a performative construct, weakens the engagement with indigenous traditions. More care should be taken to utilize the body as a vehicle for interaction with Aztec religion, rather than an instrument for its overdeterminization. This is to acknowledge that understanding the Aztecs is only achieved from one's own cultural context. My intention, however, is to highlight a disjunction between us and them, rather than present an all too simplistic assimilation, in such a way as to impinge upon contemporary understandings of religion and material life.

In the next two chapters, I will explore an indigenous hermeneutics of occupation by examining four ritual descriptions recorded in Nahuatl and dedicated to Tlaloc from the *Florentine Codex*. These are I-Atl cahualo, VI-Etzalcualiztli, XIII-Tepeilhuitl, and XVI-Atemoztli. These rituals satisfy a number of criteria for the purpose of this study. First, they all were specifically dedicated to the *tlaloque*. Second, they all addressed particular landscape referents that focused human action. Third, they were recorded in Nahuatl, which, when translated, gives a fuller sense of the significance of these actions. Fourth, Sahagún's text on these rituals, because of its centrality in Mesoamerican studies, offers a useful point of contrast between the indigenous hermeneutic of occupying the land, which it records, and a colonial hermeneutic of conquest, which it assumes. Care has been taken in chapter 3 to situate these events within the context of other ritual occasions. In chapter 4, however, I leave both the confines of the ritual context and Sahagún's text to articulate more general understandings of the Aztec world from those meanings gleaned from the ritual descriptions.

NOTES

1. This comes from the work of Tim Knab, *Words Great and Small: Sierra Nahuatl Narrative Discourse in Everyday Life*, unpublished manuscript, 1983, which is cited in Johanna Broda, "Templo Mayor as Ritual Space," in *The Great Temple of Tenochtitlan: Center and Periphery in the Aztec World*, edited by Johanna Broda, Davíd Carrasco, and Eduardo Matos Moctezuma (Berkeley: University of California Press, 1987), pp. 195–198. Also see Peter van der Loo, *Codices costumbres continuidad: un estudio de*

la religión Mesoamericana (Leiden, Netherlands: Indiaanse Studies 2, Archeologisch Centrum R.U., 1987), for a description of contemporary understandings of Tlaloc. For van der Loo, the gods of rain and earth constitute a thematic unit among current Mixtec and Nahua people that directly connects to pre-Columbian texts.

2. Probably included are Otomi and Mixtec in particular.

3. As Karttunen says, "The derivation of this name is unclear. The singular form, which is the personal name of one deity, is not related in a regular way to the plural form, which refers to the company of rain gods. The plural form could be based on TLALLOH 'something covered with earth' if geminate reduction were to apply, reducing the LL to L, but the final-C of the singular would remain unaccounted for." Frances Karttunen, *An Analytical Dictionary of Nahuatl* (Austin: University of Texas Press, 1983), p. 276.

4. See Rémi Siméon, *Diccionario de la lengua Nahuatl o Mexicana* (Mexico City: Siglo Veintiuno editores, 1977), pp. 602–603. Also see J. Richard Andrews, *Introduction to Classical Nahuatl*, textbook and workbook (Austin: University of Texas Press, 1975), p. 478.

5. See Fray Bernardino de Sahagún, *Florentine Codex: General History of the Things of New Spain*, 12 books, 13 parts, edited and translated by Arthur J. O. Anderson and Charles E. Dibble, Monographs of the School of American Research, number 14 (Salt Lake City: University of Utah Press, 1951–1982), book 7, p. 21.

6. See Fray Diego Durán, *Book of the Gods and Rites and the Ancient Calendar*, edited and translated by Fernando Horcasitas and Doris Heyden (Norman: University of Oklahoma Press, 1971), p. 154. This translation is interesting in light of a recent discovery of a ceremonial grotto underneath the Pyramid of the Sun at Teotihuacan, the city where Tlaloc made his first iconographical appearance. The ceremonial architecture there is based on subterranean chambers that were the first sites of Tlaloc devotion. See Doris Heyden, "An Interpretation of the Cave Underneath the Pyramid of the Sun in Teotihuacan, Mexico," *American Antiquity* 40, no. 2 (1975): 131–147.

7. The final -*c* as the postposition meaning "in," however, is a postposition that is never compounded with *ohtli*. Thelma Sullivan, "Tlaloc: A New Etymological Interpretation of the God's Name and What It Reveals of His Essence and Nature," *Proceedings of the 40th International Congress of Americanists* 2 (Genoa: Tilgher, 1974): 213.

8. The title of chapter XXIII is "Donde se trata del Dios Tlaloca Tecuhtli, llanado Neptuno, de los Dioses, sus compañeros; y de los errores de estos Indios, acerca de estos Dioses." See Fray Juan de Torquemada, *Monarquía Indiana*, 4 vols. (Mexico City: Editorial Porrúa, 1969), vol. 2, p. 44.

9. I am not marking the long vowels on Nahuatl words in this book. Even though the length of each vowel is critical for translation, in this text I have decided to move toward readability. In my dissertation—*The Matter of Understanding: Ritual Ecology and the Aztec Tlálocán Landscape*, Ph.D. dissertation, University of Chicago, 1992— vowel lengths are marked. For an example of the significance of vowel length, see Karttunen, *An Analytical Dictionary of Nahuatl*, p. 237, for a discussion of *teuctli*, "lord," which is incorrectly spelled *tecutli* or *tecuhtli* in many of the sources.

10. This quote from Torquemada is in Thelma Sullivan, "Tlaloc: A New Etymological Interpretation," p. 213.

11. See Edward Seler, *Gesammelte Abhandlungen zur Amerikanschen Sprach-und Alterhumskunde*, 5 vols. (Graz, Austria: Akademische Druck-und Verlangsanstalt, 1960), vol. 2, p. 443.

12. Pulque is an alcoholic drink derived from the sweet sap of the maguey cactus. This beverage had many important ceremonial uses and was also employed metaphorically to exemplify fruits of the earth. Seler's use of the word has many interesting cultural inflections.

13. See *Códice Borgia*, facsimile, commentary by Eduard Seler, 3 vols. (Mexico City: Fondo de Cultura Económica, 1963), vol. 1, p. 85. According to Seler,

> [e]l vocablo está derivado de tlaloa un verbo que, unido con el pronombre reflexivo, suele usarse, por cierto, en el sentido de "apurarse, correr," pero que propiamente tiene el significado de "brotar." Por lo menos hay que este verbo usado reflexivamente aparece en contextos en que sólo se puede traducir por "brotar."

Also see Maria-France Gueusguin, "Tlaloc 'celui qui fait germer' et sis subordonnés les tlatoque," dissertation for E.P.H.E. (Paris: Institut d'Ethnologie, Museé de l'Homme, microfiche, 1971), for an analysis of texts and iconography of Tlaloc from the perspective of Seler's translation of the name.

14. *Mo-tlalo-t-ehua* is compounded as *mo-*, the third-person singular reflexive pronoun; *tlaloa*, "to run, flee, sprout"; *-ti-*, a ligature joining the two verbs; and *ehua*, "to rise, depart, get up." Although *tlaloa* always occurs with a reflexive object, it is not reflexive in meaning but is actually an intransitive verb. See *Códice Borgia*, vol. 1, p. 85, note 40.

15. Thelma Sullivan, "Tlaloc: A New Etymological Interpretation."

16. In this context there would be no long vowel over the *a*. Tlaloc should have a long *a* following Sullivan's analysis, which features the earth element (*tlalli*) in the deity's name.

17. See Thelma Sullivan, "Tlaloc: A New Etymological Interpretation," p. 215, regarding the importance of the Olmos grammar.

18. Ibid., p. 216.

19. See Angel María Garibay, *Teogonía e historia de los Mexicanos: tres opúscolos del siglo XVI* (Mexico City: Editorial Porrúa, 1965), p. 103. Cited in Sullivan, ibid., p. 216.

20. Thelma Sullivan, "Tlaloc: A New Etymological Interpretation."

21. See Inga Clendinnen, *Aztecs, an Interpretation* (Cambridge: Cambridge University Press, 1991), p. 183.

22. *Códice Chimalpopoca: Anales de Cuauhtitlan y Leyenda de los Soles*, translated by Primo Feliciano Veázquez, edited by Walter Lehmann (Mexico City: Imprenta Universitaria, 1945), p. 339.

23. Kay Read has recently translated this passage, tending to downplay the transforma-

tive aspect to which Thema Sullivan alludes. While the *tlaloque*, in Read's analysis, are described as being of particular colors, as in the various colors of maize, the text seems to clearly indicate that maize, chia, and amaranth are stolen from them. It would seem that the *tlaloque* at once embody characteristics of foodstuffs as well as own them (personal communication).

24. See Miguel Covarrubias, *Indian Art of Mexico and Central America* (New York: Knopf, 1957). In figure 22, he graphically charts the relationship of Mesoamerican rain gods. Also see Peter T. Furst, "Jaguar Baby or Toad Mother: A New Look at an Old Problem in Olmec Iconography," in *The Olmec and Their Neighbors: Essays in Memory of Matthew W. Stirling*, edited by Elizabeth P. Benson (Washington, DC: Dumbarton Oaks, 1981), pp. 149–162. Others have suggested that what has been consistently viewed as the "baby jaguar," particularly regarding the giant basalt heads, are actually proof of African influence in the New World previous to the colonial period. See Ivan van Sertima, *They Came Before Columbus* (New York: Random House Inc., 1976).

25. See Cecilia F. Klein, "Who Was Tlaloc?" *Journal of Latin American Lore* 6, no. 2 (1980): 155–204, for a detailed account of the chronology of Tlaloc iconography that, in her hands, achieves a complexity not attained by his presence in the written sources. Also see Esther Pasztory, "The Aztec Tlaloc: God of Antiquity," in *Smoke and Mist: Mesoamerican Studies in Memory of Thelma D. Sullivan*, edited by J. Kathryn Josserand and Karen Dakin (Oxford: B.A.R. International Studies, 402[i], 1988), pp. 289–327.

26. See Hattula Moholy-Nagy, "A Tlaloc Stela from Tikal," *Espedition* 4, no. 2 (1962): 27.

27. Lindsay Jones, *Twin City Tales: A Hermeneutical Reassessment of Tula and Chichen Itzá* (Niwot: University Press of Colorado, 1995).

28. See Friedrich Katz, *The Ancient American Civilizations*, translated by K. M. Lois Simpson (New York: Preager Publishing, 1972), pp. 43–55.

29. See Rene Millon, *Urbanization at Teotihuacan, Mexico: The Teotihuacan Map* (Austin: University of Texas Press, 1973).

30. For a more in-depth analysis of this orientation compared with other Mesoamerican sites, see Anthony F. Aveni, "Concepts of Positional Astronomy Employed in Ancient Mesoamerican Architecture," in *Native American Astronomy*, edited by Anthony F. Aveni (Austin: University of Texas Press, 1977), pp. 3–19. In the present context, the diagram of Teotihuacan and its orientational scheme (figure 2.2) is very helpful. Also see Aveni's discussion of Teotihuacan and the importance and mechanics of the Pleiades in Anthony F. Aveni, *Sky Watchers of Ancient Mexico* (Austin: University of Texas Press, 1980), pp. 222–226 and 30–35. Also see page 223 for a good diagram that helps illustrate the present discussion.

31. There is a wide spectrum of opinion about the precise function of the "pecked circle." According to Aveni, opinions among specialists vary from their being ceremonial markings done in ritual, to game boards, to architectural benchmarks, to the esoteric designs of ancient, pre-Columbian astrologers, or any combination thereof (personal communication). Aveni has convincingly discussed the cosmological significance of the quadripartite structure of the pecked circle and how the count of indentations, in most cases, closely matches the division of various Mesoamerican calendar counts. See Anthony F. Aveni, Horst Hartung, and B. Buckingham, "The Pecked Cross

Symbol in Ancient Mesoamerica," *Science* 202 (1978): 267–279; and Anthony F. Aveni and Horst Hartung, "New Observations of the Pecked Cross Petroglyph," *Lateinamericka Studien* 10 (1982): 25–41.

32. A heliacal rising is defined by Aveni as "[t]he annual reappearance of a bright star in the predawn sky." Aveni, *Sky Watchers of Ancient Mexico*, p. 109.

33. The *-can* is a locative suffix denoting the place of Tlaloc both physically and mythically. It can also refer to the temple of the deity. See Esther Pasztory, "The Tlalocan Complex," in *The Murals of Tepantitla, Teotihuacan* (New York: Garland Publishing, Inc., 1976), pp. 58–103, for a description and analysis of these murals.

34. See Esther Pasztory, *The Iconography of the Teotihuacan Tlaloc*, Studies in Pre-Columbian Art and Archaeology (Washington, DC: Dumbarton Oaks, 1974), vol. 15, p. 3.

35. Ibid., p. 18.

36. This is known as Tlalteuctli in the Aztec context and is the embodiment of creation in the *Histoire du Mexique*. See Garibay, *Teogonía e historia de los Mexicanos*.

37. See Pasztory, *The Murals of Tepantitla, Teotihuacan*, p. 19.

38. Rubén Cabrera Castro, Saburo Sugiyama, and George Cowgill, "The Templo de Quetzalcoatl Project at Teotihuacan, a Preliminary Report," *Ancient Mesoamerica*, 2 (1991): 77–92.

39. These investigators hypothesize that the interior burial chambers may have contained the remains of a person or persons of high status, while military retainers were placed in burials around the periphery facing outward, as if to guard the interior contents of the temple.

40. Doris Heyden, "An Interpretation of the Cave Underneath the Pyramid of the Sun in Teotihuacan, Mexico," *American Antiquity* 40, no. 2 (1975): 131–147.

41. Philip P. Arnold, "Parallel Consumptive Cosmologies," in *Mesoamerica's Classic Heritage: Teotihuacán to the Aztecs*, edited by Davíd Carrasco, Lindsay Jones, and Scott Sessions (Niwot: University Press of Colorado, 1999).

42. Alfredo López Austin, Leonardo López-Luján, and Saburo Sugiyama, "The Temple of Quetzalcoatl at Teotihuacan, Its Possible Ideological Significance," *Ancient Mesoamerica* 2 (1991): 93–105.

43. Saburo Sugiyama, "Worldview Materialized in Teotihuacan, Mexico," *Latin American Antiquity* 4, no. 2 (1993): 103–129.

44. Fray Alonso de Molina, *Vocabulario en Lengua Castellana y Mexicana y Mexicana y Castellana* (Mexico City: Editorial Porrúa, 1977), pp. 58v and 59r. For a discussion of time and social organization, see Kay Almere Read, *Time and Sacrifice in the Aztec Cosmos* (Bloomington: Indiana University Press, 1998).

45. Oral presentations by Eduardo Matos Moctezuma and Linda Manzanilla at Teotihuacan, Mexico, February 1995.

46. See Johanna Broda, "Las fiestas Aztecas de los dioses de la luvia: una reconstruccíon según las fuentes del siglo XVI," *Revista Española de Antropología Americana* 6 (1971): 245–327. See also Broda's, "El culto Mexica de los cerros y del agua," *Multidiscipline* 3, no. 7 (1982): 45–56; and "Ciclos agrícolas en el culto: Una problema de la correlación del calendario Mexica," in *Calendars in Mesoamerica and Peru: Native American Computations of Time*, edited by Anthony F. Aveni and Gordon Brotherston (Oxford: B.A.R. International Series 174, 1983), pp. 145–164.

47. The term *Chichimecatl* refers to a person from one of the many groups of northern Mexico who were considered related to the Aztecs, because they migrated from that area. In Nahuatl, however, *Chichimecatl* is used as a general term to signify both barbarism and "noble savage." Karttunen, *An Analytical Dictionary of Nahuatl*, p. 48.

48. This division can also be methodologically linked to Smith's use of the terms "locative" and "utopian" in the history of religion. See Jonathan Z. Smith, "Earth and Gods," in *Map Is Not Territory: Studies in the History of Religions* (Leiden, Netherlands: E.J. Brill, 1978), p. 128.

49. See Jacques Soustelle, *La pensee cosmologique des anciens Mexicains, représentation de monde et de l'espace* (Paris: Hermann & Cie, 1940), p. 49.

50. These fir branches were also collected at various times of the year as penitential offerings to Tlaloc. See chapter 3.

51. Among the contemporary Nahua of the municipality of Ixhuatlán in Vera Cruz, shamans still communicate with the rain dwarfs, who appear as elderly little men wearing fine black clothing with rubber sleeves. They carry walking sticks, swords, or chains in their hands. As clouds travel from the Gulf of Mexico inland, they strike and rattle their implements.

> The rain dwarfs appear to be metaphors for the dark clouds that blow in off the Gulf at the start of the rainy season. As the clouds rise to surmount the Sierra they cool and drop their precious moisture. Several people told me that the pilhuehuentsitsij are black, "like the clouds."

From Alan R. Sandstrom, *Corn Is Our Blood: Culture and Ethnic Identity in a Contemporary Aztec Indian Village* (Norman: University of Oklahoma Press, 1991), p. 250.

52. Broda's examination of this important text is distinct from its use by Sullivan. Broda emphasizes the contractual nature of human and *tlaloque* relations expressed in this story. See *Códice Chimalpopoca*, translated by Primo Feliciano Veázquez.

53. While many translate this as "the pimply one," Karttunen indicates that the condition of this deity is much more serious than a case of acne. Karttunen, *An Analytical Dictionary of Nahuatl*, p. 159.

54. Toltecs of the city of Tollan were a post-Classic civilization in the central Mexican region (900 C.E. to 1150 C.E.). Much of Aztec mythology originates from this civilization. Key figures include Quetzalcoatl and Tezcatlipoca and the antagonistic relationship between them. They acted as mythic prototypes for priest and warrior classes among the Aztecs. See Davíd Carrasco, *Quetzalcoatl and the Irony of Empire: Myths and Prophecies in the Aztec Tradition* (Chicago: University of Chicago Press, 1982); Miguel León Portilla, *Aztec Thought and Culture*, translated by Jack Emory Davis (Norman:

University of Oklahoma Press, 1963); Michel Graulich, *Quetzalcoatl ye el espejismo de Tollan* (Antwerp: Instituut voor Amerikanistiek v.z.w., 1988); and Burr C. Brundage, *The Fifth Sun: Aztec Gods, Aztec World* (Austin: University of Texas Press, 1975).

55. Sahagún, *Florentine Codex*, book 11, p. 247. Interestingly, the passage goes on to mention that rivers run from Tlalocan from the goddess Chalchihuitlicue, "she of precious green stone skirt," probably referring to the mountain slopes of evergreen forest that skirt the mountainsides. This passage expresses the androgynous nature of the deity.

56. For the most complete and authoritative discussion of the Tlaloc complex, see Henry B. Nicholson, "Religion in Pre-Hispanic Central Mexico," in *Handbook of Middle American Indians: Guide to the Ethnohistorical Sources*, edited by R. Wachope (Austin: University of Texas Press, 1971), vol. 11, pp. 414–420.

57. The Lake of Mexico was actually a system of five lakes, of both salty and sweet water, that extended throughout the Valley of Mexico. See the discussion of the lakes and their significance in chapter 3.

58. This is translated from the Nahuatl by Dibble and Anderson using Sahagún's Spanish gloss as their guide. Sahagún, *Florentine Codex*, book 1, p. 22.

59. According to Siméon, *Diccionario de la lengua Nahuatl*, p. 766, *Xilonen* is divided into *xilo-tl*, "tender ear of green maize," and *nene-tl*, which according to Karttunen, *An Analytical Dictionary of Nahuatl*, p. 168, translates as either "female genitals" or "image/doll." She goes on to say, "Since the two senses of this item are at some distance from each other and both distant from the senses of the attestations, it is possible that more than one lexical item is represented here and they may differ phonologically." Also see Karttunen, p. 325, for long vowels on *xilo-tl*. Both of these senses of maize (reproductive and representative) were significant during the rituals.

60. Among the Nahua today there is still a pulque-making industry. On 22 June 1989 I had the opportunity to visit Santa Catarina del Monte and San Miguel Tlaxpan with Robert Bye and Edelmira Linares, ethnobotanists from Jardín Botanico, Universidad Nacional Autonoma de México. We visited a family of *pulqueros* who had been harvesting their maguey fields for generations. We were introduced to three generations of harvesters, their techniques, and their home brew.

61. In the Introduction to *The Great Temple of Tenochtitlan: Center and Periphery in the Aztec World* (Berkeley: University of California Press, 1987, p.1), Johanna Broda, Davíd Carrasco, and Eduardo Matos Moctezuma graphically portray the events and significance of this discovery and excavation for Mexicans:

> In the early morning hours of 21 February 1978, electrical workers laying down lines behind the Cathedral of Mexico City uncovered the edges of a huge round stone with unusual carvings on it. When archaeologists from the Instituto Nacional de Antropología e Historia (INAH) visited the site and made a preliminary excavation, they realized that a major piece of Aztec sculpture had been found. Their excitement was enhanced by the fact that this stone, depicting the ritually dismembered body of the goddess Coyolxauhqui, was the most significant Aztec monument to be discovered since 1790, when the now famous Aztec Calendar Stone was

unearthed several blocks from the site. It appeared that the discovery signified more than simply another addition to the heavy, awesome collection of monuments in the National Museum. This discovery hinted of a new era in both public awareness and scholarly research regarding Aztec religion and society. Further excavation of the immediate area uncovered six rich ritual offertory caches containing statues of gods, human skulls decorated with obsidian eyes, ancient masks, and sea shells. It had been known that this was the site of the Templo Mayor (Great Temple) of Tenochtitlan, but previous excavations had barely touched the corner and fringes of the ceremonial precinct. The astonishing richness and significance of this discovery rekindled interest in the Templo Mayor and the ancient capital, and within a month a major excavation of the shrine, Proyecto Templo Mayor, was ordered by the president of Mexico, Miguel López Portillo. Since February 1978 Eduardo Matos Moctezuma has served as general coordinator of the project, and the excavation was successfully concluded in November 1982.

62. Broda elects to use the term "cosmovision" borrowed from the common Spanish and German usage. As she says, it "denotes the structured view in which the ancient Mesoamericans combined their notions of cosmology relating to time and space into a systematic whole. This term is thus somewhat more specific than the English terms 'cosmology' and 'worldview.' " "Templo Mayor as Ritual Space," p. 108. Her usage of this term suggests a more narrow field of application than cosmology due to its being more fixed to a specific cultural context with more directly traceable functional characteristics. She first defined her methodological approach, and the term "cosmovision," in her article "Astronomy, *Cosmovisión*, and Ideology of Pre-Hispanic Mesoamerica," in *Ethnoastronomy and Archaeoastronomy in the American Tropics*, edited by Anthony F. Aveni and Gary Urton (New York: *Annals of the New York Academy of Sciences* no. 385, 1982), pp. 81–110.

63. See Eduardo Matos Moctezuma, "The Templo Mayor of Tenochtitlan, History and Interpretation," in *The Great Temple of Tenochtitlan: Center and Periphery in the Aztec World*, edited by Johanna Broda, Davíd Carrasco, and Eduardo Matos Moctezuma (Berkeley: University of California Press, 1987), pp. 15–60, for a complete catalog of these offering boxes. Also see Debra Nagao, *Mexica Buried Offerings: A Historical and Contextual Analysis* (Oxford: B.A.R. International Series 235, 1985), for an overview of Mexican burial offerings as well as an analysis of burials at the Templo Mayor.

64. A "philosophy of nature" assumes that the Tlaloc cult was primarily an ideological complex. This study attempts to depart from this view by focusing on the *practice* of hermeneutics. See Johanna Broda, "Geography, Climate, and the Observation of Nature in Pre-Hispanic Mesoamerica," in *The Imagination of Matter: Religion and Ecology in Mesoamerican Traditions*, edited by Davíd Carrasco (Oxford: B.A.R. International Series 515, 1989), pp. 139–153.

65. See López Luján's *The Offerings of the Templo Mayor of Tenochtitlan*, translated by Bernard R. Ortiz de Montellano and Thelma Ortiz de Montellano (Niwot: University Press of Colorado, 1994), pp. 144–145. Mircea Eliade also remarked that offerings found at the Templo Mayor constituted a language of the sacred during a visit to the Mesoamerican Archive and Research Project in Boulder in 1984 (personal communication).

66. Including Xiuhteuctli-Huehueteotl, the "old god of fire, turquoise and the year."

67. "And in order for it to rain, the god of water [Tlalteuctli, or Tlaloc] created many tiny helpers, who were in the rooms of the house [Tlalocan]. They have *alcancías* [clay money boxes] in which they carry water from the barreños in one hand, and sticks in the other. When the Rain God orders them to rain somewhere, they take their containers and sticks and shower down the water as they are ordered. When they break the container with their sticks, it thunders and when there is lightning, it had been held inside or was a part of the water container." In Garibay, *Tegonía e historia de los mexicanos*, p. 221.

68. López Luján, *The Offerings of the Templo Mayor of Tenochtitlan*, p. 221.

69. Ibid., p. 206. Evidence for famine comes from the condition of bones in Offering 48. Twenty-one of the skeletons (50 percent) had signs of hyperostosis, a defect caused by malnutrition, and five others seem to exhibit birth defects (p. 200).

70. Broda, "Templo Mayor as Ritual Space," p. 101.

71. *teoatl* means "divine" or "god water."

72. "Sky" or "heavenly water."

73. See Sahagún, *Florentine Codex*, book 11, p. 247.

74. See Broda, "Templo Mayor as Ritual Space," p. 105.

75. For example, according to M. Merleau-Ponty's *Phenomenology of Perception* (London: Routledge and Kegan Paul, 1962), p. xix: "Because we are in the world, we are *condemned to meaning*, and we cannot do or say anything without its acquiring a name in history."

76. See Lawrence E. Sullivan, "Body Works: Knowledge of the Body in the Study of Religion," *History of Religions* 30, no. 1 (1990): 86–99, for a review of the contemporary studies of religion and the body. Peter Brown's book, *The Cult of the Saints: Its Rise and Function in Latin Christianity* (Chicago: University of Chicago Press, 1981), explores how body parts of the "glorious dead" in early Christian communities acted as focal points upon which the survival of the early church was based. Relics, into our present area, have acted as a medium of exchange in Christendom. Also his *The Body and Society: Men, Women, and Sexual Renunciation in Early Christianity* (New York: Columbia University Press, 1988) examines the role of monastic aestheticism as a paradigm for Christian identity and bodily life. Ioan P. Couliano examines the understanding of the interaction of bodies and imagination in his *Eros and Magic in the Renaissance*, translated by Margaret Cook (Chicago: University of Chicago Press, 1987). The Renaissance sciences of the imagination embraced prepsychological realities that promoted an investigation of corporeal reality through imaginative constructs. Gary L. Ebersole, *Ritual Poetry and the Politics of Death in Early Japan* (Princeton, NJ: Princeton University Press, 1989), investigates the place of funerary ritual orations in cultural and social formation. Michel Perrin, in his *The Way of Dead Indians: Guajiro Myths and Symbols*, translated by Michael Fineberg and Michel Perrin (Austin: University of Texas Press, 1987), takes a look at Guajiro burial practices and how ritual activities for the dead correspond to a mythic landscape. Ann Grodzins Gold, in *Fruitful Journeys: The Ways of Rajasthani Pilgrims* (Berkeley: University of

California Press, 1987), has likewise written about cults of the dead among contemporary village Hindus who make pilgrimages to "sink flowers" (bones of the dead) in the Ganges. Francis Zimmerman, in *The Jungle of the Aroma of Meats: An Ecological Theme in Hindu Medicine* (Berkeley: University of California Press, 1987), has examined medieval Hindu curing practices as recorded in the Charaka-Samhita, which links bodily healing directly to ecological realities of the various environments throughout the subcontinent. Joseph W. Bastien's study of the Aymara of Bolivia, *Mountain of the Condor: Metaphor and Ritual in an Andean Ayllu* (Prospect Heights, IL: Waveland Press, Inc., 1978), proceeds from a basic mountain-body metaphor that renders occupation of the Andes landscape meaningfully and physically possible. This metaphoric model is also utilized in healing activities by traditional practitioners (Bastien, "Qollahuaya-Andean Body Concepts: A Topographical-Hydraulic Model of Physiology," *American Anthropology* 87 [1985]: 595–611). Philosophically, Yuasa Yasuo's *The Body: Toward an Eastern Mind-Body Theory*, edited by Thomas P. Kasulis, translated by Nagatomo Shigenori and Thomas P. Kasulis (Albany: State University of New York Press, 1987), is a challenge to phenomenological schools of thought by integrating traditional Japanese notions of praxis into the process of reflection.

77. According to López Austin, these bands are pairs of natural opposites. See Alfredo López Austin, *The Human Body and Ideology: Concepts of the Ancient Nahuas*, 2 volumes, translated by Thelma and Bernard Ortiz de Montellano (Salt Lake City: University of Utah Press, 1988), vol. 1, p. 59. Also see Jill Leslie McKeever Furst, *The Natural History of the Soul in Ancient Mexico* (New Haven, CT: Yale University Press, 1995), for a view that emphasizes the soul's interconnections with the natural world.

78. López Austin, *The Human Body and Ideology*, p. 60.

79. Ibid., p. 163. López Austin adds that among some contemporary Nahua people this number is expanded to thirteen by adding two ear passages, two armpits, the urinary tract, and the fontanel. The connection between bodily design and temporal origination is a significant one, taken up in more detail later. See Elizabeth Boone, "Migration Histories as Ritual Performance," in *To Change Place: Aztec Ceremonial Landscapes*, edited by Davíd Carrasco (Niwot: University Press of Colorado, 1991), pp. 121–151.

80. As Sahagún says, "Blood . . . our gushing forth, our growth, our life is blood . . . thick, fat, animating, our life; it reddens, moistens, drenches, fills all the flesh with mud, it gives it growth, it surges to the surface, it covers people with earth . . . it strengthens people, it fortifies people greatly." Quoted in López Austin, *The Human Body and Ideology*, vol. 1, p. 168.

81. Ibid., p. 173.

82. Ibid., p. 190. Among contemporary Otomí, the heart is also seen as the animistic center of the body. Called *mbui*, it is located between the heart and stomach and is the seat of vital energies associated with the emotions, which in the Aztec case is associated primarily with the liver. See Jacques Galinier, *Pueblos de la Sierra Madre: Etnografía de communidad Otomí* (Mexico City: Instituto Nacional Indigenista, número 17, 1983), pp. 441–442.

83. The translation of *in ixtli in yolloti* has been given by Garibay and León-Portilla as "face and heart," referring to a human being while emphasizing his animistic life.

López Austin, however, translates this as "the eyes, the heart," which is linked directly to allusions of sensation and perception.

84. López Austin, *The Human Body and Ideology*, vol. 1, p. 197.

85. Ibid., p. 192.

86. Galinier reports that *tona* is likewise an important component of the soul among the Otomí. He goes on to say, however, that they make a clear distinction between *tona* and *nahual*, as does López Austin for the Aztec. See Galinier, *Pueblos de la Sierra Madre*, p. 431.

87. See López Austin, *The Human Body and Ideology*, vol. 1, p. 205.

88. See Karttunen, *An Analytical Dictionary of Nahuatl*, p. 134.

89. It is Aveni's contention that the human gestation period, combined with other climatological and celestial cycles, offers one of the most compelling justifications for the 260-day *tonalpohualli* (personal communication). Also see Peter T. Furst, "Human Biology and the Origin of the 260-Day Sacred Almanac: The Contribution of Leonhard Schultze Jena (1872–1955)," in *Symbol and Meaning Beyond a Closed Community: Essays in Mesoamerican Ideas*, edited by Gary H. Gossen (Albany: State University of New York Press, 1986), pp. 69–76.

90. Among the Maya of Momostenango, Guatemala, "shamans" or "priests" learn to read signals of lightning that runs through their blood, tissue, and muscles. This corresponds to the actions of sheet lightning over the lakes at the four corners of the world. Divination takes place at several different earth shrines, or earth openings, during which the diviner feels their pulse, and also that of the patient's, to interpret it as a message of the movement of lightning in the blood. "As one priest-shaman explained it, 'These shrines are like a book where everything—all births, marriages, deaths, successes, and failures—is written down.' " See Barbara Tedlock, *Time and the Highland Maya* (Albuquerque: University of New Mexico Press, 1982), p. 80. Also see chapter 3, "Shamanic Priests and Priestly Shamans," and chapter 6, "The Blood Speaks," of the same volume.

91. There have been some significant advances in our contemporary understanding of Aztec medical practices. Using the work of López Austin, Bernard R. Ortiz de Montellano has classified herbs used specifically for illness sent by Tlaloc ("Las hierbas de Tláloc," *Estudios de cultura Náhuatl* 14 [1980]: 287–314) as well as tying basic Aztec concepts of physiology to cosmological realities ("The Body, Ethics and Cosmos: Aztec Physiology," in *Imagination of Matter: Religion and Ecology in Mesoamerican Traditions*, edited by Davíd Carrasco [Oxford: B.A.R. International Series 515, 1989], pp. 191–209). See also his *Aztec Medicine, Health, and Nutrition* (New Brunswick: Rutgers University Press, 1990), which combines his own mastery of biological and chemical attributes of plants and the body with ethnohistorical and religious texts.

92. Some women were known to use the concoction *macacoatl*, which was taken from the steeping of snake parts. A man who drank this would then be driven to sexual relations with four to ten women, then die of being too dried up of all his vital juices. See Clendinnen, *Aztecs, an Interpretation*, p. 167.

93. The principle of energetic relations is the central organizing feature of Christian Duverger's work. His theories of cosmic entropy have been used in an analysis of the

Mesoamerican ball game and human sacrifice. See his *L'Èsprit du Jeu chez les Aztèques* (Paris: Mouton Èditeur, 1978) and *La flor letal: Economía del sacrificio Azteca*, translated by Juan José Utrilla (Mexico City: Fondo de Cultura Económica, 1983).

94. Among contemporary Nahuas, "heart" is expressed by the term *yol, yuhlu*, or *yoll(o)*, or *ánima*, or *alma* in Spanish. Among the contemporary Tzotzil Maya, the equivalent is *ch'ulel*, which encompasses both the Nahua *tonalli*, as that which travels to the outside, and the *teyolia*, which is seated in the heart and does not leave the body while living but after death goes to another world. See López Austin, *The Human Body and Ideology*, vol. 1, p. 230 and, in particular, p. 429, note 123.

95. Among contemporary Indian people, the negative emanations in the form of bad air (*mal aire*) are usually associated with dead bodies or contact with the dead. See Hugo G. Nutini, *Todos Santos in Rural Tlaxcala: A Syncretic, Expressive, and Symbolic Analysis of the Cult of the Dead* (Princeton, NJ: Princeton University Press, 1988), p. 35. Among the Otomí, *aire malo* is also associated with the earth spirits and the wind that comes out of caves. See Galinier, *Pueblos de la Sierra Madre*, p. 445. Similarly, among the Nahua of Vera Cruz, wind spirits are the cause of disease-causing illness. See Sandstrom, *Corn Is Our Blood*, pp. 321–322.

96. López Austin, *The Human Body and Ideology*, vol. 1, p. 347.

97. Ibid., p. 346. According to López Austin, the ancient Nahuas created a language for addressing the hidden forces upon which life was substantively and meaningfully predicated. This was called *nahuallatolli*, or "the language of the hidden," to communicate with those beings whose presence was imperceptible but real. *Nahuallatolli* was also used in the day-to-day offences of humans against other beings. The example given is of a person who chops down a tree then asks for its forgiveness.

98. Etymological interpretations vary greatly with regard to Xiuhteuctli. *Xihu(i)-tl* can either mean "year," "grass," "precious green stone" (with the particular association to heat), or "comet." Generally, scholars translate this god's name as "fire lord," with some preferring "old lord." Aveni translates it as "celestial fire god," in *Sky Watchers of Ancient Mexico*, p. 157, which corresponds with my translation of "year lord."

99. Anthony Aveni, "The Aztec City and the Sky," in *Conversations with Anthony Aveni: Archaeoastronomy and the History of Religions*, edited by Davíd Carrasco, Philip Arnold, Lawrence Desmond, and Rebecca Herr (Boulder, CO: Mesoamerican Archive and Research Project Working Papers, no. 1, 1985), pp. 3–4.

100. Aveni, *Sky Watchers of Ancient Mexico*, pp. 156–157.

101. López Austin, *The Human Body and Ideology*, vol. 1, p. 358.

102. Davíd Carrasco, "Templo Mayor: The Aztec Vision of Place," *Religion* 11 (1981): 257–297.

103. Davíd Carrasco has described the reinvigoration of the cosmos through human sacrifices performed at the Templo Mayor as "world making," "world centering," and "world renewing." See his *Religions of Mesoamerica: Cosmovision and Ceremonial Centers* (San Francisco: Harper & Row, 1990), pp. 19–23.

3 Rituals to Tlaloc

This chapter will primarily focus on four descriptions of ritual practices to Tlaloc as described and recorded by Sahagún in the *Florentine Codex*. These four events took place during the agricultural calendar year, which was composed of eighteen twenty-day "months" and addressed the "hidden" yet substantive conditions of human existence.[1] Tlalocan was intimately involved with particular material manifestations (wood and its products, water, birds, rain, plant life, etc.) that oriented Aztec ritual actions. They actively sought to engage the worldly phenomena that were associated with Tlaloc in order to secure connections, on the one hand, between seen and unseen realities (and therefore the underlying basis of material existence); and, on the other hand, with places that meaningfully oriented their occupation of the Valley of Mexico.

There were at least two important dimensions in rituals to Tlaloc: first, an active engagement with the substantive conditions of life; and, second, the anthropological dimension of articulating an orientation for a meaningful occupation of that world. Both dimensions were embodied by Tlaloc. An Aztec understanding of the Valley of Mexico was promoted by a performative articulation of their place in a participatory cosmos.[2]

Nine of the eighteen monthly festivals[3] were directly associated with rain deities. A tenth, XIV-Quecholli ("sweeping neck bird of red feathers"),[4] was also associated with the mountain cult, which was also concerned with a historical geography of the Aztec past. The nine festivals were I-Atl cahualo ("water left"), II-Tlacaxipehualiztli ("human flaying"), III-Tozoztontli ("small vigil"), IV-Huei tozoztli ("great vigil"), VI-Etzalcualiztli ("eating bean stew"), VII-Teucilhuitontli ("small festival of the lords"), VIII-Huei teucilhuitl ("great festival of the lords"), XIII-Tepeilhuitl ("mountain festival"), XVI-Atemoztli ("water descends"), and XVIII-Izcalli ("this house").[5] Because four of these ceremonies as described in Sahagún deal directly with the *tlaloque* and have a geographical emphasis (I-Atl cahualo, VI-Etzalcualiztli, XIII-Tepeilhuitl, and XVI-Atemoztli), the following discussion of Tlaloc rituals will focus on these monthly feasts.[6] The Nahuatl used to describe the ceremonies approximates an Aztec understanding of their relationship to the Valley of Mexico.

The entire *Florentine*, including ritual descriptions from Book II, were skillfully translated into English over a period of thirty years by Dibble and Anderson. While this has made the *Florentine* available to English speakers, it is difficult to get a deeper understanding of the rituals by just reading translations of the Nahuatl.[7] Therefore, to revivify a sense of the various meanings of these rituals, I have elected to retranslate the ceremonies and to keep as close to the sense of the Nahuatl as possible.[8] What follows is an account of the events taken from the Nahuatl in the *Florentine*. This chapter is an examination of the textual description of each of the four rituals. This will help to clarify the sequence of events, the various focal points of the rituals, and some of the context in which the rituals took place. In chapter 4, I will widen the scope of the analysis to include other ecological and archaeological materials and then discuss the rituals in relationship to landscape phenomena.

I-ATL CAHUALO—WATER LEFT; DROUGHT

As its name suggests, I-Atl cahualo was a ritual that addressed drought. Its other name, Quahuitl ehua, "raising up poles," refers to staffs of paper banners raised on houses and hilltops during this festival. This indicated that sacrifices of children, considered the most precious offering, were being performed at specific points in the valley. Children were given as gifts to the *tlaloque* in order that proper amounts of rain would be released from the interior of the mountains.[9]

The ritual of Atl cahualo proceeded primarily with reference to well-defined ceremonial places. At specific spots in the landscape, offerings were given to Tlaloc in various forms. It was the correspondence between these offerings and the places that oriented the action described in the *Florentine*.

The condition for Atl cahualo, and hence its name, was drought; the time of year when the water had left the earth. Poles raised during

3.1. I-Atl cahualo, redrawn from the *Códice Matritense del Real Palacio*.

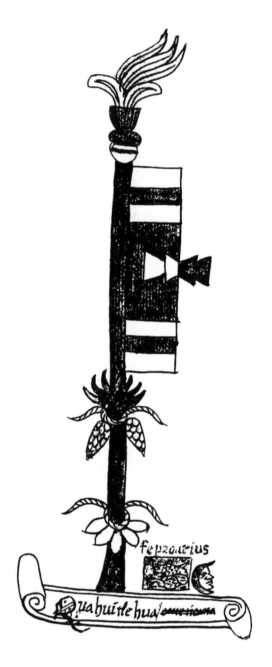

3.2. I-Atl cahualo/Quahuitl ehua, redrawn from the *Tovar Calendar*, Juan de Tovar.

the ceremonies were decorated with paper banners spotted with rubber. The festivities that were directed to the *tlaloque* occurred during the first half of the month (ten days) and continued until the presentations of captives and sacrifices commenced, thus associating it with the second month, Tlacaxipehualiztli.[10] Some sources indicate that child sacrifices to Tlaloc started before Atl cahualo and continued throughout the next several months until the end of the drought.[11]

Sacrificial offerings were referred to as "debt payments." *Nextlahualiztli* means "someone's debt payment," which, according to López Austin and Dibble and Anderson, was the most often used metaphor for human sacrificial offering.[12] Implied in this understanding of sacrifices to Tlaloc was that these gifts were payment for "goods" received and that human life (or blood) was the medium of exchange. The concept of "debt payment" to Tlaloc suggests that there was a necessary reciprocity of relations between the deity and the Aztecs, a reciprocity that was substantiated and promoted through the course of I-Atl cahualo. An Aztec understanding of debt, however, cannot be equated with a profit-based economic model. In a sacrificial context, the "debt" is the gift, or an understanding that human survival is dependent on an appropriate reciprocal relation with the deity. A monetary economic structure does not fit this sense of sacrifice.

People would "pay the debt" to Tlaloc on mountaintops and transform their offerings into paper streamers. The children sacrificed were referred to as "human paper streamers," and, according to Dibble and Anderson, some paper streamers may actually have been surmounted by a representation of a human head symbolizing the children.[13] This is the only place in the *Florentine Codex* where human sacrifice is referred to as "human paper streamers."[14] A correspondence between the life of the sacrificial children and the paper streamers was emphasized. The papers themselves were spattered with rubber and fastened to long poles called *cuenmantli*, or "poles of worked land." The *cuenmantli* were freshly cut and had sprouts, probably in groups of three, distributed up the pole. These displayed the signs of life and were explicitly connected with the sacrificial children and the upcoming planting season. Moreover, the sacrifices were given to the *tlaloque* at seven particular places in the landscape.

The criteria for choosing children are difficult to determine exactly. They were referred to as being precious or costly. While it has been written that they were slave children selected for the Tlaloc sacrifice, it is also possible that these were children of the nobility, or, perhaps, that they achieved a noble status due to their being chosen. They always had two cowlicks that, according to Nagao, represented both the horns of the *tlaloque* and the mountains in which they resided.[15] López Austin links cowlicks to an abundance of *tonalli*, which was stored in the head (as grain was stored in their granaries called *cuezcomatl*) and would be released with sacrifice. According to the *Leyenda de los Soles*, the *tlaloque* were the original owners of maize.[16] Indeed all of the staples for human subsistence were stolen from Tlaloc by Nanahuatl.

Another criteria for choosing the children was that their day-sign be good. As discussed in the previous chapter, orientation within the cycle of the solar year was critical for understanding each human's place both cosmologically and socially. *Qualli*, in this case, could translate as good, meaning comestible, or "good to eat." The children who were transformed into nobility, fertility, landscape, etc., became food for the *tlaloque*. As the text says, "The *tlaloque* happily received them and were pleased and contented with the offering."

At each person's home, at the *calmecatl* (or men's houses), and on the major temples of the *calpolli* (barrios of the city), poles with paper streamers were raised. In addition to their being raised at the actual site of offering, various other significant communities would thus acknowledge their connection with the sacrificial children. During the ritual, various places were linked to each other through the significance of raising the poles.

Seven sites are mentioned as the places where sacrifices were made. First was Quauhtepec, "tree mountain place." The name of the male child who died there was Quauhtepetl, or his name corresponded with the place where he was sacrificed. His paper costume was black or dark green. The second was called Yohualtecatl, "night dweller," which was also the name of the male child who died at this place. His costume was black-and-red striped, which symbolized sacrifice and rain. Third was Tepetzinco ("honored hill place"). There a female child named Quetzalxoch, "feather flower," who was dressed in blue, was sacrificed. Fourth was Poyauhtlan, "dark color place," which is the Nahuatl name for a peak called La Malinche today, and which is east of the Valley of Mexico. At Tepetzinco, however, there was an altar to Poyauhtlan that probably resembled the actual peak. There a boy was offered who was named Poyauhtecatl ("dark dweller") and who was covered with rubber. Fifth was a place in the middle of the saltwater lake called Pantitlan, "the place of banners," where another boy was offered named Epcoatl ("shell snake"). He was adorned with pearls or shells. The sixth place was Cocotl, which can be translated alternatively, depending of the etymology, as "pimple," "windpipe," or "mourning dove." This boy's costume was like the costume of Yohualtecatl, the second place mentioned, with one side painted red and the other painted black. The seventh place was Yiauhqueme ("his sacrificial garment"), where the child sacrificed had that same name. His costume was stained black.

In all seven of these places, a direct correspondence was established in the text between the location and the life of human children. Renaming children according to the place they were to be sacrificed indicated that they were to be identified with that location. The linguistic device yetiuh ("it goes to be," or "they go being something") was used to describe the renaming process. Yetiuh suggests that through this activity of sacrificial transformation a necessary and substantive link was established between the child's life and a specific place.

According to Pomar, these children were from seven to eight years old. Motolinía also tells of how a three- or four-year-old would be sacrificed after planting the fields by town authorities. Unlike the warrior sacrifices at the Templo Mayor with hearts extracted, they were instead beheaded on a stone that was anointed with blood. It was understood that this was required to avoid famine.[17]

Their costumes were opulent symbols of water, fertility, and wealth. Their headbands were crammed with queztal feathers at the precise location of their cowlicks. These feathers were an insignia of wealth and prosperity for the Aztecs. They came from the resplendent trogon, which was native to the southern lowlands of Mexico.[18] In Book XI of the *Florentine*, Sahagún recorded a description of the *quetzaltototl.* Its most precious feathers were the tail feathers, which were a rich green color ("herb-green," "very green," "fresh green," "turquoise-colored"). In addition, these feathers bent like wild reeds (which were important ritual items in VI-Etzalcualiztli) and glistened in the light. In this context, however, they are also associated with corn tassels, or corn flowers, which develop before the cob of the maize plant. Adornment of the head in this fashion duplicated a particular agricultural moment: the flowering stage of maize. The headdresses designated the sacrificial children as noble, or those connected with wealth, which corresponded to the early agricultural stages of maize.

People followed the procession of the children by hanging necklaces of precious green stone around their necks. In Book XI, Sahagún describes common characteristics of *chalchihuitl*, or the precious green stone. Similar to the quetzal feathers, its primary attribute was its deep green color ("herb-green," like amaranth). It was understood to have the ability to attract moisture and was associated with wealth and nobility when worn as a necklace or bracelet.[19] With these children being literally covered with green stone jewelry and quetzal feathers, their status within Aztec society was as honored nobility. Various elements of their costume were seen to attract moisture, thus conjoining water and agricultural fertility as the sources of their wealth.

The children were also covered with rubber into which was set amaranth, a staple in the Aztec daily diet. Rubber was worn on their faces and feet and was also considered to be an honored and valuable ornament. Like green stones and quetzal feathers, rubber adornments also had their associations with water. The children were carried in procession on litters, a mode of travel reserved only for the most revered nobility in Aztec society. The litters were surrounded with quetzal feathers ("quetzal feather housed"). Attached to the children's costumes were paper wings or leaves. Wrapped and encapsulated in their most potent symbols of wealth, these children were paraded to the seven sites of their death to be offered to Tlaloc. As they proceeded though the city and countryside, the sound of conch trumpets filled the air.

The emotional appeal of this procession, however, was not celebration but rather sadness. The response of the people through which the children moved was that of compassion. This opulent display of wealth and nobility was intended to make people cry. This dimension of the ritual indicated that there was an emotional intimacy between the children and the people that perhaps indicated that they were not purchased for the event, but rather part of the community. The sacrifices were meant to cause pain and elicit tears from all those present, which directly associated the ritual with rainfall.

All night long the children and priest kept a vigil at a place called *ayauhcalli*, or "the mist house." The priests were of two classes: 1) Tlamacazque, or serving priests, and 2) Quaquacuiltin, or head-offering priests, who were the old and honored Tlamacazque. Their continued honored status required that they not abandon their duties during the night, such as forgetting an offering to the fire or falling asleep. If they were to fall asleep, they would no longer be respected or feared. If the children cried continuously during the vigil, this was a sign of rain. While tears of the crowd showed compassion for the children about to die, it was the children's tears themselves that were directly associated with rain. Water generated from the eyes had a direct correspondence with the release of water by Tlaloc. The more the children cried, the more contented the people became. This must have been a paradoxical range of emotions for the participants.

Other signs were closely scrutinized during this time. If during the ritual someone contracted dropsy, or any disease associated with the retention of fluids, the rain would be held back. The term for this illness is formed from the root *itia*, "to have someone drink," which refers to a body being full of fluid. A diseased body that could not release water signaled that a relationship with Tlaloc had only been partially established.

At the end of his description, Sahagún tells us that birds were particularly potent rain signs. First was the *cuitlacochini*, or "excrement sweeper," commonly known as the curve-billed thrasher, named by the song it sings.[20] Second was the *pipixcan*, or "harvesters," which is currently known as the Franklin's gull. The root of this name is *pixca*, "to harvest maize," and these birds were known to enter the

Valley of Mexico at harvest time from the sea. Third was the *necuilic*, "bent or twisted one." These are currently known as the sparrow hawks that eat mice and lizards. After eating, they suck air to get their water, and by doing so were seen as knowing the wind and the time of frost. The appearance of these three birds indicated very important moments in the agricultural cycle. The *cuitlacochini* corresponded to spring and a time when stores of maize were at their end, the *pipixcan* to harvest after having left the sea, and the *necuilic* to frost and the close of the growing cycle. Moreover the *necuilic* sucked water from the air, which associated him directly with Tlaloc as the one who "raises" rain into the air in the form of clouds and mist from his home in the mountain.

Activities during II-Tlacaxipehualiztli were centered around the presentation of captives taken in war through mock battles staged on a circular stone, which led to their eventual death and flaying. This was a festival to the deity Xipe Totec, "the flayed one," who represented mature maize and the sun. Fray Diego Durán links the rites of II-Tlacaxipehualiztli with ceremonies to the *tlaloque* by referring to paper banners covered with rubber found at caves and sanctuaries on the mountains, as during I-Atl cahualo. Also offerings of copal (an incense made of tree resin) were given to the *tlaloque*, or *tepictoton*, "little molded ones," who were dressed in paper costumes.

According to Motolinía, III-Tozoztontli also included the sacrifice of nine child slaves between the ages of five and seven to Tlaloc.[21] They would deposit the bodies of these children in a cave. Sahagún also mentions sacrifices of children during this month.

IV-Huei tozoztli took place when the silk on the young ears of corn was beginning to develop.[22] In addition to other calendrical events, the growth of maize signaled a great festival for the goddess of maize, Chicomecoatl-Cinteotl. The Aztecs would offer the goddess reeds, corn, and other types of plants. Sahagún mentions this month as the last in which they sacrificed children, indicating that this was the end of drought and the beginning of the rainy season.

According to the accounts of some, they assembled the children whom they slew in the first month, buying them from their mothers. And they went on killing them in all the feasts which followed, until the rains really began. And thus they slew some in the first, ... the second ... the third ... [and] the fourth (months): so that until the rains began in abundance, in all the feasts they sacrificed children.[23]

The most important ceremonial event to Tlaloc during this month, however, is described by Durán.[24] Events during this annual ceremony were simultaneously conducted on the summit of a high mountain to the east called Tlalocan and in the great salt lake, Texcoco. In his description of Tlaloc Durán says:

First of all, it must be noted that the idol is known as Tlaloc and was venerated and feared throughout the entire land. The whole country was dedicated to his service—lords, kings, noblemen, and the common people. His permanent home was in the same temple of the great Huitzilopochtli, next to him, where a special chamber had been erected ... This same name of the god was given to a lofty mountain ... Today this mountain is called Tlalocan, and it would be difficult to say which received its name from which—the god from the mountain [or the mountain] from the god because on the whole sierra the clouds become cold, the storms of thunder, lightning, thunderbolts, and hail are formed.[25]

The physical mountain was identified as the principal point of access to the paradisiacal world of Tlalocan inside the earth. Temples on Mount Tlalocan arbitrated between worlds and highlighted Tlaloc's connection to the valley landscape. According to Durán, the events on Tlalocan during IV-Huei tozoztli were the most magnificent ceremonies performed to Tlaloc during the entire year. Nobles from all the cities under Aztec control gathered at Tlalocan. With the rising sun a child in a covered litter, probably similar to the those described in I-Atl cahualo, was sacrificed to Tlaloc amid the swell of music from conch shells and log drums. The altar of sacrifices, which was arranged in the same manner as the one at the Templo Mayor, is described in some detail.

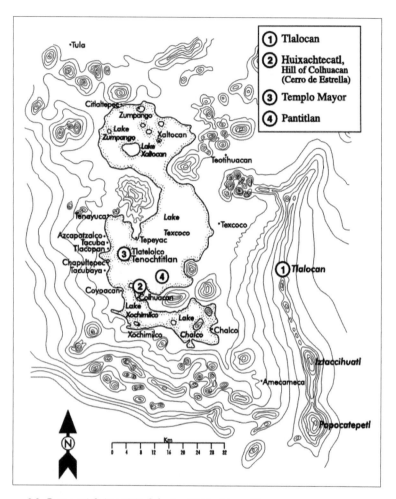

3.3. Ceremonial sites visited during IV-Huei tozoztli.

In the middle of this room upon a small platform, stood the stone idol Tlaloc . . . Around [Tlaloc] were a number of small idols, but he stood in the center as their supreme lord. These little idols represented the other hills and cliffs which surrounded his great mountain. Each one of them was named according to the hill he stood for.[26]

Children were sacrificed to Tlaloc on an altar that also included various deities of the surrounding landscape. The altar on Tlalocan can be seen as a deified map of the valley; an articulation of the hidden world upon which material existence was predicated. Sacrifices at this altar/ map directly linked a human world with Tlalocan. The media of this ritual communication were child sacrifices and food offerings. Nobles also brought gifts of cotton mantles, feathers, and food from cities all over the land. In their assemblage on Tlalocan the nobles themselves and their gifts embodied a map analogous to the deified map of the altar. With their presence they too articulated an undergirding feature of the human subsistence, just as did the altar of Tlalocan. Over the course of a full day, the nobles would make their offerings and then depart, leaving guards to assure that the offerings were not stolen by Tlaxcalans.

In Tenochtitlan the people were preparing for the return of Moctezuma, the Tlahtoani ("principal speaker"), from Tlalocan. They cut a tree from the Hill of Colhuacan, today known as Hill of the Star (Cerro de Estrella). They sought the tallest, fullest, and most beautiful tree and tied the branches carefully to its trunk. When it was securely bound, they cut down the tree in such a way as to prevent it from touching the ground. They would return with the tree amid rejoicing, songs, and merrymaking. The tree was placed in a deep hole in the courtyard of the Tlaloc temple. The tree was called Totah, "our father," because it was situated in the center of four smaller trees.[27] From each of these four trees, which formed a square, a twisted straw rope was strung to Totah. On these ropes were hung huge tassels of grass or straw, the same material as the rope itself. These cords were said to represent the penance and harshness of life led by those who served the gods. They were often used for the practice of autosacrificial bloodletting.

When the mock forest had been assembled, the priests adorned themselves and carried a girl of either seven or eight on a covered litter so that no one could see her. This was similar to the boys' procession on Tlalocan. She was dressed in blue, representing the lake and other springs and creeks. On her head was a garland of red feathers with a tuft of blue feathers (probably *quetzalli* feathers). She was set down in the mock forest in front of Totah and sang to until news arrived that the offerings on Tlalocan had been completed. When the nobles had arrived from Tlalocan, they took the child in the litter and the Totah, which had been re-bound, and set off into the lake by canoe. The music and singing were continuous and the innumerable canoes, filled with as many people as wanted to come, embarked into the lake. They arrived at a place in the middle of the lake called Pantitlan ("banner place"), where the lake was said to drain. At this place they set Totah into the mud near the lake's opening. They then took the small girl and slit her throat with a small spear that was used for killing ducks. Her blood was allowed to flow into the water. She was then cast into Pantitlan and the lake swallowed her. Other offerings were then cast into the whirlpool, such as jewels, stones, necklaces, and bracelets—things similar to those offered at Tlalocan and during I-Atl cahualo. Everyone returned in silence, but the ceremonies continued as farmers tilled and sowed their fields. Celebrations also took place along rivers, springs, and streams.

Symbolic representations of the landscape (like the altars on Tlalocan; the simulated forest in the ceremonial plaza at the Templo Mayor; the assembly of nobles, and the placement of Totah in the lake's opening) ritually organized the valley and oriented the Aztecs within a meaningful place. Tlaloc ritual, while involved in the material exchanges of blood and food, also articulated correspondences of various kinds of seen and unseen places. Simultaneous to giving gifts, rituals to Tlaloc also articulated a mode by which the Aztecs meaningfully occupied the Valley of Mexico.

The lake was called Tonanhueiatl, "our great mother the lake," and was the most important source of sustenance of the valley.[28] The girl sacrificed at Pantitlan was dressed and treated as the deity Chalchihuitlicue, "she of a skirt of precious greenstone," the most revered female goddess associated with the *tlaloque*. Likewise, the boy sacrificed on Tlalocan was associated with Tlaloc. She was sacrificed with an instrument used for killing lake fowl and in that act she was brought into a closer association with the death of aquatic animals (an important food resource). Pantitlan, like Tlalocan, was defined by the actions of the Aztec in their offerings to the *tlaloque*.

As with other rituals to Tlaloc, IV-Huei tozoztli dramatically developed correspondences between elements of water and blood. Tlalocan was the place of origin for earthly water and from it would issue continued life and, by extension, wealth. Offerings at Mount Tlalocan were given directly to Tlaloc, particularly in the form of a male child's blood. The nobles then descended from Tlalocan, duplicating the flow of water from the sierra to the lake. They then embarked in canoes to the center of the lake to offer the blood of a female child at the place where water entered the earth. The ritual encompassed two distinct yet reciprocal points in the landscape—one, Tlalocan, the highest point in the valley's hydrological cycle and where water entered the human realm, and the other at the lowest point in the valley's water cycle and where it reentered the earth, leaving the human domain.[29] Blood given at both of these points in the hydrological cycle constituted appropriate openings in the earth for offerings. Giving the lifeblood of humans at specific points in the ritual landscape articulated a reciprocity between living beings—humans and the earth. Both gave up part of their lives for the perpetuation of other living beings, and were therefore locked in a substantive reciprocal relationship with one another.

Sacrificial events, at potent communicative points in the Aztec landscape, were an exchange of food. The practice of offering food also required an interpretive vigilance because signs of approval or disapproval would appear from Tlalocan. While the medium of communication was based in a practice of exchanging food, the consequences of rituals to Tlaloc were to make the Aztecs watchful of signs sent from an unseen world, which resulted in their being meaningfully oriented to the valley ecology.

Durán describes the buildings of Tlalocan as being surrounded by a brilliant white enclosure with eight-foot walls. In this enclosure, as among other altars, was the altar to Tlaloc with a stone-lined pit of standing water. Pomar says that the idol at this site was the oldest of New Spain and that the Toltec people made it.[30] The Aztecs, upon arriving in the valley, found this statue and came to venerate it as the "God of the Waters." It was fashioned from a light white stone such as pumice, though somewhat harder and heavier. It sat on a square slab of stone and faced the east, in the direction opposite the walled causeway leading to the enclosure, and toward sunrise.

Currently, on the top of what is known today as Mount Tlaloc, there are the remains of a rectangular foundation of ancient stone walls that were covered with plaster. This mountain has been the subject of recent surveys. Wicke and Horcasitas were able to verify some of the statements of Pomar made four hundred years earlier.[31] An analysis of pot shards confirms that the Toltec occupied this site in 1000 C.E. It has also been rumored that child sacrifices may have continued up until as recently as 1887.

Aveni has also surveyed the site and has taken transit measurements of the remaining architectural remains.[32] The causeway leading to the ceremonial enclosure deviates 11° north of west (west being defined by the setting sun at equinox). This deviation exactly matches the orientation of the skewed notch between temples to Tlaloc and Huitzilopochtli at Stage II of the Templo Mayor.[33] Moreover, sunset on 29 April 1500 C.E. would have occurred directly along the entrance of the causeway as viewed from the ceremonial precinct. This date falls within the latter half of the month IV-Huei tozoztli. Over long distances (forty-seven kilometers) the Aztec consciously aligned their major ceremonial complexes of Tlalocan and the Templo Mayor with reference to each other and particular celestial events.[34] A conjunction of sky and landscape was a "ritual theater" that dramatized an underlying cosmological structure.[35] Human ritual action within this landscape articulated the nature of the relationships between elements that came into play.

VI-ETZALCUALIZTLI—EATING BEAN (MAIZE) STEW

The festival of VI-Etzalcualiztli was held during the sixth month of the agricultural year. Because of the length of this description, we can deduce that Sahagún's informants were particularly familiar with the events of this month's festivities. According to Motolinía, VI-Etzalcualiztli took place when there was abundant water and when maize was fully formed.[36] The central focus of this month-long ritual was the feast of *etzalli*, a bean/maize stew, and from which the month derived its name. This was a highly regarded ceremonial dish that was prepared and shared among people of Tenochtitlan. The ritual highlighted, however, the violent nature of food consumption by human and other beings. This was articulated in a variety of ways during the course of the ceremonies. Sahagún's description of this ceremony was organized into a framework of successive four-day segments, which peaked with the day-long festival of Etzalcualiztli.[37] The analysis that follows, like Sahagún's description, will be organized by the four-day intervals.

Etzalcualiztli began four days prior to the sixth month. For four days the priests began their fast, the Tlamacazque (from the root *maca* meaning "to give something to someone"), or serving priests, went to harvest reeds from a place in the northern end of Lake Texcoco called Citlaltepec, "the place of the star hill." They sought a special type of reed that grew in the saltwater lakes of the Valley of Mexico. The reeds were called *aztapilli*, which translates as "noble heron" and thus links this particular water bird (probably referring to the heron's legs) to this type of reed. These reeds were recognizable for their white bases and were round, long, and slender; much like the whiteness of a heron that inhabited these marshes whose legs were long and slender. *Aztapilli* must also have grown in very large fields within the lake because another name for them is given as *tomimilli*, or "many reed fields."[38]

The Tlamacazque violently seized and pulled the reeds from their watery moorings. They were then bound around the middle in bunches and wrapped in a blanket. This technique of binding the reeds was similar to the capture of wild birds. The Tlamacazque loaded themselves up with the "captured" reeds and carried the bundles by tumpline, or as common laborers and slaves.

The road between Citlaltepec and Tenochtitlan was very quiet during their trip. No one would travel during this time for fear of being robbed and beaten by the Tlamacazque. If they would happen upon a traveler, the priests would beat, trample, and whip them severely and leave them for dead on the side of the road. A *tlalmecatl*, or "earth cord," was regularly used as a device for measuring land, but during this month may have been used to severely beat travelers.[39]

3.4. VI-Etzalcualiztli, redrawn from the *Tovar Calendar*, Juan de Tovar.

During this time, the Tlamacazque inspired great fear in people because, in addition to the beatings, they would also take all of a person's
clothes and belongings, even tribute destined for Moctezuma.
Moctezuma so revered the priests and their penitential lives, however,
that he did not (or could not) seek retribution. After arriving at the site of
the ceremony in Tenochtitlan, the priests stretched out the reeds and, by
using maguey roots and maguey fibers, weaved them together into mats
for sleeping and sitting. These mats were a sign of nobility and in many
primary texts denoted the Tlahtoani, or "principal speaker."

The night before Eztalcualiztli began, all the priests, including the Tlamacazque and novices, crowded themselves into their houses (the *calmecac*). The mats were stretched out and the Tlenamacac, or "the fire offering priest," adorned himself. He put on a sleeveless jacket that was colored and used only by priests. He also took the *matacaxtli*, which is described by Dibble and Anderson as a maniple made from the skin of

3.5. VI-Etzalcualiztli, redrawn from the *Códice Matritense del Real Palacio.*

a wild beast, and he draped it over his left arm.[40] He took up the copal incense pouch and firebrand and offered incense from the entrance of the temple courtyard to the four directions.[41]

The Tlenamacac then entered the temple and sat on a reed mat facing the offering fire, or brazier. He very carefully placed four balls made of maize dough in the fire. None of his movements could disturb the pile of maize dough balls that he was forming. His offering established an order that could not be compromised. If one of the balls were to roll from its place the Tlamacazque who surround him would abuse him saying, "We have caught you rolling them over." In their turn each of the Tlamacazque made offerings to the same brazier, filling it with food. Specifically mentioned are large tomatoes, leafy tomatoes, and chili peppers. As this was done, all the priests watched closely to see that nothing rolled, moved, or was dislocated in any way. If someone should carelessly make an offering, they were seized and "they [made] a sign on him." Constructing the fire offering was not taken lightly. A watchful crowd made sure that all was secure in assembling the sacrificial pile of food, and those who disrupted the offering were severely beaten.

Likewise, the bodies and garments of the priests had to be in a very particular order during the offerings. If dirt, a spider's web, or wool fibers were seen on a priest's head or cloak, the priest would be seized and also "marked with a sign." If someone stumbled or hurt themselves accidentally, the same thing would occur. For four days they lived in this careful manner under the threat of a violent beating. During this time they lived carefully and with prudence. Ordering the offering required the strictest adherence to watchfulness and active attention to the task at hand. Only the Quaquacuiltin, or "head offering priests," were allowed to eat these offerings. Even though the offerings were made of maize, tomatoes, etc., the rest of the priests had to do without food.

Close to midnight of the fourth day, a conch shell, associated with the sea, was blown. All the priests undressed and cut their ears with thorns and maguey spines. The offerings of food had shifted to the letting of blood. All priests went to the lake and bathed themselves as conch trumpets, flutes, and whistles were blown. On their backs they carried tobacco pouches on rope necklaces. They were led by the Tlenamacac, whose fire of copal and penitential offerings was said to be frightening to behold. The Quacuilli led the people with his *ayochicahuaztli*, or "water vessel fortifier," also know as *nahualcuahuitl*, or "sorcerer's staff." It was a large rattle that was wide and long, and whose magical properties seemed to lie in its ability to strengthen water. Potency over the substantive conditions of life defined wealth in Aztec society and was predicated primarily on one's control over water. In this context, it was the Quacuilli, the most revered penitents among the priests, who could wield the *ayochicahuaztli*. Only they, it would seem, possessed sufficient means or authority to strengthen water and directly engage the watery deities at the edge of the lake.

All the Tlamacazque, who resided in the *calmecac* ("house of whips or penitence"), or the men's houses, participated in these events. All the *calmecac* were emptied of their inhabitants.[42] All but four singers and musicians remained in the deserted houses playing the lateral log drum, the water drum, the gourd rattle, and the conch shell trumpet. The houses stood empty of men but were full of sound.

A procession of penitents continued to the lake shore where they usually bathed at a place called *ayauhcalli*, or the mist house. This place was also an important place of vigil during I-Atl cahualo. At *ayauhcalli*, the Tlamacazque would lay down wet and naked. They were very cold and trembled continuously with fear and cold. A revered priest (Quacuilli) then told them that "this is the place of the snake's wrath, the place of the mosquito who takes blood, the place where ducks gather, and the place of the thunderous *aztapilli*." It was a fearsome place full of obstacles to human existence. It was a place of cold and fear. Yet it was also a place of water and sustenance, which made human life possible. Because the regions of the lakes were associated with the goddess Chalchihuitlicue, she of a skirt of precious greenstone, the *ayauhcalli* was also a female/cold place, and thus in opposition to the male priests.[43]

The priests then entered the water splashing and splattering about with their feet and hands. Like the singers and musicians in the *calmecac*, the priests made a lot of noise. They imitated the speech of several different water birds and by means of sound came to experience, or taste, what it was like to be water birds. They spoke like the *pihpitztin*, or "the blowers," which was a gull characterized by its whistle or screech. Other priests spoke like the *acacalomeh*, or "water birds." These were either of the stork, ibis, or spoonbill family and are described as eating water life.[44] Some spoke like the *aztatl*, which was the white heron, or egret.[45] This was an honored water bird as its name, mentioned above, was associated with the mats woven of reeds. The fourth bird mentioned was *axoquen*, or "the little blue heron." It smelled of the rotten fish that was its primary food source.[46] The last bird that the priests imitated was the *tocuilcoyotl*, the "coyote crane," now called the brown crane. It was long and stringy like the others previously mentioned.[47] Splashing in the cold water while making the noise of water birds gave the Tlamacazque the "taste" of birdness. This was not the usual dwelling of human beings, but it was the "site of abundant water" necessary for human existence. By emulating the birds of water whose life was tied to the lake, the priests forged a relationship with the place of the goddess Chalchihuitlicue: the Lake (a place of abundant water, wealth, and fertility).

Birds, in this context, were important intermediaries between human penitents and the *tlaloque*. The connection with the *tlaloque* was formed by sound and speech. The languages of water fowl were therefore indigenous but, unlike that of Nahuatl, which was associated more with agricultural fields, it was indigenous to the water. The priest's activity of communicating with the watery landscape was accomplished by articulating a nonhuman language and movement, thus bringing the total Aztec community closer to an unseen watery realm. The Otherness of the watery world of water fowl and deities had to be overcome momentarily by the ritual devotions of the priests. The Otherness of the lake, the *tlaloque*, and the birds were directly involved with human sustenance and survival.

For four days they splashed and imitated birds in the water. On the eighth day of VI-Etzalcualiztli, from this liminal state of speaking as water birds, the priests emerged playing their flutes completely naked. The absence of adornment indicated their liminal state, which was brought with them from the lake. They again filled the *calmecac* and sprawled out on the mats cold. All night they slept cold making noises, grunting, and complaining. Some lay as if they were dead.

In the middle of the ninth day the Tlenamacac again adorned himself. He offered incense to "warm" the many temples. Then the beginning of the feasting began. People gathered to exchange mole, or chili sauce. This went on for four more days. Like the priestly offerings during days one through four, people were watchful for anyone who spilled their mole. Even if a single drop reached the earth they would seize the transgressor and give them a severe penalty. Also during this time, the general community gathered penitential reeds and branches and bound them about their middle and stacked them in all the temples. They also searched for branches and broke them up for their temples. If someone lost their way, stumbled, or hurt themselves during these gatherings, they were then also punished. Or if someone lagged behind the group or did an incomplete job of collecting the reeds, then they became a captive. Only by offering a gift to the captor could they be freed. Specific gifts mentioned are the *totolin*, or "turkey;" breechcloth; cloak of cotton or maguey fiber; or a cotton sheet. Gifts for the release of a captive were considered costly and, therefore, only available to rich people. For poor people, wooden vessels of maize dough offering were ransom enough.

Ransom for the release of captives required gifts of specifically named domestic goods. In particular is mentioned the turkey. In direct contrast to the water fowl with which the Tlamacazque had been engaged with for four days, the turkey was essentially a domestic animal who inhabited dry land. In a description of the turkey in Book XI, Sahagún discusses many of its attributes in considerable detail. It was regarded as a servant whose feathers were thick and round.[48] Its wings were heavy so it was not regarded as a flyer. Like humans, it ate maize and cooked greens. Four herbs are mentioned as staples of its diet: 1) *tonalchichicaquilitl*, a bitter herb that aids in digestion and grows in grasslands and forests; 2) *cuanacaquilitl*, a lettuce specifically used for bird feed; 3) *coyocuechtli*, or "coyote dust," also good for children suffering from a sore throat; and 4) *tetzitzili*, which was a vine with blossoms and spines. Many of these turkey greens were also regarded as important for humans. In nearly every feature the turkey was seen in opposition to water fowl. Both types of birds were edible, but had dramatically distinctive characteristics. The turkey was large and fat, with heavy feathers, and could not fly. The water fowl were generally lean, stringy, of delicate plumage, and could fly. The principal difference, however, was that the turkey was a "servant" and the water fowl were wild. All of the water birds mentioned were migratory animals whose status, with reference to the landscape, was essentially dislocated. They were present in the valley only by virtue of the vicissitudes of the season, the climate, and water availability. All birds referred to during the ritual occupied distinctive parts of the Aztec landscape and were therefore incorporated into ritual action at different moments.

After these four days, no other gifts were accepted for the release of the captives. This marked the beginning of the feasting period. All over Tenochtitlan and its subject lands, people (the *macehualli*) would make *etzalli*, described as a bean and maize stew. This was a communal activity because everyone shared in the making and eating of the stew. They also enjoyed themselves by dancing the *etzalli* dance, which began at midnight. Brave warriors, in particular, would enter people's homes seizing the *eztalli* pot and threatening violence either to the home or to the women if they were not fed.

When dawn broke again, the Tlenamacac adorned himself. He put on the sleeveless colored jacket, over which he would put on the *ayauhquemitl* ("mist cloak"), which was also called the *ahuachquemitl* ("dew cloak"). In pictorial codices, it is shown to have been made of a netting that was associated with moisture given by the *tlaloque*. He was adorned with motmot feathers, which were derived from a very colorful water fowl, and a pleated-paper neck ornament was worn at the nape of the neck. His forehead was painted blue and was spread smooth with iron pyrite, which was also used in making ceremonial mirrors. He carried a special incense bag that was hung with shells and filled with *yauhtli*. *Yauhtli* was a plant with medicinal properties that was often used during fire-offering ceremonies. It helped heal people with chills and was taken in an infusion, or it was added to water and rubbed on the hands. *Yauhtli* was a water herb.[49] It was used with water, to overcome the chilling effects of water (just like the priest's penitential activities in the *ayauhcalli*, or mist house) and was therefore appropriate to be used to make offerings to water.

In addition, the Quacuilli carried the *ayauhchicahuaztli*, "mist fortifying rattle," by his neck. While the rattle mentioned earlier referred to a vessel of water, this rattle, however, was explicitly connected to mist, which thus linked the costume of the Tlenamacac (wearing the mist, or dew, cloak) with the instrument. The rest of the Tlamacazque carried waterlike rubber figures in the likeness of human beings and copal incense figures in the shape of pyramids. The tops of the figures were adorned with quetzal feathers and were called *quetzal-miyahuayotl*, "quetzal feather maize tassels." At the sound of the conch trumpet all assembled on the road. Costumes, instruments, offerings, etc., all signaled the culmination of the various themes addressed during earlier points of the ceremony. These included, water, moisture, birds, music/sound, etc.

The captives (who were taken during the vigils in which offerings were made) were then held by their necks and breechcloths by the priests while presented to the community. The priests then fell on the captives, muddying them in rain puddles on the water's edge. They struck the captives at Totecco, or "the place of our serpent." The Tlenamacac offered burned paper, copal, and rubber to the gods while incensing the reed beds with *yauhtli*, while other priests continued to beat the captives. They attempted to drown the captives in the lake. It was expected that the captives would fight and attempt to flee the scene. Some fainted and were left on the shore for dead. Many captives swallowed the bitter salt water and vomited. After the sounding of the conch shell and the return to the *calmecac*, the captives were collected by their families and then returned to their homes to eventually be restored to health.

Beginning with the uprooting of reeds and despoiling of travelers, acts of violence throughout this ceremony were conducted by priests with almost random wild abandon. With the dispersal of captives to their homes, the violent acts that were perpetrated by the Tlamacazque ceased. Ritual violence dramatized for the Aztec both how suffering was an intrinsic feature of life and also how one could easily become a victim of violent activity simply by virtue of where one found oneself. Actions of the various priests articulated an understanding of the paradox of how the destruction of life was involved in the continuance of human existence.

With the return of the Tlamacazque to their various *calmecac*, another four-day period of fasting began called *netlahcahzahualiztli*, "my bean daytime fast." Priests rested on reed mats, taking no more captives and doing no more feasting. Before the final day, the senior priests were adorned by the novices. Again they were arrayed with paper ornaments called *tlaquechpanyotl* ("paper neck ornaments") and *amacuexpalli* ("pleated paper neck ornaments") worn on the head, and necklaces of the pelican flower.[50] Their foreheads were colored blue, which was specifically linked with the goddess Huixtocihuatl, the elder sister of the *tlaloque* and the goddess of salt.[51] This element of their costumery articulated an intimate connection between the body and the great salt lake. The Tlenamacac seized the incense bag, which was made of ocelot skin and adorned with seashells hanging in the four directions. The Tlamacazque also held a paper incense bag on which were painted representations of the jaguar, ocelot, duck, and the duck called *atzitzicuilotl* ("water splatter"). The last of these was identified as the northern phalarope, or sanderling, which in Book XI was a water bird with a long, pointed, slender bill.[52] It was understood to be from the province of Anahuac, or where the Aztecs originated and where they got their name. The incense bags were full of the herb *yauhtli*. The Tlenamacac led the throng to the Tlaloc temple and he was also adorned with quetzal feathers. His face was coated with rubber and he wore a sleeveless painted jacket. He also wore a rainstorm mask, or his Tlaloc water mask. Reference was made to his long and tangled hair, which fell loosely to his waist. The procession was accompanied by a loud noise that was made by the Tlamacazque.

At the Tlaloc temple, the Tlenamacac stopped the procession to scatter the *aztapilli* reeds and another herb called *quequezquic* ("something that causes an itch"). The latter was an edible herb that grew outside of the Valley of Mexico in the Huazteca region to the east. He also scattered the fruit of the nopal cactus and *yauhtli*. He then placed four precious green stones at the temple, which was reminiscent of the placing of the four offering balls of maize. He was given a wooden hook colored blue and beat the stones while turning himself about. More *yauhtli* was scattered and he was then given the *ayochicahuaztli*, the water fortifying rattle, which he shook vigorously. It was understood that he offered it as a sacrifice to Tlaloc's temple. Then they all returned to the *calmecac*. The locus of the ceremony had shifted from the landscape of the lake to the temple precinct in the center of Tenochtitlan. The priests directly entered the temple precinct of Tlaloc only on the final day of IV-Etzalcualiztli.

At night the ritual activities continued on top of Tlaloc's temple, called Tlalocan, where the priests sang and played the lateral log drum, the conch trumpet, and the water reed trumpet. The lateral log drum was described as making low noises like that of grunting wild animals. A variety of animal sounds were integrated into the festivities of IV-Etzalcualiztli: aquatic birds and beasts of prey were mentioned in particular.

At midnight, "when the night was split in two," the human representatives of Tlaloc were sacrificed. First were the prisoners who were bent down over the sacrificial stone. Then the debt payments, or blood offerings, were burned. These offerings also included unblemished precious green stones and rubber balls that were black or dark-colored. The priests seized the heart from the opened chest of the prisoner and placed it in a blue vessel covered with rubber called *mixcomitl*, "the cloud vessel."

Many people came to see this event with artemisian flowers in their arms, which they pushed to the ground or whipped toward the water, or whipped ahead of themselves at their children. The latter movement was to keep worms from infecting their children with acne, which was also associated with Tlaloc. In Book XI, these flowers were described as being medicinal.[53] They were used to reduce an overabundance of phlegm in the system, to reduce a fever, and cleanse the urine. They were prepared as a hot drink and also to help relieve colds.

The priests then emerged from within the Tlalocan, bringing with them the offerings of paper banners, painted maguey fiber cloaks called *ayauhixo* ("mist face"), precious green stones, quetzal feathers, and copal incense shaped as people. Central to all of these offerings was the *mixcomitl*, which contained the human hearts. The priests then proceeded to a place called Tetamazolco ("people's toad place") on the water's edge and they boarded canoes that were filled with people and offerings. The assemblage then rowed out into the lake to Pantitlan ("paper banner place"), which also figured prominently in the festival of I-Atl cahualo and IV-Huei tozoztli.[54] The poles used to propel the boats were of considerable interest. They were colored blue and adorned with rubber. This may have been because the poles were in direct contact with the lake and again were intermediary between the watery domain of Tlaloc and human beings. Until this point, the *tlaloque* were propitiated from the shore, but now they were addressed in the very middle of the lake. At Pantitlan the Tlenamacac stood in their canoes while conch trumpets sounded. They then cast the *mixcomitl* of human hearts in front of the *cuenmantli*, the poles from which paper banners flew and which were placed there during various previous rituals, and into the water. As the *mixcomitl* entered the water, people observed a turbulence that was generated from below the surface of the water. It was described as a bubbling, roaring, and blistering. All three terms also are used in descriptions of a boiling cooking pot. Food, particularly cooked food, organized the mode by which offerings were given to Tlaloc.

Finally, paper streamers and precious green stones were hung on wooden staffs in the middle of the lake. Other offerings were also cast into the water with the *mixcomitl*. The ritual concluded when the Tlenamacac offered four paper banners with incense at the edge of Pantitlan, which thus completed the offerings to the waters.

Activities during IV-Etzalcualiztli were organized in reduplications of the number four. This referred to the four cardinal directions in the sense that these activities oriented the Aztec people to the world. For example, offerings of smoke and balls of maize to the four cardinal directions articulated and arranged their space. Likewise, it engaged the wide expanse of space so as to be more actively connected with a Tlalocan landscape. The monthly activities were also arranged in four periods of four days leading to the *etzalli* feast. There were also four days that preceded the month and four days after the feast, which framed the central sixteen-day period.[55]

The ceremony ended at dawn when the boats docked and the Tlamacazque bathed on the shore. There they washed the blue from their foreheads and beat any priests who had managed to avoid the monthly festivities. When they returned to their *calmecac*, the priests took the reed mats and threw them out at the back of the house, thus ending the events of IV-Etzalcualiztli.

A consequence of devotions to Tlaloc and associated deities during this month was that it clarified the relationship between eater and eaten; between the consumers and their food. This relationship was worked out with reference to particular places and living beings. As with XIII-Tepeilhuitl and XVI-Atemoztli, this ceremony articulated a spatial relationship involved in the consumption of food. Priestly activity during IV-Etzalcualiztli, however, focused on the lake ecology. During most of this time the priests were seen as wild, violent, and generally antagonistic to human beings. Their identification with the nonhuman world of the *tlaloque* identified them as mediators between worlds to secure the nourishment of a living landscape for human beings.

Similar to VI-Etzalcualiztli was the feast of VII-Teucilhuitontli, which was dedicated to the female deity Huixtocihuatl: "salt woman." She was the patron of salt makers of the lake beds. An impersonator was adorned with a yellow face paint made of maize blossoms, a paper cap full of quetzal feathers like maize tassels, gold earplugs that were like squash blossoms, and a shift and skirt designed like waves of water, with a border designed with green stones to represent billowing clouds. On her ankles were golden bells or rattles, and on her calves were ocelot skins also adorned with bells. Her sandals were sided with loose cotton yarn that included flecks of raw cotton. She carried a shield painted with water lilies, upon which yellow parrot feather pendants were made into tassels like the forepart of a locust. These were also made of eagle feathers and down, pieces of quetzal feathers, and the breast and tail feathers of parrots. Her reed staff was decorated with papers that were spattered with liquid rubber. This staff had various cuplike flowers placed in three areas, with each one containing *yauhtli*, a flower of the anise herb used for ceremonial and medicinal purposes, and each was crossed with motmot feathers. Elements in her costume directly linked her with water, moisture, animals, and maize.

During a ten-day period, Huixocihuatl danced in a crouched position while swinging her shield around in a circle. She leaned on her staff while thrusting it to the ground to mark the rhythm of the dance. The community of salt makers would gather to dance and sing for her in the manner of women, including old women, mature women, and maidens recently matured. The women, arrayed with flowers on their heads, would cry and lament loudly in high voices. Huixtocihuatl would go among them in their spectacular processions.

After ten days, male priests adorned themselves similar to Huixtocihuatl and climbed to the summit of the Tlaloc temple at the Templo Mayor. There they sacrificed captives to the *tlaloque*. The impersonator of Huixtocihuatl was the last of the sacrifices. She was laid over the sacrificial stone and her chest was opened in such a way as to gush the blood up high in the air—"it was as if it showered; it was as if it boiled up." Her heart was put in a green stone jar while trumpets were blown to signal the beginning of a feast. During this time there was a great amount of drinking and celebration. Insults received during this time would be resolved and forgotten.

The goddess of salt, elder sister of the *tlaloque*, was described in Sahagún's account as embodying several of the symbolic elements of maize and, more generally, food plants that were coming to fruition during this time of the agricultural year. Her costume was the Aztec definition of wealth and prestige. This ritual was primarily a celebration of female creativity and its associated violence. Mature women were the impersonator's entourage—those capable of bearing children and perpetuating human life. Fruits of the earth (connected with the nurturing effects of the lake), coming to fruition, corresponded with the powerful creative capacities of women. Likewise, it was primarily through the medium of female song and dance that this unique creative ability manifested itself.

According to Broda, VIII-Huei teucilhuitl, "great feast of the lords," like VII-Teucilhuitontli, revolved around the cult of maize, the sun, and the underworld.[56] This ceremony took place in July when young maize germinated and the sun made its underworldly journey. During this festival, maize deities were addressed with particular emphasis on Xilonen. This was a time of hunger, when winter foods were running low, but was one not as serious as a famine. Throughout this festival, food was dispensed by the nobility of Aztec society. The ceremonial banquets of warriors and lords during VII-Huei teucilhuitl expressed an economic reciprocity between the inhabitants of subject towns and their rulers. By linking the rain cult and the cult of maize, the sun, and the underworld, the same process of reciprocity was activated at both cosmological and social levels. The correspondences of blood and water, which we have discussed as elements of rituals to the *tlaloque*, expressed social position—the *tlaloque* were to humans as the lords of Tenochtitlan were to subject towns and peoples. Maize, as the basic food, was the foundation of social authority.

XIII-TEPEILHUITL—FESTIVAL OF THE MOUNTAINS

Although XIII-Tepeilhuitl was a "festival of the mountains," the focus for activities during this month was actually on the various representations and images of mountains. These were either fashioned from food or embodied by different sacrificial victims. It is chiefly this feature of the ritual that will serve as my point of departure to analyzing the meaning of this ritual.[57] For both I-Atl cahualo and XIII-Tepeilhuitl, debt payment in the form of offerings or human sacrifices to Tlaloc was central to the ritual action. The principal distinction, however, was that the human sacrificial offerings during XIII-Tepeilhuitl were of adults, being primarily female, rather than children, who were also adorned to represent specific deities.

Within their homes, people gathered the necessary materials to make images of serpents and the wind. According to Sahagún, these were wooden serpentine figures fashioned from tree roots and made in honor of the mountains. The wind images were called *ecatotontli*, or "little wind," and were covered with *tzoalli*, a ground amaranth that was mixed with a sweetener and used in ceremonies. The people organized them "mountain-like," or in a fashion reminiscent of the valley topography. During XIII-Tepeilhuitl, a particular *tzoalli* was made from a type of amaranth called fish or ash amaranth.[58] The important qualities of the amaranth used seemed to have been that it be a food staple for human beings, that it be small like a grain of sand, and that it correspond in significant ways to water. Fish amaranth fit all these criteria.

The Aztec also made representations of mountains for people who had died. In particular, they made images of those who had

3.6. XIII-Tepeilhuitl, redrawn from the *Tovar Calendar*, Juan de Tovar.

died in the water or who had been struck by lightning. A bolt of lightning was associated with whipping, like the punishment of penitents in the *calmecac*, or threshing grain.[59] Lightning was directly associated with the *tlaloque* and was understood to emanate from Tlalocan. People who had died in these ways and were not burned would be fashioned into an image of a mountain from *tzoalli*. Torquemada adds that this was done as a memorial, but it seems more likely that the dead, like the priests, were intermediaries between human beings and the *tlaloque*.

The following day the people bathed themselves along with the mountain images.[60] Water was used to bath either the people, the images and their platforms, or all of them together. A correspondence was established between images of those slain by Tlaloc, primarily in water, and the activity of bathing in water. Accompanying the bathing was the music of flutes, also called *cocotl*, and the conch shell trumpet. Another sort of bathing occurred after this point at the *ayauhcalco*, or mist house. With reed shoots, people washed the faces of the images at the shore of the lake and some of the people took the images to places on the lake where they regularly bathed.

People then returned to their homes and continued to make more of the images late into the night. The images were referred to with an indefinite personal pronoun, indicating that they had the status of being alive. The process of making and adorning the images also had the

3.7. XIII-Tepeilhuitl, redrawn from the *Códice Matritense del Real Palacio*.

meaning of giving birth to, or engendering, a human being. During the course of constructing "mountains" of the dead, the Aztecs were giving life to those ancestors who had died for Tlaloc. The images were adorned with rubber masks and the *tzoalli* of fish amaranth. Mentioned specifically was fashioning the mouths of the images; an important site of consumption. According to Sahagún's Spanish gloss, two faces were made on each of the mountain images: one of a person and the other of a snake.[61] On top of the mountain images were fitted paper banners and other paper structures on which were placed crossed heron feathers.

The representations of the mountain/dead were then arranged in a circle, or on round platforms, on top of reeds called *aztapilli*, which were also used in VI-Etzalcualiztli. The reeds were described in Book XI as being cylindrical and salty, thus associating them directly with the salt lake.[62] A ceremonial meal was then laid out in front of the images, which consisted of fruit tamales, dog meat, and turkey. Incense was burned. A sumptuous meal was given to the family and the mountain images. Also music, dancing, and drunkenness were offered to the mountain images.

Then five women and one man who personified the mountains were sacrificed. They were named: 1) Tepexoch, "mountain flower"; 2) Matlalcue, "dark green skirt"; (3) Xochtecatl, "flower dweller"; (4) Mahahuel, "black corn stalk" and the representative of maguey; and 5) Milnahuatl, "field of agreeable sound," possibly a reference to the Nahuatl language. The sixth was male and was a representative of the snake. They were all richly arrayed with paper headdresses and rubberized cloth and were then carried by litter in a great procession by singing women. The women were also arrayed in fresh skirts and blouses as well as feather adornments. Up until this point, this was to be a female affair with female bearers and female offerings.

They put down the litters and ascended the temple of Tlaloc. Then the representatives were stretched over the sacrificial stone and their hearts were extracted. The bodies were then rolled down the stairs of the temple. After offering their lives as representatives of mountains, they were rolled down Tlaloc's mountain-temple, or Tlalocan. At the bottom they were taken to the *tzompantlan*, or "head row place," where there was a rack of the skulls of those taken in sacrifice. Probably the Quaquacuiltin (head-taking priests) would cut off the heads of the representatives and string them on the *tzompantli*. Their bodies were then taken to the various *calpulcos* and divided among the people. Durán tells us that they were then cooked into a stew of maize and beans and eaten by the entire community.

At the same time, or immediately after this event, they destroyed the mountain images of the dead made of amaranth and placed them in storage. In their storage areas, the images withered and dried out. The dried images were as hard as wood or as the stone and earth of the mountain. Eventually, they were also eaten, as all had to be totally consumed.

Again a correspondence between landscape, food, and the human body was established through ritual action. Just as the human representatives were sacrificed, divided, and consumed, so too were the mountain images of food destroyed, made hard, and consumed. Human life and agricultural fruits were linked in a correspondence with one another so as to orient a practical engagement with Tlalocan. Intermediaries between the human world and Tlalocan were dead family members.

All the paper adornments of the mountain images of the dead were then placed on the circular reed platforms and the clothes of the human sacrifices were hung where the stew was eaten in the *calpulco*. These paper and clothing adornments were left for a year, after which they were taken down and scattered at *ayauhcalco*, the mist house, at the lakeside. As with eating, the distribution of adornments from the representatives of the mountains underscored another connection between the human beings and the *tlaloque*. A consumptive correspondence was made during this feast between the human body and the body of land. The dead, associated with Tlaloc, were the intercessors for the maintenance of a living reciprocity between landscapes. An active engagement with the *tlaloque* was achieved through the activity of ritualistic eating. As we have seen before, the earth was an eating landscape. During XIII-Tepeilhuitl, it was the human act of eating that articulated ritual activity.

XVI-ATEMOZTLI—DESCENDING WATER

During the festival of XVI-Atemoztli, the meaning of human consumption was again brought to the forefront.[63] During this time of year, there was a greater incidence of thunder, lightning, and other climatological phenomena on mountains that were associated with the activity of the *tlaloque*. At this time, the Aztec made the *tepictoton*, or "little molded ones," from wood, paper, rubber, and amaranth in the images of the *tlaloque*, the servants or dwarfs of Tlaloc who oversaw the emerging rainstorms. These images were given food and then "killed" by the Tlamacazque. Their hearts were torn out and placed in greenstone vessels, just like in human sacrifices. The *tepictoton* were then eaten in a solemn feast with pulque, a fermented beverage made from the maguey plant. The ceremony gradually gave way to a drunken revelry. Like XIII-Tepeilhuitl, it focused primarily on a consumptive activity, but unlike the previous ceremonies the referent for this activity was eating the bodies of the *tlaloque* themselves and no human sacrifices were performed.

XVI-Atemoztli, "descending water," was named for its being the time of year when rain first started to fall. At this time, water, or the *tlaloque*, were said to descend from the mountains.[64] Thus rain and the *tlaloque* were active during that particular time of the year. The ritual was oriented around the construction, destruction, and consumption of the *tepictoton*, who represented the mountain deities. Likewise, action relating to these representatives will serve as the primary focus of my analysis.

At the Tlaloc temple, the Tlenamacac, or fire-offering priest, began his ceremonial duties. In a rigorously focused manner, he maintained a resolute self-absorption until the rainstorms began to rumble loudly over the valley. The timing of the festival was contingent on the force of the weather. When the rainstorm had reached an appropriate force, he emerged into the temple courtyard. *Moquetztiquiza* translates as "he emerges raising himself" and refers to the action of the Tlenamacac emerging from his penitential enclosure. It also referred to the "emergence" of rain, which, residing inside mountains, was seen to rise and emerge from under the earth through the mouths

3.8. XVI-Atemoztli, redrawn from the *Tovar Calendar*, Juan de Tovar.

3.9. XVI-Atemoztli, redrawn from the *Códice Matritense del Real Palacio.*

of caves. The priest, in this description, embodied the movement of rainclouds sent by the *tlaloque* in order that the earth might be replenished.[65]

The priest wielded an incense burner that was very large and made of wood that rattled. Upon the handle was carved a snake's head that rattled at its center, or heart. He offered the incense to the four directions in various places while rattling the censer as he went. In each temple precinct, he offered the incense, which had a warming effect in these places and also built confidence in the people. As during VI-Etzalcualiztli, offering incense in this fashion had the effect of generating heat in the world. Moreover, with this heat a confidence in the human community was generated. With this confidence in the effect of his offering, he summoned the *tlaloque* and requested that rain be sent.

[114]

Then people began molding the images of the mountain gods. For five days they stocked themselves up with paper, rubber, obsidian (volcanic glass), and maguey fiber. The markets were busy during this time selling materials for the feast. While fashioning and adorning the mountain gods, people would abstain from bathing with soap and sleeping with the opposite sex. For most of this twenty-day period people lived a penitent existence, concealed away in their homes, while fashioning the molded mountain images. They also made many paper banners splattered with rubber, which were hung on poles and arranged in rows. These poles were hung with the paper banners from top to bottom and then raised in the center of the temple courtyard.

The Tlamacazque, or serving priests, also made paper costumes for the *tepictoton* in the various *calmecac*, or men's penitent houses. When the paper adornments were finished, they carried the *tepictoton* to the houses, accompanied by the fanfare of the *teponaztli*, lateral log drums, and the *ayacachtli*, gourd rattles. Celebration of the *tlaloque*'s descent was accompanied by joyous sounds that contrasted with the introspective, self-contained demeanor needed while fabricating the images. The procession emphasized, in sonic imagery, the emergence of climatological phenomena from inside the earth.

Mountain images were fashioned out of the same substance as those of deceased relatives during XIII-Tepeilhuitl. While the image substantively remained the same, or similar, it shifted from representing the ancestors to representing the deities of water. The ancestors in XIII-Tepeilhuitl were those who had been taken by Tlaloc, and in this context became substituted for, or transformed into, the various *tlaloque*.

The *tepictoton* referred to specific mountains as well as other significant places in the landscape. Thirteen specific places are mentioned. They are: 1) Popocatepetl, "great smoking mountain"; 2) Iztactepetl, "white mountain," or Iztaccihuatl, "white woman"; 3) Tlaloc, "he who is the embodiment of earth"; 4) Yohualtecatl, "night dweller"; 5) Quauhtepetl, "tree mountain"; 6) Cocotl, or Cocohtli, either "pimple," "windpipe," or "mourning dove"; 7) Yauhqueme, "sacrificial garment"; 8) Tepetzintli, "honored hill"; 9) Tepepolli, "great hill"; 10) Uixachtecatl, "thorny tree dweller"; 11) Chicomecoatl, "seven snakes"; 12) "Chalchihuitlicue, "skirt of precious green-stone"; and 13) Ehecatl, "wind." All these sites were fashioned by the Aztec into an image, or representative, so as to articulate a specific relationship with that place.

Then the *tepictoton* were arranged and fed. They were given an abundance of small, thin tamales. They were served with small wood bowls that were filled with various sauces and clay bowls that were filled with chocolate. They were fed at four different times during the night. They were also offered two greenstone pots of pulque that were actually made from a soft green squash split in two. The seeds and pulp were removed and it was filled with pulque. All night long they sang, blew flutes, and blew the conch trumpet for the *tepictoton* while making oblations. It was the particular responsibility of the youths to drink during this time until they were drunk.

The nature of the connection between the mountain images and humans was clarified through the course of ritual feeding. A reciprocity was based on an exchange of food. The arranged *tepictoton* were the articulation of a landscape, or a representation of a "deified map" similar to that described during IV-Huei tozoztli, and which the Aztec had to successfully and meaningfully occupy. Their creation of mountain offerings secured a communicative link to a larger landscape. Meaningful occupation of the Valley of Mexico required active engagement with the places of Tlaloc.

At dawn a weaving stick was thrust into the "hearts" of the *tepictoton*. Then their heads were bent over and broken. Their hearts were extracted and placed in the green gourd vessel. They were symbolically killed. All the various adornments were collected and assembled in the Tlaloc temple courtyard and burned. As during XIII-Tepeilhuitl, the wood and green-gourd vessels containing the "hearts" of the *tepictoton* were left at the *ayauhcalco*, or mist house, near the edge of the lake. Then people were summoned to eat the *tepictoton* and everyone was served the bodies of the mountain deities. The women brought abundant dried maize in their skirts and the people would eat and drink until satiated and drunk. At the beginning of the rains, this was a time of unmitigated gluttony. The point of the festival was to consume all that one could. Human beings consumed the very bodies of those deities from which rain came. The final action of the ceremony of XVI-Atemoztli revealed the relationship of humans to the landscape: eating. At the end the paper banners were again tied to poles in the courtyard to signify the debt payment to the *tlaloque*.

According to Durán, XVIII-Izcalli means "growth."[66] For Siméon, it translates as "return to the heat," referring to the heat of the sun.[67] This was a dry time of the agricultural year and required that offerings be made to the *tlaloque*. Also during this time parts of the body, particularly those of children, were pulled to promote growth. A special tamale of boiled amaranth leaves mixed with maize was prepared for this festival. The feasts were to honor two particular mountains. The first was Tlalocan and the second Matlalcueye, a peak in the nearby province of Tlaxcala. During the rituals, a boy and girl who represented these mountains were sacrificed. Blood and food were given to promote growth during this sowing season. Durán also links the rites during this month with those of the first month, I-Atl cahualo.

According to Broda, human sacrifice to the *tlaloque* was not just an offering but actually represented the god's life. This was not devotion as in a conventional sense, but a contractual arrangement. Rituals were the mediating activities between mythic and material realities in the forms of the word, song, dance, costume, liturgical objects, offerings, and above all, human sacrifice.[68] Human material well-being depended on the *tlaloque*. Although hidden from direct human contact, the *tlaloque* were material beings and various phenomena, like mountains and weather, were taken as proof of their existence and activity in the world. Places and phenomena were given by these deities. Mountains were not just the place where the *tlaloque* resided, but were embodiments of the water deities. The mountain rituals during the final part of the calendar year anthropomorphized these deities for purposes of communicating with them.[69]

These nine festivals can be seen as generally falling into three groups. First were those festivals that included child sacrifice, chiefly concerned with agricultural success and ample rainfall. Second were festivals that included impersonators of the *tlaloque* sacrificed to promote growth of tender maize. Third were the festivals to the *tlaloque*, or *tepictoton*, who were images of various mountains fashioned from maize and amaranth. This third festival type was performed both to alleviate diseases attributed to the *tlaloque* and to lessen violent storms in the lakes, thereby reducing watery deaths. All the rites included an understanding of magical imagination, in Broda's parlance, in which "like produces like."[70] Moreover, these were festivals for common people and priests. They were not the more spectacular sacrificial practices of the sun or warrior cult. According to Broda, magical imagination was the basis for plentiful and successful life in the valley from a indigenous viewpoint, not an elite one. This is not to say that nobles did not participate. According to the *Relación Breve*, it was they who made the difficult climbs to the mountaintops to make offerings to Tlaloc.[71] Motolinía indicates that it was the children of nobles who were preferable as sacrifices to Tlaloc.[72] The nobility necessarily incorporated the indigenous cult into state activities in order to locate their basis of authority.

Framing the Tlaloc cult strictly in terms of its sociological effects for authorizing Aztec presence in the valley, however, abbreviates our understanding of the consequences of these rituals. In the previous examination, careful attention has been given to illustrating the interplay of practice and interpretation of the Aztecs. Overemphasizing culture as the object of study obfuscates a dynamic interplay between the landscape and the practitioner. An interpretation of the Tlaloc religion as oriented to a material landscape, rather than a system of beliefs, gives us a more authentic sense of it as an indigenous hermeneutic of occupation. Thought and environment, it seems, were not discrete, rarefied objects for the Aztecs, but were systems involved with the activity of human beings. Reflection on their community's place in a cosmos was discovered through divination, while acting appropriately with reference to other living beings. As with Sahagún, moving too quickly to capture the broad contours of the Other's "cosmovision" on paper tends to erase from view their hermeneutical practice that constituted the basis of a meaningful orientation to the world.

The subject of chapter 4 is how rituals to Tlaloc and the *tlaloque* are to be involved in a phenomenal world. The structure that Sahagún has imposed on these rituals (i.e., a chronological one) suggests one way that they fit with each other. The Aztecs, however, were more concerned with addressing ritual themes with reference to spatial arrangements. Each of these ceremonies occupied a particular place in the agricultural calendar that corresponded to various stages of maize production and food acquisition. There are particular points of reference, however, that keep recurring. What follows is an examination of Tlaloc's body as it was tied to particular material sites of Aztec ritual activity.

NOTES

1. As López Austin says, "The Nahuas created a form of expression for addressing hidden invisible beings, often very close to them, but hidden behind a barrier that could be crossed only under very special conditions. This speech was called nahuallatolli, 'the language of the hidden.'" Alfredo López Austin, *The Human Body and Ideology: Concepts of the Ancient Nahuas*, 2 vols., translated by Thelma and Bernard Ortiz de Montellano (Salt Lake City: University of Utah Press, 1988), vol. 1, p. 346.

2. Tzvetan Todorov, in *The Conquest of America*, translated by Richard Howard (New York: Harper Torchbooks, 1984), pp. 69–70, discusses the differences in communicative strategy between the Aztecs and the Spanish. He characterizes the former as a "human to world" strategy that primarily acknowledges a connection between people of the Valley of Mexico and deities who also inhabit that space. Johannes Wilbert, in "Eschatology in a Participatory Universe and Destinies of the Soul Among Warao Indians of Venezuela," in *Death and Afterlife in Pre-Columbian American*, edited by Elizabeth Benson (Washington, DC: Dumbarton Oaks, 1975), p. 163, n. 1, borrowing the term "participatory universe" from F. Helitzer, "The Princeton Galaxy," *Intellectual Digest* 3, no. 10 (1973): 25–32, applies it to the worldview of the Warao of Venezuela. As he says, "[it is] essentially similar to what the Warayo think of the interdependence or mutuality that exists between man and the supernatural world."

3. The Mesoamerican calendar is a complicated subject and will be more directly addressed below. The agricultural calendar was composed of eighteen "months" of twenty days each (= 360 days). At the end of the monthly calendar round, there was a five-day interval called Nemontemi and known to be an unlucky time. During the course of each of these eighteen "months," there was a festival for a particular deity or constellation of deities. For a complete and concise discussion of the Mesoamerican calendar, see Aveni, "The Mathematical and Astronomical Content of the Mesoamerican Inscriptions," in his *Sky Watchers of Ancient Mexico* (Austin: University of Texas Press, 1980), pp. 133–173. See also Johanna Broda, "Ciclos agrícolas en el culto: Una problema de la correlación del calendario Mexica," in *Calendars in Mesoamerica and Peru: Native American Computations of Time*, edited by Anthony F. Aveni and Gordon Brotherston (Oxford: B.A.R. International Series 174, 1983), pp. 145–164.

4. According to Karttunen, in *An Analytical Dictionary of Nahuatl* (Austin: University of Texas Press, 1983), p. 207, while this is a bird of red plumage, the phrase refers to its characteristic of a sweeping motion of its neck rather than its feathers. According to Andrews, in *Introduction to Classical Nahuatl*, textbook and workbook (Austin: University of Texas Press, 1975), p. 465, this is a bird variously referred to as a macaw, flamingo, or the roseate spoonbill.

5. Roman numerals preceding the names of the festival months indicate where they fall in the eighteen-month sequence.

6. See Fray Bernardino de Sahagún, *Florentine Codex: General History of the Things of New Spain*, 12 books, 13 parts, edited and translated by Arthur J. O. Anderson and Charles E. Dibble, Monographs of the School of American Research, no. 14 (Salt Lake City: University of Utah Press, 1951–82), book 2, pp. 42–46; 78–90; 131–133; and 151–154. I have relied on Dibble and Anderson's translations in addition to my own to gain a fuller sense of the meaning for much of the action.

7. During the course of my translation of these texts from the Nahuatl, I found that Charles Dibble and Arthur Anderson's translations were very reliable. While their intention was to render the Nahuatl into a smooth English equivalent, my intention was quite different; to examine the varieties of meanings found in the lexical items. Here I wish to express my gratitude to Dibble and Anderson for their fine and rigorous translations, upon which I had to rely when the Spanish gloss strikingly contrasted with the Nahuatl account.

8. Perhaps it is desirable at this point to reflect on the impossible task of translation. My experience in working with Nahuatl suggests that there is rarely a one-to-one correspondence between a Nahuatl phrase and an English translation. One challenge to translation is the oral nature of Nahuatl, where meaning is transmitted in specific contexts that are inherently performative. Second, and resulting from the first, is that Nahuatl has a referential basis (see my discussion of Hanks in chapter 1) in which meaning is always framed with respect to whom one is talking to or about, etc. Third are the cultural restraints of my ability to meaningfully frame a Nahuatl utterance. This is nothing more or less than a restatement of an important anthropological dictum that we can only know the world from our cultural vantage point. In my case, that vantage point is distinctly different from the Aztecs'.

9. See my "Eating Landscape: Human Sacrifice and Sustenance in Aztec Mexico," in *To Change Place: Aztec Ceremonial Landscapes*, edited by Davíd Carrasco (Niwot: University Press of Colorado, 1991), pp. 219–232, for a brief analysis of this ceremony.

10. These were the sacrifices that took place for Xipe Totec, the Flayed One, and included the presentation of captives. Scholars have connected this with other gods and rituals for new maize. See Henry B. Nicholson, "Religion in Pre-Hispanic central Mexico," in *Handbook of Middle American Indians: Guide to the Ethnohistorical Sources*, vol. 11, edited by R. Wauchope (Austin: University of Texas Press, 1971), pp. 422–424.

11. According to Johanna Broda's "Las fiestas Aztecas de los dioses de la lluvia: una reconstruccíon según las fuentes del siglo XVI," in *Revista Española de antropología*

Americana 6 (1971): 268, the sacrifice of children began in the sixteenth month and ran through to the fourth month, when the rains really had taken hold.

12. See López Austin, *The Human Body and Ideology*, vol. 2, p. 292.

13. Added to *teteuh*, "paper streamers," is *tlaca*, "person," rendering these children as "human paper streamers."

14. Special thanks goes to R. Joseph Campbell and his "Florentine Project" for supplying indexes listing the frequency with which *amatl* and *tetehuitl* appear in the *Florentine*.

15. See Debra Nagao, "The Planting of Sustenance: Symbolism of the Two-Horned God in Offerings from the Templo Mayor," *RES Anthropology and Aesthetics* 10 (1985b): 5–27.

16. See Karttunen, *An Analytical Dictionary of Nahuatl*, p. 159.

17. See Broda, "Las fiestas Aztecas de los dioses," pp. 274–275.

18. See Sahagún, *Florentine Codex*, book 11, p. 19.

19. Ibid., p. 223. This stone was neither jade nor turquoise but a more common gem sometimes called jadeite.

20. It is also the name for a black maize that has been infected by a fungus that is considered a delicacy among contemporary Nahua. Jane Rosenthal, personal communication.

21. See Broda, "Las fiestas Aztecas de los dioses," p. 277.

22. See Fray Torbio Motolinía (de Benavente), *Memoriales o libro de las cosas de Nueva España y de los naturales de ella*, edited by Edmundo O'Gorman (Mexico City: Universidad Nacional Autónoma de México, 1971), p. 65.

23. See Sahagún, *Florentine Codex*, book 2, p. 8.

24. See Durán, "Chapter VIII: Which Deals with the Idol Named Tlaloc, God of Rain, Thunder, and Lightning, Who was Revered by All the People of the Land. The Name Means Path Under the Earth or Long Cave," in *Book of the Gods and Rites and the Ancient Calendar*, edited and translated by Fernando Horcasitas and Doris Heyden (Norman: University of Oklahoma Press, 1971), pp. 154–171.

25. Ibid., pp. 154–156.

26. Ibid., p. 156.

27. This would be Totah[-tli] according to Karttunen, *An Analytical Dictionary of Nahuatl*, p. 214.

28. According to Fernando Horcasitas and Doris Heyden, "The lake, giving moisture to the corn fields and teeming with edible things such as algae, mosquito eggs, water plants, shrimp, fish of a dozen varieties, frogs, ducks, and other birds, such as wading birds, was really the mother of ancient Mexico-Tenochtitlan. The Aztecs saw her as Our Lady Tonan, who suckled her favorite children with her lake milk." Durán, *Book of the Gods and Rites*, p. 168, note 4.

29. See Philip P. Arnold, "The Aztec Ceremonial Landscape in the Valley of Mexico: Implications of Examining Religion and Environment," M.A. thesis in Archaeology (Institute of Latin American Studies, University of London, 1986), p. 32.

30. Juan Bautista Pomar, "Relación de Texcoco," in *Relaciones de Texcoco y de los señores de la Nueva España* (Mexico: S. Chavez Hayhoe, 1941), pp. 14–16.

31. See Charles Wicke and Fernando Horcasitas, "Archaeological Investigations of Monte Tlaloc, Mexico," *Mesoamerican Notes* 5 (1957): 83–96.

32. In addition to Aveni there have been some recent intensive surveys of this site. Stanislaw Iwaniszewski and Iván Sprajc, over the course of several years of surveying the central Mexican landscape, have developed a map to further elaborate the relationship between sites ("Field Reconnaissance and Mapping of the Archaeological Site at Mt. Tlaloc," December, 1987). Unfortunately this map remains unpublished (personal communication). In addition, Richard Townsend and Felipe Solis Olguin have conducted surveys of Mount Tlaloc and traced iconographical relationships with other sites in the valley. See Richard Townsend, "The Mt. Tlaloc Project," in *To Change Place: Aztec Ceremonial Landscapes*, edited by Davíd Carrasco (Niwot: University Press of Colorado, 1991), pp. 26–30. For a very useful and compact analysis of the connections between mountain ecology and pre-Columbian sites, see Stanislaw Iwaniszewski, "La arqueología de alta montaña en México y su estado actual," *Estudios de cultura Nahuatl* 18 (1986): 249–273.

33. See Anthony F. Aveni's "The Aztec City and the Sky," in *Conversations with Anthony Aveni: Archaeoastronomy and the History of Religions*, edited by Davíd Carrasco, Philip Arnold, Lawrence Desmond, and Rebecca Herr (Boulder, CO: Mesoamerican Archive and Research Project Working Papers, no. 1, 1985), pp. 1–8. Also see Anthony F. Aveni and Sharon Gibbs, "On the Orientation of Ceremonial Centers in Central Mexico," *American Antiquity* 41 (1976): 510–517.

34. See Anthony F. Aveni, "The Role of Astronomical Orientation in the Delineation of World View: A Center and Periphery Model," in *Imagination of Matter: Religion and Ecology in Mesoamerican Tradition*, edited by Davíd Carrasco (Oxford: B.A.R. International Series 515, 1989), pp. 85–102.

35. Other studies by Mesoamericanists have reinforced this view. See Rudolph van Zantwijk, *The Aztec Arrangement: The Social History of Pre-Spanish Mexico* (Norman: University of Oklahoma Press, 1985). R. Thomas Zuidema has found many analogous relational systems in the ancient Inca capital of Cuzco. See *The Ceque System of Cuzco: The Social Organization of the Capital of the Inca*, International Archives of Ethnography, supplement to vol. 50 (Leiden, Netherlands: E.J. Brill, 1964). The *ceque* system was an elaborate system of sight lines that ran from the ceremonial center to the horizon and organized the social and religious landscape, as well as other media, including textiles (*quipu*). See also R. Thomas Zuidema, "The Inca Calendar," in *Native American Astronomy*, edited by Anthony F. Aveni (Austin: University of Texas Press, 1977), pp. 219–259.

See Gary Urton, *Crossroads of the Earth and Sky: An Andean Cosmology* (Austin: University of Texas Press, 1981). His study of a contemporary Quechua-speaking community has linked the cosmological circulation of water through the earth and landscape to revolutions of the sun and Milky Way. The horizon astronomy, in this case, perpetuates the circulation of life-sustaining fluids. See Lawrence E. Sullivan,

"Astral Myths Rise Again: Interpreting Religious Astronomy," *Criterion* 22 (1983): 12–17, for a review of recent literature and avenues of approach to indigenous calendar systems and their ritual significance.

36. See Motolinía, *Memoriales o libro de las cosas*, p. 45. Also see Broda, "Las fiestas Aztecas de los dioses," pp. 282–298, for an overview of this ceremony.

37. Broda has the festivities of the month beginning on the tenth day. My analysis indicates that for all the events recorded to fit into the twenty-day interval the actions would have had to begin four days before the first day of the month. Dibble and Anderson's translation also indicates that this was the case.

38. These reeds were gathered at three specific sites: 1) Temilco, "place of stony fields," 2) Tepexic, "place of cliffs," and 3) Oztoc, "place of caves." These three places refer to distinct geographical features that were identified with the *aztapilli*. The first refers to nonagricultural fields, or wild fields; the second to a mountainous place jutting out of a plain; and the third to a space interior to the earth. All were probably descriptive of particular locations now unknown.

39. A *tlalmecatl* directly translates to mean "earth cord," which was used for measuring property. It could be that the Tlamacazque actually used such an earth cord to whip and rob the travelers of the road. It is used in this context, however, to refer to the great distance this fear traveled among the people.

40. Referring to *matacaxtli*, the corresponding Spanish text says that it lay over the arm as an ornament and was made from the skin of a wild beast (jaguar or ocelot) in the manner of a maniple used in the mass. See Sahagún, *Florentine Codex*, book 2, p. 76, note 25. Etymologically, this word is difficult to trace. According to Andrews, *Introduction to Classical Nahuatl*, pp. 450 and 467, *ma-*, or "hand," precedes *tacaxtli*, or "trough at the base of a tree" or "root ball of a tree." Unfortunately this latter element is unaccounted for in any of the other dictionaries I have used and Andrews gives no citation for his translation.

41. The process of adorning throughout this ritual is referred to as *mochichihua*, which has the root *chihua*, meaning "to make, create, engender, or beget something or someone." By adding a reflexive *mo* to this verb, the sense of it is "to make oneself," or "to engender oneself." By assembling his costume, the fire priest thus created himself. Likewise, Dibble and Anderson translate *moxixitinia* as "his undressing himself by taking off his ceremonial garments." However, this refers to his destroying or undoing himself, and could also refer to some form of autosacrifice. The sense is that by assuming his ceremonial garments, the Tlenamacac gave himself life, and by relinquishing these garments he destroyed that same life.

42. The emptiness of these schools is emphasized by referring to them as "scraped out," as one would do to the inside of a gourd or squash.

43. Although it is not my intention here, there could be a very interesting reading of VI-Etzalcualiztli based on the interplay of gender symbolism. Important here, however, is that the ritual activity seems to address the female aspect of water and fertility, Chalchihuitlicue, and not Tlaloc per se. They are connected, though, as seen in the dynamics of the hydrological cycle in IV-Huei tozoztli or expressed in their kinship associations as wife/husband or sister/brother.

44. A *cacalotl* is identified as Jabiru mycteria (Lichtenstein) of the stork and wood ibis family, or as Plegadis guarauna L. of the ibis and spoonbill family. According to Sahagún, "it is a black waterfowl and an eater of water life. Its legs are long and black and it has a sharp curved bill." See Sahagún, *Florentine Codex*, book 11, p. 43.

45. The *aztatl* is identified as the Leucophoyx thula by Molina, *Vocabulario en lengua Castellana y Mexicana y Mexicana y Castellana* (Mexico City: Editorial Porrúa, 1977), and is probably the snowy egret. *Aztatl* however refers generally to heron, which includes egrets for the Aztecs. According to Sahagún, "it is also called *teoaztatl*—divine heron. It is white like snow. Its back is rounded, dry and old looking; its neck is long and stringy and curved; its bill is pointed, long and black; its legs are long, stringy and black; and its tail is stubby." See Sahagún, *Florentine Codex*, book 11, p. 28.

46. *Axoquen* is identified as Florida caerulea (Linnaeus). "It is called the little blue heron and it resembles the brown crane in its color because it is ashen and grey. It smells like fish, rotten and stinking fish." See Sahagún, *Florentine Codex*, book 11, p. 28. Rémi Siméon, *Diccionario de la lengua Nahuatl o Mexicana* (Mexico City: Siglo Veintiuno editores, 1977), p. 51, describes this as a type of parrot with white plumage.

47. The *tocuilcoyotl* is identified as Grus canadensis (Linnaeus) and is called a brown crane. According to Sahagún, "its bill is long, like a nail and dart-shaped. The head is chili-red, the body ashen, and the neck long. It is tall and the legs are stringy, long, and black, like stilts. It is edible and good to taste." See Sahagún, *Florentine Codex*, book 11, p. 27. Siméon, *Diccionario de la lengua Nahuatl*, p. 712, suggests that this may be rendered something like "coyote crane."

48. *Totoli* is translated by Dibble and Anderson as "turkey." See Sahagún, *Florentine Codex*, book 11, pp. 53–54, where there is a lengthy discussion of the *totoli*. It is identified as Meleagris gallapavo (Linnaeus) and the male turkey is called *huexolotl*, "great male servant." It is also called *ihhuiquen*, "feather garment," *ihhuiquentzin*, "honored feather garment," and *xiuhcozca*, "grass or turquoise necklace."

> It lives at home, near by people. Its feathers are thick and tail round. It has wings but is heavy and not a flyer. It is edible and leads all the meats; very tasty, fat, savory. It molts. It is glistening white, ashen, tawny and some smoky. It eats ground maize, roasted maize and cooked greens. Of these it eats *tonalchichicaquilitl* [probably Oenothera lacinata], *cuanacaquilitl* [which seems similar to the *coyocuexi* (book 11, pp. 137–138, note 12)], *coyocue(chtl)i* [which cannot be unidentified], and *tetzitzili*. The male turkey is big, has air sacks, wattles, has a big breast and long neck. It has a necklace of coral. The head is blue and dewlapped. Its eyelids are cylindrical and swollen. It spreads its tail feathers at an attack and tramples others underfoot. Its rounded protuberance is pliant, leathery, and soft. If one hates another this protuberance is fed to the other in chocolate or a sauce to render them impotent. It eats many things including maize, tortillas, tamales, chili, and greens. It dies quickly from a lack of salt. A hen is of average size with a low back. She has a necklace and is coral-headed. She is mounted by the cock to create eggs. She sits and is tasty and healthful, fat, fleshy. She gathers the eggs and hatches her young and gathers them under her arm.

A turkey's development is also described: "a drop forms; it thickens; a covering forms, a shell forms. The egg is laid. When it falls, [the shell] is still soft; then it quickly hardens in the air. It is settled over; it is warmed. It breaks open, hatches, becomes colored. The little poult, the poult is a molted one; it becomes round. The young turkey cocks, the young turkey hens mature, form air-sacs, develop wattles." See Sahagún, book 11, pp. 53–54.

According to Sahagún (book 11, p. 137), *tonalchichicaquilitl* grows in the dry lands, in the grasslands and the forest. "It is an ashen color and bitter. It remedies diseases of internal fever, aids digestion, especially during the fast. It means sun warmed bitter greens." *Coyocue(chtl)i* "is said to be soft, stalky and has blossoms that are fragrant. It is not to be eaten by children because it irritates the throat." It can be translated as "coyote dust," and appears as a form of lettuce whose seeds are born through the wind and translates as "bird greens" (p. 139). *Tetzitzili* "is said to be a cord-like plant that creeps and sends out feelers. It also has blooms and spines which are sharp." It is also known as *tzompachquilitl*, "top hay greens." *Tetzitzili* means something like "people's bells, herbs." (p. 197).

See also Doris Heyden's recent exploration of the symbolism of this bird in "Guajolote, guajolote, en realidad ¿quién eres?" in *Códices y documentos sobre México, Primer Simposio*, edited by Constanza Vega (Mexico City: Colección Científica, INAH, 1995), pp. 173–192.

49. See Sahagún, *Florentine Codex*, book 11, p. 145.

50. This is identified as Aristolochia grandiflora. The literal meaning may be "medicine staff." See Karttunen, *An Analytical Dictionary of Nahuatl*, p. 256.

51. Huixtocihuatl was the goddess of salt, who was also honored during the festival VII-Tecuilhuitontli, which was the festival directly following VI-Etzalcualiztli.

52. This is identified as the northern phalarope (Lobipes lobatus) or as the sanderling (Crocethia alba). See Sahagún, *Florentine Codex*, book 2, p. 87, note 35. Sahagún (book 11, p. 28) describes this bird as "round-backed, with a bill long and pointed, needle-like, stilt-like, broom-like, and slender. Its place of dwelling is the province of Anahuac. It has a white breast, is heavy fleshed, fat, and greasy."

53. Sahagún, *Florentine Codex*, book 11, p. 165. This is identified as Artemisia mexicana and described by Sahagún as "small and stalky with ashen and slender branches. It is like the wormwood of Castile. Its foliage is ground up and crumbles in the hands. It cures many things as when one has much phlegm settle in him, when he is dizzy he drinks it thickened. It throws off the fever and cleanses the urine. It relieves head blisters. And when one is anguished in his heart, or a humor is oppressive, the center stalks of *iztauhyatl* and *quauhyayahual* are ground up. The center is white and somewhat sweet. One can drink this hot, with water. This also relieves the cough." This was a popular herb sold in the markets by medical specialists. Also book 10, pp. 85–86.

54. In descriptions of this place, poles of paper banners and other ceremonial items characterize this place.

55. Aveni has suggested that constant reference to 4-, 8-, and 16-day intervals may be organized in such a way that specific events were designed to land on significant day names (personal communication).

56. See Johanna Broda, "The Sacred Landscapes of Aztec Calendar Festivals: Myth, Nature, and Society," in *To Change Place: Aztec Ceremonial Landscapes*,

edited by Davíd Carrasco (Niwot: University Press of Colorado, 1991), p. 82.

57. According to Nutini, XIII-Tepeilhuitl was the model for the contemporary Day of the Dead celebrations throughout central Mexico. Hugo Nutini, *Todos Santos in Rural Tlaxcala: A Syncretic, Expressive, and Symbolic Analysis of the Cult of the Dead* (Princeton, NJ: Princeton University Press, 1988), p. 56.

58. The first, as described in Book XI, was a food that looked like fish roe. "It was yellow and round like a stone or grain of sand." The second is described as resembling the Spanish goosefoot and was a large butterflylike herb with ample branches of green leaves at its top, and seeds that were sandlike and which were round and white. The name of ash amaranth is either *cocotl* or *cocohtli*, and can mean either "pimple," "throat/windpipe," or "mourning dove." This was also the name of the sixth of seven sites mentioned in I-Atl cahualo where children were sacrificed. See Sahagún, *Florentine Codex,* book 11, p. 286.

59. See *huitecoc,* bolt of lightning, in Karttunen, *An Analytical Dictionary of Nahuatl,* p. 90. This is in the verbal form of *huitequ(i)*—"to get whipped, whip or beat someone," "to thresh grain." As in Dibble and Anderson's translation, the sense is of one who had been struck by lightning.

60. Dibble and Anderson translate this to mean "that people bath them" (the images). There seems to be a confusion about the prefix *te-* and whether it is the subject or object of the sentence. To my mind, it is the object of the action. Moreover, this is backed up by Eduard Seler in *Einige Kapitel aus dem Geschichtswerk des Fray Bernardino de Sahagún aus dem Aztekischen bersetzt,* edited by Caecilie Seler-Sachs, Walter Lehmann, and Walter Krickeberg (Stuttgart: Strecker and Schroeder, 1927), pp. 190–191, in which he maintains that the people are washed. Sahagún has a very different sense of the action, in which the people bath the reed mats upon which the images rested. See Sahagún, *Florentine Codex,* book 2, p. 131, note 7.

61. According to Sahagún, *Florentine Codex* (book 2, p. 132, note 9), the corresponding Spanish says that on each mountain two faces were made. One of the person and the other of a snake.

62. Dibble and Anderson say that Sahagún's corresponding Spanish text indicates this round place as being a circular jar resting in grass.

63. See chapter 6 for a more thorough analysis of this festival.

64. They would say that there was growling and thunder in the rainstorms on the mountains. The word *tititl,* used to denote thunder, was also the name of the festival of the seventeenth month, which followed XVI-Atemoztli (Siméon, *Diccionario de la lengua Nahuatl,* p. 549). Meaning "contraction," or "stretching," according to Torquemada, *tititl* refers to the forces of contraction due to cold and hail on the sierra during this time of year that would generate an odd yet consistent drizzle. In this sense it refers to thunder, or the contraction associated with shifting weather on the sierra (Sahagún, *Florentine Codex,* book 2, p. 155, note 1).

65. The use of the reflective in *moquetztiquiza* may indicate that this action was accomplished with reference to the self; it was a matter of self-reflection in the service of community survival.

66. See Durán, *Book of the Gods and Rites*, pp. 465–468. He is probably deriving this meaning from the verb *(i)zcalia*: "to hatch, revive, be restored, or nurture someone." Karttunen, *An Analytical Dictionary of Nahuatl*, p. 123.

67. See Siméon, *Diccionario de la lengua Nahuatl*, p. 234.

68. "[L]os medios para su representación eran la palabra, el canto, el baile, los atavios, los objectos litúrgicos, las ofrendas y sobretoda, los sacrificios humanos." See Broda, "Las fiestas Aztecas de los dioses," p. 319.

69. The place of sacrifice in ritual has been examined from several points of view. It is not my intention to present a new general theory of human sacrifice from the Aztec case, but rather to situate it in a series of substantive reciprocities. For Walter Burkert (*Homo Necans: The Anthropology of Ancient Greek Sacrificial Ritual and Myth*, translated by Peter Bing [Berkeley: University of California Press, 1983]), sacrifice must be seen in the larger sociological context of violence and authority. He ties sacrifice to the violence of hunting, which was primarily a communal activity. Sacrifice is the remembrance of hunting activity that forges a "guilt-bond" similar to Sigmund Freud's conception of the "primal horde" (*Totem and Taboo: Resemblances Between the Psychic Lives of Savages and Neurotics* [New York: Vintage Books, 1946], pp. 162–164). Also see Marcel Detienne and Jean-Pierre Vernant, eds., *The Cuisine of Sacrifice Among Ancient Greeks*, translated by Paula Wissing (Chicago: University of Chicago Press, 1989); René Girard in *Violence and the Sacred*, translated by Patrick Gregory (Baltimore: Johns Hopkins University Press, 1977); and Freud's explanation of familial violence as the basis of sacrifice. Sacrifice, for Girard, keeps distant the familial violence that is sometimes too close.

Taking a different viewpoint is E. E. Evans-Pritchard, who, in *Nuer Religion* (Oxford: Oxford University Press, 1956), describes cattle sacrifice as ridding the community of evil. As with Robertson Smith (*Religion of the Semites: The Fundamental Institutions* [New York: Meridian Books, 1957]), Evans-Pritchard sees this as a process in the action of community formation through the use of a scapegoat. For me, however, Evans-Pritchard's view of religion becomes more understandable when paired up with his book *The Nuer: A Description of the Modes of Livelihood and Political Institutions os a Nilotic People* (Oxford: Oxford University Press, 1940). In this earlier study of the economic and ecological existence of the Nuer, the intimate relationships between men and their cattle are explored within a larger constellation of material concerns. Likewise, Henri Hubert and Marcel Mauss, in *Sacrifice: Its Nature and Function*, translated by W. D. Halls (Chicago: University of Chicago Press, 1967), give a useful description of sacrifice in terms of its functional attributes within a given social context (Vedic India). They end by determining that it is a contractual agreement between realms of being that revitalizes a sense of human boundaries. This is not so much a theory of sacrifice as an analysis of what it accomplishes.

All of these authors, as well as many more, contribute to our general understanding of the significance of ritual sacrifice. Elements of violence, authority, community, reciprocity, etc., are all present in the Aztec case. Less attention has been place, however, on the interpretive attributes of human sacrifice as it expresses fundamental biological realities. Rather than reduce Aztec sacrifice too quickly to the disembodied world of theory I will be satisfied with a descriptive rendering of its place in a Tlalocan landscape. This is to highlight the interpretive underpinnings of Aztec human sacrifice as embedded in an embodied landscape as well as embedded in my attempts to deal with this phenomenon.

70. Here Broda is employing the Frazerian model of magic and therefore embraces a traditional concept of a fertility cult, which is different from the hermeneutical approach I have set out. Indeed, much of her analysis seems to be based on the notion of sympathetic magic expressed by Sir James George Frazer in "Chapter III—Sympathetic Magic," in *The Golden Bough: A Study in Magic and Religion*, abridged edition (New York: Collier Books, 1950), vol. 1, pp. 12–55.

71. See Fray Bernardino de Sahagún, "Relación breve de las fiestas de los dioses," translated by Angel María Garibay, *Tlalocan* 2, no. 4 (1948): 289–321.

72. Broda, "Las fiesta Aztecas de los dioses," p. 325.

4 The Ritual Cosmology of Tlalocan

Even the most cursory glance at rituals dedicated to Tlaloc, Chalchihuitlicue, and the *tlaloque*, as discussed in chapter 3, reveals a tremendous amount of performative detail. It is, therefore, presumptuous to assert that any single interpreter can claim to have understood the meaning of all the various elements. This is particularly the case when the data are presented in an abbreviated textualized form. Any speculation about the significance of these events has to take into account the highly circumscribed character of their having been presented in an ethnographic book—the *Florentine Codex*. Therefore, this chapter will widen the scope of the textual descriptions to include ecological, archaeological, and experiential phenomena. Activities mentioned by the *Florentine* will act as our guide to understanding certain features of the Aztec landscape. Descriptions of rituals to Tlaloc examined in Sahagún's text have been reorganized in this chapter around specific material points of reference that guided cultic activity and that will therefore guide our exploration of Tlalocan.

First, we will look at a series of correspondences (usually between bodies of various beings) that were expressed in rituals to Tlaloc. Then we will widen those correspondences to see how specific material realities were involved with human sustenance and occupation of the

Valley of Mexico. Understanding an Aztec hermeneutics of occupation requires reflection on the meanings of the material points of reference that oriented human practice. Material realities, integral to human survival, acted as focal points for Aztec understanding as well as points of contact between human beings and the world. They are discussed here in the hope that various understandings of material life can moderate between the modern scholar and pre-Columbian people.

EARTH BODY

As discussed in chapter 1, the *Codex Fejérváry-Mayer* is a pre-Columbian "map" of an interactive place/time.[1] Spatial arrangements of the cosmos were articulated with reference to the progression of daily events, thus uniting place and time. Rituals reinforced this arrangement by physically uniting space and time in bodily activity; both individual and communal. The landscape was an event—its material life was seen as an activity rather than a state of being. Occupation of the land was thus organized through human ritual actions. Ritual occupation was cosmogonic (i.e., an essentially creative activity) because it participated in those processes perpetually involved in the ongoing regeneration of life.

Half of the ritual events during the agricultural year were dedicated to Tlaloc. We have looked at several of them in some detail. The strategy of these rituals was to actively build correspondences between beings. While the human body was the focus of much of the ritual action during these rituals (e.g., human sacrifice), the referent of action was the Valley of Mexico, which was understood by the Aztecs to be the living being Tlaloc. For example, in the ritual descriptions, and particularly during I-Atl cahualo, the term *yetiuh* was used to denote correspondence. *Yetiuh*, meaning "goes being" or "goes to be," is from the verbs *ye*, "to be," and *-tihu(i)*, "to go to do something," and thus expresses a connection between existence and action.[2] *Yetiuh* was a linguistic device used to describe how a child's life, through sacrifice, came to be conjoined with a place. In the *activity* of ritual, one living being "goes to be" another quality of being. In paragraph 8 of Sahagún's account of I-Atl cahualo, we read, "Quauhtepec: and with

those who were dying there, the same place went being, Quauhtepetl."
Through the ritual activity of sacrifice at this place the child's life and
being were transformed into other states of being. Human activity naturally and ritually was bound to violence, thereby promoting correspondences between living beings. Sacrifice articulated those correspondences, and also implied that these activities were communicative. In I-
Atl cahualo, the life of the child corresponded to, or was in substantive/
communicative connected with, a place, or opening, in the Tlalocan landscape. To some extent, this relationship was expressed in place names.

Several distinct places are mentioned in these texts as either locations of ritual action or significant landscape referents for action, but
before we can investigate these places in context we must get a sense of
the lay of the land.[3] The Valley of Mexico is a high volcanic valley (at
least 2,234 m above sea level) at approximately 20° north latitude (i.e.,
in the tropics).[4] It is ringed by high sierra peaks to the east, south, and
west. To the north are a series of low rolling hills. During the pre-
Columbian era there was, within the valley, a system of shallow salt-
and sweet-water lakes. These lakes were the basis of all life in the valley, including that of the Aztec empire.[5] Within the valley there is a
radically varied topography in which several ecological zones exist.
This diversity is specifically incorporated into the sites of sacrifice during I-Atl cahualo.

In I-Atl cahualo seven sites are mentioned where children were
sacrificed. They are:

1. Quauhtepec ("tree mountain place")
2. Yoaltecatl ("night dweller")
3. Tepetzinco ("honored hill place")
4. Poyauhtlan ("color-darkened place")
5. Pantitlan ("banner place")
6. Cocotl ("pimple," or "windpipe")
7. Yiauhqueme ("his sacrificial garment")

Today, Quauhtepec is a mountain peak located almost directly
north of central Mexico City in what is now known as the Guadalupe

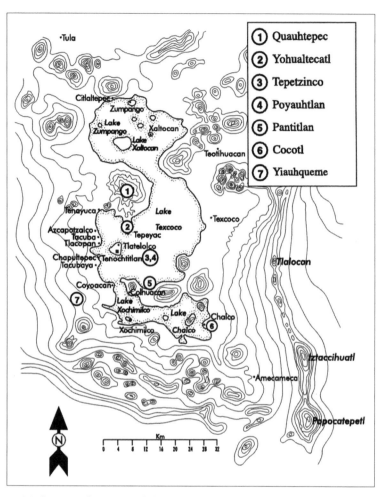

4.1. Ceremonial sites visited during I-Atl cahualo.

range. This range juts out into the valley from the mountain range to the west. It is defined ecologically as belonging to the sierra region (2,750 m and above). The Aztec chiefly exploited this zone for its wood and quartzite, which were used for building materials. Wood products were also used for various other goods, including paper making, which was used extensively during rituals to Tlaloc. Today, on its summit and north side, there is a substantial cover of conifer forests, while on the south flank, facing what was once Tenochtitlan, are a series of terraced maguey fields.[6] Within this single site are at least two utilization areas. Maguey was (and is) primarily used in making pulque, a fermented alcoholic beverage of which large quantities were consumed during ritual occasions. The cactus's spines were used for bloodletting as well as sewing and basket making. The maguey deities, as discussed in chapter 2, were also associated with the *tlaloque*.[7]

Today, Yohualtecatl is a hill located just north of the Guadalupe shrine.[8] Sitting on this high hill gives one a commanding view of Mexico City. During Aztec times, this hill would have been surrounded by water on three sides.[9] It is defined as middle piedmont (2,350–2,500 m), a place where rainfall agriculture was practiced, in addition to some mining.

Tepetzinco was a small island in the middle of the saltwater Lake Texcoco. It was understood to be a very important place of residence for the nobility of Tenochtitlan. Hot springs heated by volcanic activity inside the earth spouted out of the ground and transformed the place into a system of baths. Several important temples and shrines were located on this island, making it a regular stop in a number of ritual events. As with the previous two sites, this was also a very good vantage point because it was situated in the middle of the lake and in the middle of the valley directly east of Tenochtitlan.[10]

Poyauhtlan is actually a peak in the Tlaxcala region east of the valley, which is known today as La Malinche. On the flank of Tepetzinco was an altar to this mountain.[11] This was one in a series of mountain altars, discussed below, that were the focus of a number of ceremonial activities throughout the valley.

According to Durán, Pantitlan was known alternatively as where the lake drained into the earth or from where it spouted into the air.[12] It was situated in the southern end of Lake Texcoco and, being little more than a sand bar, was primarily identified by the large poles that surrounded the opening (hence the name "banner place").[13] Simultaneously, this is the lowest point in the valley and one of its richest resource areas. The salt lakes of the valley were a yearly migration stop for a large variety of geese and ducks. Many different kinds of fish, frogs, polliwogs, mollusks, turtles, and aquatic insects and their larvae were harvested seasonally in large nets. Wild rice and blue-green algae (called *tecuitlatl*, "their excrement") were saltwater vegetable resources. Reeds and water grasses were also gathered for mat and basket making. Salt was manufactured along the lake shore and was a lucrative trade item throughout Mesoamerica.[14]

Cocotl is a small hill that rises abruptly out of the deep soil alluvium. It divides the fertile Amecameca sub-valley region from what were once the sweet-water lakes Chalco and Xochimilco in the southern valley region. The Amecameca Valley is one of the most fertile nonirrigated areas of the valley. Being situated in the drainage of the volcanoes Popocatepetl and Iztaccihuatl, it receives a constant nutrient flow from eroding volcanic material.[15] On the other side of Cocotl, to the west, in the shallow sweet-water lakes, were the famous *chinampas* or raised fields. Nutrient-rich mud was scooped from the bottoms of the lakes and placed on a crisscrossed arrangement of reeds. Deep canals were created between the *chinampas* where fish, algae, and other water plants grew. The nutrient-rich canal water was splashed onto the *chinampas,* which would then produce astounding yields of maize, squash, beans, flowers, medicinal herbs, tomatoes, chiles, etc. Many investigators assert that this highly organized arrangement of *chinampas* constituted the material basis for the expansion of the Aztec empire.[16]

Yiauhqueme cannot be readily identified today. According to Calnek, its approximate location lies near Santa Fe (Acolxochic) in the district of Tacubaya, between the lower and middle piedmont regions (2,255–2,350 m and 2,350–2,500 m, respectively) on the western slope of the valley.[17] In this area, wooded hills are cut by seasonally running waters. It was chiefly utilized for wood resources and for hunting wild game.

These seven sites cut across the major ecological resource areas of the valley: vertically from the high sierra to the lake system, and horizontally from the hilly piedmont to the alluvial plain. In addition, the physical situation of these sites also suggests an importance in the Aztec calendrical arrangement. First, and most obvious, the ritual circumambulation of I-Atl cahualo may have begun in the north and then moved clockwise to the east, south, and west.[18] According to Aveni, the fact that this ritual began in the north is interesting given that in a number of other cases in Mesoamerica (most notably Teotihuacan, Tenayuca, and Ihuatzio in the Mexican highlands) prominent mountains can be found north of these ceremonial precincts. Perhaps these mountains acted as a northern point of orientation and a dramatic backdrop, or model, for the sacred buildings one finds at the centers of these cities.[19] Aveni believes that the north-south axis of Tenochtitlan may have had some cosmological meaning. The orientation of the north avenue, leading from the Templo Mayor (as well as the orientation of the Templo Mayor itself) and across the lake, is within 1.5° of the orientation of Quauhtepec (4.5° east of north).[20] Over the distance of 17.5 kilometers, a spatial correspondence between the ceremonial center of the Aztec and the northern horizon was established through the construction of an avenue.

In addition, Tepetzinco, the third site mentioned in the *Florentine*, is oriented on the horizon, as viewed from the Templo Mayor, twenty days, or one Mesoamerican "month," north of equinox sunrise. This means that sunrise over Tepetzinco would occur one month after the spring equinox and one month before the fall equinox. This point becomes significant due to another relationship established between the location of the hills of the Mount Tlaloc range and the sunrise position twenty days south of the equinox, with respect to the Templo Mayor. In another study, it was found that Cerro Yeloxochitl, which is south of Mount Tlaloc in the same range, lies one month (twenty days) before spring equinox on the horizon, or on the other side of the equinox from Tepetzinco.[21] If the equinox occurred over Mount Tlaloc as viewed from the Templo Mayor, then sunrise over Tepetzinco and Cerro Yeloxochitl would have been seen one Mesoamerican "month" before and after equinox.

Sunrise during I-Atl cahualo may have occurred in the direction of Pantitlan, the fifth site of the ritual. The coincidence of a solar event directly over this important watery source may have also been integrated into the ritual. The winter solstice sunset on the horizon may have also corresponded with the final site mentioned; Yiauhqueme.

While not all of the sites are accounted for in their associations with the sun as gauged from the Templo Mayor, there are enough accounts to suggest that there was some calendrical significance featured in the ritual circumambulation. Celestial phenomena (particularly the sun) corresponded with significant points in the landscape *from the perspective of the center*. Current understandings of space and time seem at odds with this because, from an Aztec ritual understanding, time and place were realities meaningful only when in correspondence with one another, and then only from a given point of view. Interpretations of various phenomena were necessarily included in the reality of Aztec place/time.[22]

At these seven places the lives of children were sacrificed to Tlaloc. The Templo Mayor, according to Broda, was the principal earth opening. As she says, "[O]n a mythological level Templo Mayor, the sacred mountain, was the earth itself, the earth as a voracious monster devouring human victims and blood. At the same time, the earth contained regenerative forces that linked it to agricultural growth and fertility in general."[23]

Like the Templo Mayor, the seven sites mentioned in I-Atl cahualo, as well as other sites mentioned in other rituals, were mouths of a voracious earth monster. In I-Atl cahualo, the sacrificial blood and souls of children were said to be "happily received." The *tlaloque* wanted them, and when they were given their sacrifices it was said that "they [were] very content, thus they [were] well pleased." The bodies of these seven children were food for the *tlaloque*, who reciprocated by releasing climatological elements from the openings of the earth. The flesh and bones of children corresponded to the earth. Tlaloc's flesh and a child's body constituted a correspondence whose relationship was physically circumscribed through the sacrificial event. This correspondence concretely expressed the reciprocal relationship of human body and earth body. The earth body (Tlaloc) physically sustained the human body through the fruits of agriculture, etc. Likewise, the fruits of the human body (children) sustained the earth body. Moreover, this exchange of the precious fruits of life corresponded to a mosaic of bodily openings in the landscape. It was at these places (mouths) that direct and substantial contact with the Tlalocan body was achieved.

VI-Etzalcualiztli, like I-Atl cahualo, begins in the north at a site called Citlaltepec ("star hill place"). Various priests associated with Tlaloc gathered a reed called *aztapillin* ("noble heron"), which grew in vast fields at Citlaltepec. Other sites are mentioned near Citlaltepec where they also gathered *aztapillin*—Temilco, "stone field place"; Tepexic, "cliff place"; and Oztoc, "cave place."

According to the survey taken there in 1973, the area around what is today known as San Juan Zitlaltepec has a large number of isolated ceremonial sites that are situated on the hilltops.[24] This city sits on what was then the shore of Lake Zumpango, with a mountainous area directly to the north whose highest peak is today called Cerro de la Estrella, or Xalpan. On virtually every hill and ridge top, the remains of ceremonial mounds were found, which have a scatters of shards that are of Late Aztec origin. Many of these sites also have the remains of temple structures (as at Quauhtepetl and Yohualtecatl). These are perched on ridges that provide commanding views of the valley. While Citlaltepec is specifically mentioned as the place were VI-Etzalcualiztli originated, the focus of the opening days of the ritual actually occurred en route between Citlaltepec and Tenochtitlan.

It is approximately forty-one kilometers between the ceremonial center of Tenochtitlan and Citlaltepec, which is directly north. Travel between these two cities would have either required traveling along the Tenayuca causeway, skirting the Guadalupe range to the east then proceeding up the lakeshore, or first going along the Tepayacac causeway and moving west around the Guadalupe range and proceeding north along the lake shore. Either going through the mountains, as discussed above, or staying close to the lake shore would have made a difference to the significance of VI-Etzalcualiztli. Based on my reading of VI-Etzalcualiztli, I think the priestly procession stayed near the lake.

The Tlamacazque, or serving priests, of Tlaloc came along the road bearing the *aztapillin* reeds.[25] They traveled on deserted roads upon their return to Tenochtitlan. If someone happened on this procession of reeds by accident, they would be beaten and robbed. Not even Moctezuma interfered with this penance. The Tlamacazque were

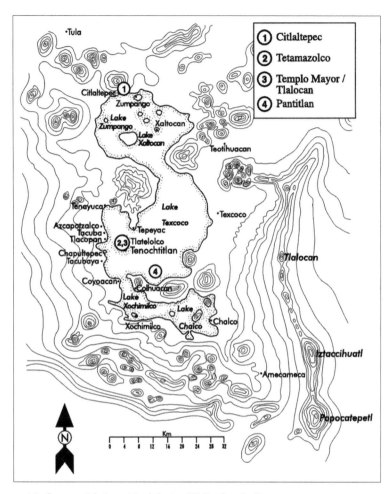

4.2. Ceremonial sites visited during VI-Etzalcualiztli.

the sanctioned wild men of the road. They were sanctioned by their penance to Tlaloc, whose authority superseded Moctezuma's. Their behavior was authoritative in that it expressed a connection with Tlaloc as an ultimate owner (or embodiment) of the landscape. While the Tlamacazque did not follow social rules, they were nonetheless recognized as appropriately acting as representatives of a Tlalocan landscape.

Several other places are mentioned in the ritual. The *calmecac*, or "young men's house," was where the priests resided;[26] the Ayauhcalli, or "mist house," was where bathing and shivering took place; Tetamazolco, the "people's toad place," was where the throng embarked with sacrificial hearts on their final trip to Pantitlan, which was located at the center of the lake. These suggest that a connection between the *calmecac* and the water's edge was established by means of various types of penance. At the water's edge, in particular, there were grand occasions that required the autosacrifice of priests. The lake shore was a powerful place in the Aztec landscape because it was a liminal boundary between worlds.

Just as the *calmecac* housed wild men in the heart of a social world (roaming loose during ritual occasions), so too the shore was the locus of a powerful conjunction of human and aquatic worlds. The watery lake environment simultaneously destroyed and sustained human life. At the shore, the Aztecs understood that it was the interaction of land (earth) and lake (water) that sustained human life—as in the *chinampa* agriculture. As we have seen in previous sections, both of these worlds were embedded in the single body of Tlaloc. At the shore were located various beings who were in direct contact with one another. While penance was appropriate on the road and shore, these sufferings were only brought to a significant close by entering into the domain of the *tlaloque*. The final activity transpired at Pantitlan, where the lake drained, which located a connection between water and earth.

In the ceremonies of XIII-Tepeilhuitl and XVI-Atemoztli, the Aztecs constructed deified landscapes. As with the altars to Tlaloc on Mount Tlaloc discussed in chapter 3, these were representations of places constructed of food in the form of a "human mountain" rather than one of stone. The human-food-mountains were then arranged in particular patterns so that they would represent a living landscape. As during IV-Huei tozoztli, these altars formed the focus of ritual activity, while at the same time articulating the conditions of occupying the valley. Ritual feeding at the altars underscored an appropriate mode of occupying Tlalocan.

XIII-Tepeihuitl was a celebration of the mountains, and of the dead whose lives were taken by Tlaloc. It was primarily a commemoration of a special class of ancestors: those who went to live with Tlaloc in his earthly paradise.[27] People who had died from drowning, from being struck by lightning, or from one of the several diseases that were associated with the *tlaloque*[28] were buried in the ground.[29] Because of their association with water, it was thought that the bodies of these victims contained a seedlike reproductive energy that had positive effects on the land, and thus required burial rather than cremation.

Their images of the dead were constructed of a sweet ground amaranth paste called *tzoalli*, which was applied to wooden staffs carved in the likeness of serpents and called *ecatotontli* ("small wind"). The wood serpents served as the bones of the images. Over this was spread the *tzoalli*.

During XVI-Atemoztli, mountain images were also fashioned, but as images of the *tepictoton*, or "little molded ones." These images were of the *tlaloque* themselves, which at this time of year were heard growling and roaring as thunder over the sierra. Again, these were mountains in human form created from *tzoalli* that corresponded to particular places in and around the valley. Mentioned in the literature are: the two volcanoes Popocatepetl, "great smoking mountain," and Iztaccihuatl, "white woman"; Tlaloc, or Tlalocan, a peak on the sierra directly east of Tenochtitlan and the home of Tlaloc; Quauhtepetl ("tree mountain"), Yohualtecatl ("night dweller"), Tepetzintli ("honored hill"), Cocotl ("pimple" or "windpipe"), and Yauhqueme ("sacrificial garment"), or five of the seven sacrificial sites mentioned in Sahagún's account of I-Atl cahualo; Tepepolli, "great hill," which rises out of southern Lake Texcoco; Huixachtecatl, "thorny tree dweller," now known as the "hill of the star"; Chicomecoatl, "seven snakes"; Chalchiuhtlicue, "the skirt of precious greenstone"; and Ehecatl, "wind," possibly on the eastern shore of Lake Texcoco at the end of the Guadalupe range.[30] Many of these mountains had been sites of sacrifice to the *tlaloque* during I-Atl cahualo and IV-Huei tozoztli.

These rituals articulated a correspondence between mountains, sustenance, the *tlaloque*, and the dead, through their manifold manifestations. Actions of the Aztecs were directed toward a living land-scape at potent periods of the year. In both ceremonies, the images were arranged in a particular order. In XIII-Tepeihuitl, Sahagún tells us, they were set out in a circular fashion. In XVI-Atemoztli, the images were fashioned with reference to specific landscape features. In both cases, the images were arranged in such a way as to be directly and actively addressed by people throughout the ritual activities. A sym-

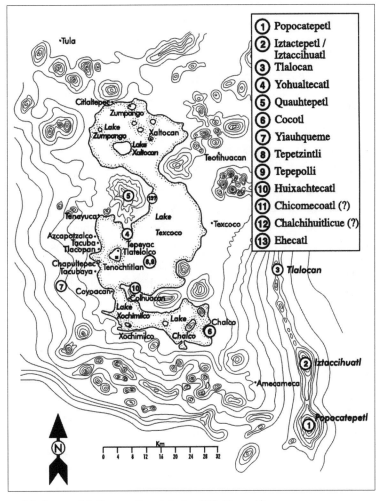

4.3. Ceremonial sites mentioned during XVI-Atemoztli.

bolic mapping of the Tlalocan landscape was duplicated at other shrines throughout the valley. Durán tells us that on Mount Tlaloc offerings during IV-Huei tozoztli were directed toward a permanent altar to Tlaloc that depicted, in stone, the human mountains that surround the earthly paradise of Tlalocan. There may have been similar sites located on the volcanoes Popocatepetl and Iztaccihuatl that demonstrate the existence of similar altars to a Tlalocan landscape.[31] At the Templo Mayor, there existed similar altars dedicated to Tlaloc. The significant difference, however, between the altars constructed during XIII-Tepeihuitl and XVI-Atemoztli and those at other sites was that these were made of food, which thereby directly associated mountain, sustenance, and body. It was incumbent that human life energies be expended in order to sustain the life of a wider cosmos.

Images were washed and fed. During XIII-Tepeihuitl it was the women who riotously celebrated the *tepictoton*'s presence while carrying the images about by litter. The presence of women was a central feature of this event, and indicated the fructifying promise of mountain veneration. During the molding of the *tepictoton*, sexual contact and bathing were forbidden. Only after the destruction of the human mountains were people required to drink and cavort in excess. In addition, like the actions of the priests along the lake during VI-Etzalcualiztli, the wild behavior of the women was an occasion for breaking conventions and boundaries.[32]

Both rituals shared a particular rhythm. In XIII-Tepeihuitl, five human sacrifices were offered to Tlaloc. Only after their decapitation and consumption were the mountain images "killed" and eaten. As in I-Atl cahualo, a correspondence between landscape and human life was one that required the violence of sacrifice and eating. Similarly, it was the death and consumption of the *tepictoton* during XVI-Atemoztli that was required for people to directly interact with Tlaloc. During these festivals a landscape was constructed of correspondences between mountainous and human life. It was then addressed in various celebratory ways and finally killed and consumed. An Aztec hermeneutics of occupation was simultaneously connected with a cosmological understanding of the creativity and violence of eating.

Combining these four rituals marked various moments in the meaningful occupation of the Valley of Mexico. First, during I-Atl cahualo children were carried to various places in the landscape that corresponded to openings of the Tlaloc body, which were significant sites of sustenance. They were then killed and their bodies were fed to the deity. During VI-Etzalcualiztli, it was the priests who traversed the landscape along the lake shore. It was their movement between potent places that integrated a plurality of existences. In addition, the hearts and blood of sacrificial victims were carried from the Templo Mayor to the center of the lake.[33] Finally, in XIII-Tepeihuitl and XVI-Atemoztli the landscape was constructed from food and it was killed, which along with human sacrifices acted as embodiments of the fructifying aspects of their world. Through various means and through specific actions, human beings were enlisted to engage their place in such a way as to articulate their proper relationship to it. They followed a temporal rhythm from drought to rainy season; then from harvest to drought again. Correspondences established and maintained through ritual action were the basis for continued life. It was in the interaction between various beings that occupied Tlalocan that formed the basis of life.

VITAL FLUIDS

Water was the primary focus for ritual actions dedicated to Tlaloc, and this fact is accounted for in a wide variety of ways throughout Sagahún's descriptions in the *Florentine Codex*. The primary purpose was to attract appropriate amounts of water—the vital fluid upon which human existence is based. Human engagement with the hydrological conditions of existence was promoted by means of actively building correspondences between various life-sustaining fluids. While water was the referent of these celebrations to Tlaloc, the appropriation of water required the manipulation of a host of other fluids that could generate the needed bodily correspondence between humans and landscape. A link was forged primarily between blood and water, which also extended to other types of fluids. What follows is an exploration of the modes by which the Aztecs would ritually organize vital fluids to promote a reciprocity with the Tlalocan landscape, thereby enlisting powerful unseen forces in order to sustain the lives of humans and other beings.

I-Atl cahualo and XVI-Atemoztli directly refer to water. I-Atl cahualo literally means "water left," or "drought," and XVI-Atemoztli means "descending water." These festivals occurred within forty days of each other at times of the year when it was critical to secure enough moisture to ensure good planting and harvest seasons. Festival times marked points in the agricultural year that fluctuated between drought and rainfall. During I-Atl cahualo, a connection with water was ritually accounted for in at least two ways. First, the arrangement of sacrificial sites corresponded to important hydrological features of the valley, and, second, water cosmology corresponded with the incidence of bodily fluids, particularly blood, which was given special status. In XVI-Atemoztli, these themes were condensed into a symbolic arrangement of the rain dwarfs, or *tepictoton*, in order to extend the significance of the correspondence of Tlaloc and bodily fluids to other properties of the landscape.

Due to volcanism, water in the Valley of Mexico was highly uncertain and dangerous. As it is now, the rise and fall of water levels are often sudden and problematic. During pre-Columbian times, fluctuations in the hydraulic level could be disastrous for *chinampa* agriculture. A strict relationship between water and earth had to be maintained. Too much water would inundate and eventually salinate the groundwater, while too little water would deplete the soils of needed moisture and nutrients.[34] For these reasons, the lake system was divided by a series of dikes to separate salty from sweet waters.[35] Tenochtitlan, in the middle of the lake system, was surrounded by sweet water and was also fed water via an aqueduct from the hill of Chapultepec.[36] The city was built up in a *chinampa*-like fashion by mucking the bottom of the lake and piling it on reeds. In this way the city was recaptured, in effect, from the watery world of the *tlaloque*. Although the lake was the source of life, it was not always kind and could easily deliver death as well as life.[37] This fact of life in the valley required that, above all, the ultimate source of water be understood.

Lake water (or "feminine" water), however, stood in sharp contrast to other types of water, particularly mountain water (or "masculine" water). Ecologically, there are three basic types of running water in the valley. First, there is that water which originates on the sierra from melting snow. Second, there is seasonal rainfall, which can appear quite violently, washing away the land and leaving deep ravines, called *barrancas*. Third, there is water that emanates from underground caverns and which, in some cases, can also occur violently and abruptly.[38] Due to their volcanic origin, some of these interior waters are hot, sulfurous, or salty. Several of these places were the sites of pre-Columbian baths. Sweet underground springs were sometimes carried over long distances through an elaborate system of aqueducts to urban centers, as was the case of a spring at Chapultepec that quenched the thirst of Tenochtitlan.[39] These springs often emanated from caves and other significant earthly openings associated with Tlaloc.

In Book XI of the *Florentine Codex*, Sahagún recorded a number of descriptions of water in Nahuatl. Due to editing, some of the manifold distinctions within Aztec hydrological categories seem to be lost. What remain are many distinct types of water that do not clearly correspond to modern categories. A consistent emphasis of the entries, however, is on the ambiguous, even violent, nature of water. For example, *atoyatl*, "running water,"[40] or "river," is described as beginning in

> [the] mountains [which] were only magic places, with earth, with rock on the surface; that they were only like ollas [granaries] or like houses; that they were filled with the water which was there. If sometime it were necessary, the mountains would dissolve; the whole world would flood.
>
> The river is [water] which flows, wells up, gushes. It is a runner; a former of rapids, of swift currents; a glider. It is that which crashes, which groans. It has man-eating animals. It is irresistible; it frightens people; it drowns people. It is that which is swift of current. It has fish; it has serpents. It wells up, it gushes, it forms rapids, it crashes.[41]

Water that originated in the untamed world of Tlaloc consumed the land and people in its descent to the lake system. Released in comparatively small amounts from its storage places within mountains, it would make its way into the human world, spreading life and death. Significantly, mountains are referred to as *ollas*, which in the human context were containers of food. Running water, in addition to its thunderous existence, contained wild animals and serpents that ate people, as well as fish that nourished them. Its appearance at once indicated the possibility of life and death.

This description goes on to say that mountain water proceeded from the womb of the goddess Chalchihuitlicue, she of the precious skirt of greenstone, who was known either as the consort, wife of Tlaloc, or sister of the *tlaloque*. The green of her skirt referred to the evergreen trees that grow on the slopes of high mountains. In addition, a relationship was established between the sea, which was directly associated with the lake because both were salty, and the land. The sea entered the land and spread underneath it, filling all its cavities and particularly the interiors of mountains and hills. In this journey salty water became potable. The activity of water, when in contact with an earthly interior, created a vital fluid appropriate for human consumption. This journey, however, was only a small segment of the circulation of water throughout the cosmos. The larger significance of water was Cemanahuac: the "place surrounded by water," which described the Aztec cosmos as completely encapsulated in a watery envelope.

Water was divided according to color, its place of occurrence, its relational properties, and the animals that resided in it, as well as other criteria (including "omen" and "shame" water). Many waters were desirable, such as *amahualli*, "flat water," or *xalatl*, "sand water." The majority of waters, however, were dangerous. For example, there was *tecuan(i)atl*, "human-eating water," so called "because it has many man-eating animals." *Tollan atl* was so named "because it passes with the city of Tollan . . . I drown; it carries me off, it drowns me it is winding." The Aztec hydrological topology promoted characteristics of water that were held between various beings of the landscape. Water was organized with reference to the relationship established by actively interacting with other properties, with the activities being primarily based in violence.

During I-Atl cahualo, the bodies and blood of sacrificial children corresponded to the various kinds of water discussed above. They were carried on litters, wearing precious green/blue stone bracelets and necklaces (associating them with wealth), to the seven sites of their death. The bracelets and necklaces of green/blue stone connected these children directly with Chalchihuitlicue. The stones' color and hardness linked elements of water and earth with the children's blood and bodies. Their costumes reinforced these correspondences. Total envelopment of a phenomenal world appeared in the ritual description in the form of children being carried "quetzal feather housed." These were feathers also of green and blue and, like the necklaces, they were highly regarded. They were attained through trading relationships with the lowlands peoples and were worked by craftsmen into elaborate headdresses, shields, and clothing.[42] Due to their connection with the deities of water and earth, these feathers were an insignia of status. The plumes were a deep blue, associated with Tlaloc and Chalchihuitlicue. Housing children, whose lives and bodies directly corresponded to the earth and its fruits, within quetzal feathers condensed a cosmological understanding. Earthly and bodily existence was encapsulated by divine/celestial water. This cosmological relationship was meaningfully constructed and promoted through ritual actions and in the accouterments that surrounded the children. During XVI-Atemoztli, the human-mountain figures were also carried on litters by women, thereby signifying their high status. As with the ritual construal of children, during XVI-Atemoztli these personified food mountains were constructed and embellished to articulate an embodied landscape (mountains) that was full of vital fluids (as altepetl, or "water mountains") and displayed an image of Tlaloc's wealth. Through these festivals, bodies, both of children and the *tepictoton*, were adorned so as to accentuate the vital fluids residing within them.

In I-Atl cahualo, the seven sites of sacrifice likewise corresponded to particular expressions of valley hydrology. Most types of waters were accounted for in the ritual circumambulation. At the sierra site of Quauhtepec, as we have seen in the case of Tlalocan in the east, there was a connection with celestial or "sky" water, primarily expressed in the form of rain. This was the largest of the mountain sites and thus the most potent container of water. It was from these earthly openings that rains would arise.[43] At the base of Yohualtecatl, in the gardens near what is now the Basilica of the Virgin of Guadalupe, there is still an enormous sweet-water spring. This spring calls to descriptions of Chapultepec. In pre-Columbian times, this was a spot that boasted a wide variety of plants and animals. At Tepetzinco, the island site in the middle of the lake that was surrounded entirely by the salt lake of Texcoco, there existed hot-water springs that were used as royal baths. Although its altar was at Tepetzinco, Poyauhtlan also referred to the darkening that occurs as rain clouds gather.[44] Pantitlan was the lowest point in the valley where salt water drained or sweet water spouted. Cocotl was located at the edge of the shore of the sweet-water lakes in the southern valley. It was also the site where water from the sierra, primarily from the volcanoes, would eventually wind its way down to Lake Chalco and where the Aztecs tended their bountiful *chinampa* fields. Yiauhqueme probably would have been situated in the drainage from the western sierra, but these were foothills that are now dramatically scarred by many barrancas. Water in this area would have been a dangerous event because it washed away the earth.

These sites expressed several correspondences between rain and lake water, or vertical and horizontal water, interior and exterior water, hot and cold water, still and running water, sweet and salt water, life-giving and death-dealing water, and male and female water.

Child sacrifices at these sites physically constituted the central theme of correspondence between human life and the earth: blood and water. The former was the bodily water and the basis of human life, while the later was an earthly, or heavenly, blood and the basis of life for Tlaloc and the earth. The reciprocal nature of life and death was a central element throughout Aztec ceremonial action. The ritual acquisition of water required paying the high price of a child's blood. Children's blood offset the costs of Tlaloc's sacrifice for human beings. Sacrifice was referred to as *(i)xtlahua,* "to pay a debt."[45] The ritual was regarded as an exchange of gifts. Unlike a monetary economy, this exchange of gifts was a liquid one. Just as blood and body interact to create life (children and mobility), so it was with the landscape. The blood of Tlaloc (water) interacted with a body (earth) to create life (animal and vegetable sustenance). Aztec rituals actively attempted to balance life's debt by reciprocating with life, thereby asserting a place in the world for human existence.

During XVI-Atemoztli, the landscape articulated by the killing of children was expanded to include other hydrological sites. Of particular importance were the peaks of the high sierra to the east. These included the volcanoes Popocatepetl [46] and Iztaccihuatl, as well as Mount Tlalocan. They are the highest peaks in the valley and visually the most impressive. The volcanoes are perpetually covered with snow and ice, something that rarely visits the valley floor in great quantities. These were the places of the *tlaloque*. It was during this month that these deities began to growl and rumble and it was these signs that revealed Tlaloc's presence, which in turn initiated the ceremonies of XVI-Atemoztli. The term *tititl*, "contraction," described these sounds, which came from the high sierra. It is also a term associated with cold and hail. Weather was subject to violent shifts on these peaks during this time of the year, and this dangerous weather was ritually linked to the violence in human-to-human combat.[47] With the cold of the winter sierra and the sound of rumbling *tlaloque*, a correspondence was signaled between violence and rain, linking these attributes through the reading of climatological phenomena.

Sonic signals, both given and received, were important elements in each of these ceremonies. During I-Atl cahualo, the success of the sacrifices was also indicated by the appearance of a bird called the *necuilic*, "the twisted one" or sparrow hawk, whose screech would signal the approach of ice and frost. In Book XI Sahagún tells us that this bird sucked the air to get its water. In both ceremonies, it was this sonic symbol from the *tlaloque* that indicated their oncoming presence in the form of snow and ice, and that highlighted potent ritual moments. During these two rituals, figures depicting attributes of the landscape (children and *tepictoton*) were likewise addressed by the playing of various instruments. Sonic relationships established an elaborate activity of signals given by the *tlaloque* and responded to by the Aztecs. Sound highlighted a liquid reciprocity between bodies.

In VI-Etzalcualiztli, there are similarly thorough descriptions of instruments dedicated to Tlaloc. It fell to a respected priest to carry the *ayochicahuaztli*, or water-fortifying rattle. Etymologically this is also linked to the turtle, *ayotl*, which means "water vessel,"[48] and was also called the *nahualcuahuitl*, or "sorcerer's staff." It was a very wide and very long hollow object of wood that would make the sound of rain when tipped from one end to the other.[49] In XVI-Atemoztli they would play the *teponaztli*, the lateral log drum, the *ayacachtli*, rattle, which has the element of water incorporated into it (*atl*), and the gourd rattle. During I-Atl cahualo, VI-Eztalcualiztli, and XIII-Tepeihuitl, as well as during other ritual feasts, conch shells were blown to signal potent moments in the ceremony. These instruments were directly connected with the absolute fertility associated with the sea. On these occasions the infusion of the seashells with the breath of a human beings articulated a direct connection with water. As in the case of all these instruments, it was through human action that a correspondence between water and other attributes of the landscape and body were perpetuated.

The ritual of VI-Etzalcualiztli expressed another type of relationship between human beings and water. Here water as a property of earthly openings was less emphasized. Instead, a polemic was developed and established between the lake and shore. There was a ritually expressed opposition[50] in which the priests would perform as intermediaries traversing between human and watery realms.[51] Strictly speaking, rather than a feeding relationship expressed between human beings and the landscape, the dynamics of the interaction between distinct human and lake worlds was articulated.

As discussed in chapter 3, the movement of the priests through the landscape indicated an intimate relationship between land and water. Although their movements within the valley can not currently be traced, it is likely that their route was plotted in such a way as to emphasize this correspondence (i.e., along the lake shore). In this fashion a relationship, in the form of an opposition between the cultural norms of Aztec society and the other world of the *tlaloque*, was reinforced as material and substantive. Requirements of this ritual relationship were expressed by specific means, usually signaled by the presence of plants or animals in one form or another.

Reeds gathered by priests, as well as feathers of the quetzal bird, were ritually tied to the blood vessels of the body.[52] The priestly activity of gathering reeds as blood vessels signaled another level of interaction between bodies based on their respective abilities to engage in the circulation of the vital fluids of water and blood. At midnight, after the initial reed gathering and offering stages of VI-Etzalcualiztli, a conch shell was sounded to signal the autosacrifice of blood let from the Tlamacazque for the deities of water. The bodies of these wild priests were opened with maguey spines to release those vital fluids, which corresponded to landscape fluids. This initiated activities at the water's edge at a place called Ayauhcalli, "mist house." After fasting and bloodletting, the priests bathed themselves in the cold lake waters. At the mist house, the Tlamacazque would do penance by submitting to shivering in the cold water, which was explicitly linked to the trembling induced by fear. Their burden was fourfold, having to do with a lack of 1) food, 2) blood, 3) warmth, and 4) security—all of which specifically referred to water. In the first case, water and food were directly equated. Blood and water likewise created a correspondence. Cold and fear were equated with an overabundance of water and inhabiting the nonhuman place of the lake.

More than a metaphorical relationship, the connection of fear and the lake was specifically alluded to by one of the head priests as he addressed the suffering throng. The lake was also a feminine place, in marked distinction to the priest's gender. According to the priest's speech, the lake was a place of anger; where the snake takes your life and the mosquito takes your blood. It was also a place where ducks gathered, not humans, and a place of the thunderous noise of reeds. While the actions of the priests during this time were accompanied by more melodious sounds of various trumpets and log drums, the lake itself issued noises that signaled fear and death to human beings.

This process of suffering drove the priests, as arbiters between human and aquatic realms, to finally inhabit a world of watery life that was not their own. This transition was also marked by sound.[53] After

[151]

they were addressed by the Chalchiuhquacuilli ("precious greenstone head-taking priests"), they entered the lake. They splashed about with hands and feet in the manner of water fowl. Their speech, a sonic symbol of human creation, was likewise transformed into the language of ducks and other water birds. Following their communicative actions, their bodies were transformed from human to lake inhabitants. For the priests, this was the climax of VI-Etzalcualiztli, which signaled a complete reformulation into another life-form directly associated with Tlaloc.[54]

The *eztalli* feast began with the eating of sauce, the juices of food, and not the food itself. Spilling any of these juices would result in being taken captive. This phase of the ritual rounded out a correspondence of fluids that was initiated with the letting of blood and the transformation into aquatic life, and then the reintegration into human form through the consumption of sauces.

Captives taken because of inattention during these rituals were submitted to a number of violent actions. These were always initiated by the adorning of the fire-offering priests, the Tlenamacac. Of particular importance in their costume was the *ayauhquemitl*, "mist cloak," or *ahuachquemitl*, "dew cloak." Another noted priest, the Quacuilli, or "head-taking priest," would carry the *ayauhchicahuaztli*, or "mist-fortifying rattle." Thus arrayed, they would oversee the brutalizing of captives taken either on the road or during the ceremonial penances themselves. These captives were dragged through mud and water at the lake shore and abused directly in the water. The place of this action was Totecco, "our serpent place." Having been identified with the serpent, as discussed previously in the priest's speech, suggested that this place was referred to as one violent to human habitation.

Along with abusing captives, sacrifices commenced with the appearance of the adorned priests. Impersonators of the *tlaloque* were killed and their hearts extracted and placed in a vessel of blue, called *mixcomitl*, "the cloud vessel." With this vessel full of hearts, the people poled into the lake and, amid a flurry of sounds from trumpets, deposited it at Pantitlan. The hearts of human impersonators would cause turbulence in the water, which signaled the acceptance of the Aztec offering. At Pantitlan the water bubbled, roared, and blistered. The terms used to describe this event are reminiscent of those describing the violent nature of water discussed earlier. The priests who adorned themselves in vestments of the *ayauhquemitl* and *ahuachquemitl* embodied Tlaloc, just as those impersonators who gave their hearts.

These terms also refer to the cooking of food in a pot identifying the hearts of humans as food for the *tlaloque*. Lake turbulence at Pantitlan underscored the violence required in feeding Tlaloc and characterized the violence inherent in human sustenance. The shore was a violent place—a necessary challenge to human habitation. Yet it was also the place of contact with the *tlaloque*. Activities during VI-Etzalcualiztli strove to overcome temporarily the Otherness of the lake, the principal site of their sustenance, so that a ritual reciprocity could be achieved.

Blood was attained at the cost of performing violent actions toward other human beings. Violence performed by the priests, both on their own bodies and on the bodies of others, further articulated their roles as intermediaries between the human and Tlalocan worlds. Priests manipulated the material conditions of life and death in such a way as to ensure that the transformation of one substance into another would promote the larger conditions of existence. Transformations of matter always involved violence. VI-Etzalcualiztli, unlike the other rituals mentioned, elaborately outlined the duties and responsibilities of the priestly office. Priests were not peripheral members of Aztec society; caretakers of a deity remote to human beings, but charged to deal directly in the material conditions of life common to all people. This required the careful articulation of correspondences between blood, water, sauce, and sound, to name but a few. Most importantly, however, a meaningful organization of these materials was effected through ritual action; an action that articulated the violent nature of biological existence while at the same time participating in the living correspondences between all beings who inhabited Aztec lands.

PLANT AND ANIMAL BEINGS

One of the most obvious and informative dimensions of these Tlaloc rituals was the active integration of various plants and animals into their ritual activity. Indeed, this is the richest area for fruitfully investigating the connection of these rituals with other symbols and rituals throughout the Mesoamerican world.[55] The relationship between humans and these other occupants of the valley was ritually expressed in their ceremonial appearances. Ritual paraphernalia, including costumery and other accouterments, musical instruments, and other objects (altars, mats, flower arrangements, images, etc.), were all made of plants and animals. It was not just the finished forms of these ritual instruments that were significant, but also how these ritual items were directly correlated to those plant and animal beings from which they came. By their incorporation into various ritual occasions a relationship was being articulated and perpetuated through the actions of the Aztec people.

VI-Etzalcualiztli most dramatically celebrated a direct connection between human and floral/faunal realms. The following analysis builds on the previous discussion of vital fluids. Just as a connection between shore and water was extended and promoted during VI-Etzalcualiztli, this connection was adjudicated largely through the participation of beings who occupied those distinct realms. In the first case, reeds were gathered from the lake, and in the second case, aquatic birds were imitated at the water's edge. In both activities, these distinct identities and realms were both challenged and reinforced in order that a meaningful context for occupation be established.

Reed gathering by the priests was a violent occasion. At Citlaltepec, they were described as seizing them, pulling them out of the lake mud and tying them around the middle in a birdlike fashion. The method of wrapping the *aztapillin*, "noble heron reeds," indicated a relationship between food gathering (i.e., collecting water fowl) and the reeds. These were "noble" reeds selected because of their length and white-colored base. In some texts, they were depicted as dramatically varying in color from dark green to white from top to bottom. Through the activity of gathering the *aztapillin*, an inverted relationship was established between the noble products of the lake world and plants of the land, namely maize. Both of these plants shared notable characteristics, including their height, coloring, and (to some degree) their uses. Both maize stalks and reeds were important materials for basket and mat weaving. They were also both involved in *chinampa* agriculture. To some degree, both were also used as food resources, but maize was considered a human food par excellence. The reed's distinction from maize, however, made it an important symbolic element in this festival, for it allowed reflection to take place through its essential Otherness. The *aztapillin* occupied a realm that was at once hostile to humans and a world upon which human life depended. It grew in the lake and thus resided in a sacred realm.[56] Maize was a plant that inhabited human space and was therefore appropriate for humans. To some degree, reeds and maize were floral inversions of one another.

A hostility to humans, embodied in the *aztapillin*, was extended on the dry land when carried by tumpline by the priests. These were the plants of hard labor (indicated by the presence of the tumpline) and their collection required that a sacrifice, in the form of human energy expelled by the penitents, be exacted. Priests, bearing the fruits of a sacred world, would punish those involved in domestic pursuits along the path they traveled. Violence always accompanied the collection of food, whether it be maize or water birds, and it was violence that was unleashed in the domestic world of the Aztecs when laborers of Tlaloc traversed their land. The priests embodied the wild domain of Tlaloc while carrying the reeds. In a social landscape, this resulted in violence against a domestic order.

These reeds were then woven into mats with back supports. Reed seats are traditional symbols of Aztec authority in the codices, and people shown seated on the woven *aztapillin*, such as Moctezuma, were understood to be rulers. Not even Moctezuma interfered with the brutish behavior of the priests because their authority superseded his. But their authority was also directly associated with the Tlahtoani's. Being identified primarily by his seat, an Aztec king's power was symbolically based on an intimate relationship with the deities. He served the deities and, like the priests, embodied the reciprocity between the human and divine worlds. He was the intercessor who extended the violence of the world, primarily through warfare, thereby ensuring an appropriate transformation and cycling of elements. By basing his place on the violent yet life-sustaining interactions between beings (as exemplified by his sitting on the *aztapillin* mat), the Tlahtoani was the primary representative and embodiment of Tlaloc among the Aztecs.[57]

At the climax of the ceremony, priests imitated water birds at the lake shore. As mentioned above, this entrance into the water was preceded by various kinds of autosacrifice including labor, fasting, fire offerings, and prayer. Only in this condition were the priests allowed to enter the salt water. For this time they would inhabit the lake. They spoke with a bird's language and motions. They splashed in the water with their hands and feet imitating the water fowl. A transformation was forcefully indicated, however, with their articulation of the bird language. In paragraph 35, Sahagún tells us that they would speak like gulls (Franklin's gulls) and water birds such as the stork, spoonbill, snowy egret, and both brown and blue herons. Through speech, these priests effected a transformation that physically linked them with the world of water beings: they became birds.

Captives would be taken at various times during the ritual. This included the taking of priests who did not commit themselves to the activities required to enter Tlalocan. During their presentation, captives could be returned to members of their family with offerings of food. Specifically mentioned was the gift of a turkey. This bird stood in contrast to those birds that the priests embodied. The turkey was a domestic fowl that stayed close to humans. It was large, heavily feathered, could not fly, and ate maize and cooked greens.[58] In other words, like maize, a turkey embodied a domesticated order. On the other hand, the priests were equated with the water birds, whose features included an ability to fly and thus migrate in and out of the valley, being thinly but beautifully feathered, eating the wild food of the lake, and having graceful and slender legs and bodies. An exchange of birds during VI-Eztalcualiztli promoted the correspondence between the *tlaloque* and the Aztecs. While Aztecs gave the turkey, the image of domestic existence, Tlaloc gave water fowl made available in human form through priestly actions.[59]

The use of paper, rubber, and wood (in poles, frames, drums, etc.) was one of the most pronounced characteristics of these rituals. One of the names for I-Atl cahualo, for example, was Quahuitl ehua, "to raise up the staff." Everywhere in the valley, particularly at the young men's houses (the *calpolli*), people raised poles decorated with rubber-spattered paper banners.

Paper was a wood product highly regarded among the Aztecs.[60] In all these ritual occasions paper was carefully placed. Traditional paper making was a labor-intensive activity that utilized many of the elements already discussed. The bark of the *amatl* tree was placed in a pool of running water.[61] The soaked and rotted wood was then boiled. The remaining pulp was then felted together with a beater called *amahuitequini*, or "paper beater," which was typically made from grooved stone. The sheets of paper were then dried. Later, Catholic priests identified paper and paper making so closely with indigenous religious practices that they virtually eradicated its production.[62]

During I-Atl cahualo, the seven sacrificial children were adorned in different-colored paper. They went to the *tlaloque* adorned with the destroyed plant life for which their lives were given. The use of paper physically collapsed the significance of the sacrificial act. Elements of earth, water, and plant life coalesced through human intervention to create paper. The reciprocal nature of life and death did not escape the Aztecs' attention. Paper was one embodiment of this process. The *tetehuitl*, or "paper streamers," that were colorfully displayed by the ritual throng directly corresponded to the *tlacatetehuitin*, or "human paper streamers," which was the name given these children.

Other elements of the children's costumes underscored this correspondence. Colors were specifically mentioned in conjunction with each child's sacrificial place name. On Quauhtepec, vestments were black or stained; at Yoaltecatl, the paper was black-and-red striped, signifying a connection with Tlaloc and bloodletting or sacrifice.[63] At Tepetzinco, the girl sacrificed was dressed in blue, which was associated with Chalchiuhtlicue and the lake water. At Pantitlan, where the child was physically given to the lake, he was named Epcoatl, "shell snake." His costume was arranged with shells or pearls that corresponded to the absolute fertility embodied by the ocean.[64] The costume of the child sacrificed at Cocotl was a variation of that of Yoaltecatl, and therefore had a similar meaning. Likewise, at Yiahuqueme the same color was used as that at Quauhtepec. As with the costumed representations of mountains and the dead given to the *tlaloque* during XIII-Tepeihuitl and XVI-Atemoztli, the instances where colored paper was used in I-Atl cahualo were generally associated with bloodletting.[65]

At each of the sites of child sacrifices, paper banners were raised on poles that were freshly cut from budding trees. As López Austin has pointed out, there is a correlation in Nahuatl, as in English, between trees and human bodies.[66] Children corresponded to the sprouting greenness or budding that was a feature of these poles.[67] This was dramatized by attaching paper leaves, or wings, to the backs of the children, linking their lives to an emerging plant life, and to the birds who bore the *tlaloque* messages at the ritual's end. The ritual tie between children and plant life articulated a message of new growth and potential.

Paper was also used in the adornment of the dead during XIII-Tepeihuitl, and of the *tepictoton* during XVI-Atemoztli. These mountain images were clothed in paper just like the children of I-Atl cahualo. Being fashioned of food, which was formed from destroyed plant life, paper was the appropriate vestment. It completed the interplay of material connections between plant and human life. After the *tepictoton* were ritually "killed" and their "bodies" stored for consumption, the paper clothing was collected and destroyed in the temple courtyard. Other offerings, including unripe squash, wood, and clay bowls full of food gifts, were also collected and burned. As the children and *tepictoton* were given by sacrifice as offerings for Tlaloc, so too were their other vestments of plant and mineral life.

Rubber also played an important part in these ceremonies. The children of I-Atl cahualo wore it on their feet, faces, and paper costumes. It was splattered on the paper banners that lined the procession route. It also adorned the *tepictoton*, "little molded ones," during the rites of XIII-Tepeihuitl and XVI-Atemoztli. Rubber, a latex sap from the rubber tree native to the Mesoamerican lowlands, was a third element in the blood-water correspondence discussed above. Its ritual use completed a cycle of sustenances in which plant life must be featured. Landscape, plant life, and human beings were locked in an eating relationship. The sacrifices of I-Atl cahualo, as well as the decorations of XVI-Atemoztli and XIII-Tepeihuitl, physically promoted this relationship. These rituals were performed to ensure adequate plant growth and harvest. Wearing rubber conflated the sacrificial theme of correspondences between life-sustaining fluids from various beings during these three festivals.

EATING AND GIVING FOOD

Landscape sites and types of food were the primary referents of the rituals to Tlaloc. Unlike the elements featured and explored above, however, food was the means by which these rituals overcame the opposition between the human and Tlalocan worlds. The necessity of food required that humans have an ability to transform the world. It was the biological means by which discrete elements of the cosmos coalesced into a substantive form to promote and sustain life. The principal emphasis, therefore, was on how food was articulated as an agent of transformation in these ritual descriptions. It was through its inherent quality of articulating the reciprocity necessary for human life that food became the most meaningful element in these festivals and their primary objective.

Two criteria were given for choosing children to be sacrificed during I-Atl cahualo. First, they had to have two cowlicks at the crown of their heads.[68] The idiom for cowlick in Nahuatl was *cuezcome*, which among contemporary Tlaxcalans refers to a large wooden-framed adobe grain storage hut that strikingly resembles a human head.[69]

[159]

The second criteria was that they be born under a good day sign. "Good," in this case, also meant "comestible." A correspondence between a human child's attributes and sustenance was established and maintained throughout the imagery of the ritual.

Children, being the fruits of the human body, were the appropriate gift to Tlaloc to commence the germination season. In exchange for the children, the Tlalocan landscape would reciprocate by releasing those elements of earth, water, and plant life, in the proper order and proportion for human consumption.

Scholars have long understood an important symmetry between human sacrifice and maize among the Aztecs.[70] In the second half of the month of I-Atl cahualo, Aztec warriors began the presentation ceremonies of their captives who were to die in the infamous gladiatorial sacrifices in the second month, Tlacaxipehualiztli. After the victim had been vanquished, his skin was donned by his captor and worn for the next twenty days. This flaying event to Xipe Totec was said to correspond to the growth of new maize.[71]

There is evidence, however, that child sacrifice during I-Atl cahualo corresponded more directly to the maize flower, or to the preproducing stage of this plant's growth. The children's headbands, for instance, were crammed full of feathery tassels of maize. As with the creation of the earth via the destruction of the goddess Tlalteuctli, there was a correspondence between the hair of a destroyed body and plant life.[72] A child's hair and head corresponded to the delicate flowering stages of maize in the agricultural cycle. During VI-Eztalcualiztli, the Tlamacazque carried figurines that represented water and were fashioned of rubber and copal incense in the shape of mountains or temples. The tops of these images were also adorned with quetzal feathers, like the children of I-Atl cahualo. They were called *quetalmiyahuayotl*, or "quetzal feather maize tassels." Again, the correspondence was promoted during the ritual between the hair of the human head and the "hair" of the maize flower.

Besides the adornment of rubber, amaranth was also applied to their faces. This small seed grain was used more centrally in the rituals of XVI-Atemoztli and XIII-Tepeihuitl as *tzoalli*. The type of amaranth used had associations to the watery world of Tlaloc in that it was said to resemble fish roe or grains of sand. It was also used in curing ceremonies that addressed illnesses associated with the *tlaloque*.[73] Being a seed as well as a food, amaranth represented the potential sustenance demonstrated in the flowery stage of maize and the lives of the children. Children's bodies were also pulled by their parents during these rites to promote their growth.

As in any community, food and eating were physical mandates of the Aztec world. The process of living in an eating landscape assumed a level of appropriate material interaction within that environment.[74] Although predicated on the idea of securing a successful harvest, rituals such as I-Atl cahualo were simultaneously occasions for meaningful dialogue with and orientation to Tlalocan.

Food was the medium of exchange that required creative transformational abilities. Its place was involved with an ability to balance the life and death processes. Unlike modern consumerist ideology, discussed in chapter 7, the interaction of life and death was of particular concern for those who inhabited the living landscape of Tlalocan—or for those who still understand land as a coherent being. With typically succinct yet stunning clarity, a contemporary Nahua group puts it this way:

> *We live HERE on the earth [stomping on the mud floor]*
> *we are all fruits of the earth*
> *the earth sustains us*
> *we grow here, on the earth and flower*
> *and when we die we wither in the earth*
> *we are ALL FRUITS of the earth [stomping on the mud floor].*
> *We eat the earth*
> *then the earth eats us.*[75]

During VI-Etzalcualiztli, four representatives of maize were sacrificed. During this time of year the tender ears of maize were already growing in the *chinampas*. Therefore, these sacrifices were dedicated to maize rather than their flowery tassels, as in I-Atl cahualo. The hearts of these sacrifices were offered to the middle of the lake as food for the *tlaloque*. Human life was once again transformed through sacrifice into that substance appropriate for the deity's sustenance. The reciprocal release of vital nutrients by Tlaloc was to follow. These events, which concluded the festival of VI-Etzalcualiztli, were indicated earlier in the description by other types of feeding activities. Because of its place in the agricultural cycle, unlike the other rituals described, VI-Etzalcualiztli was more of a thanksgiving ceremony.

One of the first duties of the priests was to offer balls of maize dough on a fire altar. These offering balls of dough were analogous to the activity of forming and cooking tortillas. Likewise, the lake's acceptance of the hearts of sacrifices at Pantitlan was signaled by a roaring and bubbling turbulence, which was linguistically connected with a pot of boiling food.

Cooking offerings to Tlaloc in the *calmecac* and feeding sacrificial hearts to Tlaloc linked these distance places. This was a regenerative activity. Likewise, in the womb a baby was understood to be surrounded by a maize gruel, just as the earth was surrounded by water. Human life was thus "cooked" into existence.[76] Preparing and eating *etzalli*, a mush of beans and corn, accompanied general dancing, drunkenness, and ribald behavior. Similar events of public drunkenness took place at the close of XVI-Atemoztli and during celebrations to the ancestors in XIII-Tepeihuitl. These human demonstrations were otherwise strictly forbidden in Aztec society. However, during this festival eating required a behavior that broke the conventions of domestic life. The Otherness of Tlalocan, promoted and embodied by the priests and the activity of consumption, was extended to the general population through the consumption food.

During both XVI-Aztemoztli and XIII-Tepeihuitl, however, we see the most dramatic articulation of the transformative properties of food and the reciprocity between life and death. Both were organized around the creation of mountains of food. A landscape of food was constructed and addressed as the substantive articulation of another reality.

In XIII-Tepeihuitl, the people initiated the ceremony by fashioning food mountains of the dead. Like the Aztec kings, they were seated on reed mats of noble status. They were then offered a meal of costly dishes, including meat (dog and turkey). Then the people themselves had a meal that was accompanied by celebration and drinking. After this ritual visit with the dead of Tlalocan, five human representations were killed and their heads were strung on the *tzompantli*, or "skull row." Their bodies then became food for various barrios of the city. The head, the container of *tonalli*, was the source of human vitality. Destruction of human life, through sacrifice and eating, signaled the destruction and consumption of the mountain images. Consumption of a human body paralleled the destruction and consumption of food mountains. Sahagún described the total consumption of destroyed human bodies, the mountain ancestors, and the destruction of their paper costumes and other ceremonial items. At some point, at some place, all life was food. In the elaboration of the constant flux of life and death, eating food was the primary transformative event. Having a place in the Aztec cosmos required that one participate in the constantly transforming quality of material life through the activity of eating.

Similarly, XVI-Atemoztli articulated a dynamic of sustenance. The representations, however, were of the *tlaloque* themselves. Mountains of food were created that conjoined features of the landscape with consumption. The *tepictoton* were the objects of celebration, and they were likewise fed and cherished. They were at once the victims of sacrifice and the embodiment of sustenance. Being the sources of wealth and life, the *tepictoton* were sacrificial victims of consumptive activity. Aztec understandings of reciprocity were primarily based on eating and giving food, which necessitated a ritual articulation of the violent consequences of life.

Food was the medium of transforming attributes of the landscape into forms suitable for bodily existence. Cosmologically, an Aztec body resulted in the intersection of vital forces that emanated from cardinal directions. Likewise, negotiating the *meaning* of food required a bodily vigilance regarding dimensions of an ongoing creation. Sustaining the body required that the Aztecs participate forcefully in an eating landscape. The consequence of consumption was violence, and this was accounted for in their rituals.

The effect of Aztec bodily existence was through their identification with an eating landscape. Correspondences between various beings were promoted through food exchanges with the *tlaloque*. Indigenous existence paid close attention to the interaction of material realities. For the Aztecs, food was the primary medium of exchange and the means by which they meaningfully occupied the Valley of Mexico. After drinking and extreme consumptive activities, the *tepictoton* were "killed," and their hearts were torn from their cores. They were completely eaten by everyone; as in XVI-Atemoztli, everyone got a piece of the bodies of the *tepictoton*.

At some point in a biological cycle of life one is either eating or eaten. This was not the sad or pessimistic outlook on the world of the Aztec, as some have suggested, but an indigenous one. Life was based on an interactive reality that food promoted in the relationship between life and death. The reciprocity between beings in the cosmos required that there be some articulation of this process; food was the vehicle of substantive transformation from one reality to another and therefore was an appropriate ritual articulation of transition between realms of being.

These Tlaloc data must be discussed with a methodological and/or ethnohistorical analysis to more completely reflect on the full range of their implications. Part II of this book focuses on the question of how to situate the *Florentine Codex* and other primary texts. Not only is Sahagún's position central to this work, but probing his place in the literature helps highlight a self-consciousness regarding our contemporary relationship to the Aztec and their landscape. All scholars of Mesoamerican traditions know the difficulties of using the colonial sources. Problems with such texts—i.e., their being produced largely by Europeans; the destruction of Native texts along with their attempts to destroy cities, cultures, and populations; and these texts' conceptual and temporal distance from contemporary life—have largely been seen as roadblocks to our understanding of the Aztecs. Rather than simply expressing confidence in Sahagún's *Florentine Codex*, which is the most complete and well-known version of his *General History of the Things of New Spain*, as a true image of Aztec life, I have incorporated into this study the questionable integrity of these sources and Sahagún himself. Conquest and colonial periods are usually presented as hurdles for Mesoamericanists without an adequate investigation of their possibilities for our coming more fully to terms with far-reaching interpretive issues. By shifting our attention from the contextual filters involved in the production of texts to the hermeneutics of occupation, I intend to account for many of these difficulties.

Second, and perhaps most significantly, reflections on the meaning of matter in radically distinctive cultural contexts requires a rigorous self-consciousness. Through the translation and interpretation of rituals to Tlaloc, many important methodological issues have been highlighted. An attempt to "locate" Sahagún is simultaneously an attempt to account for an interpretive process that includes the investigator. In chapter 5, a history of religion method is utilized to situate the work of Sahagún in a historical and hermeneutical framework. This will help outline the forces that shaped his ethnography and help clarify the colonial interaction with traditional Aztec life and culture. In the history of religion, this approach is referred to as a "methodological discussion," which not only initiates but embeds itself within an exploration of the Other. In conclusion, methodological themes are re-presented in chapter 7 by way of indicating the larger implications of this study for a contemporary hermeneutic of occupation of the Americas.

The consequences of codifying Aztec life as realities apart from contemporary interpretive efforts risks that their world, as well as our own, be rendered as transparent. Our interpretive legacy as Americans and academics can be traced to the early monastic interpreters of the New World more easily than to the Aztecs. As such, the scholarly referent for interpretation has been the production of books, which, as described in Part I, has tended to eliminate the performative dimensions of material life. Todorov has characterized this state of affairs as a self-referential hermeneutics that is tied to colonial processes of occupying the Americas. If taken self-consciously, an investigation of indigenous hermeneutical practice significantly exposes the fiction of scholarship. A hermeneutical activity of habitation approximates what Mus has called the "magical act of occupation

[by] means of gaining access to the soil as soil."[77] Ironically, by shifting the object of analysis from a purely anthropocentric to a phenomenological referent, the consequence may be a restoration of the Other's humanity along with an appreciation of the meaningful conditions of living in time and place.

NOTES

1. The Nahuatl phrase *san ie no* means the same place/time. *No* refers to both space and time as a single entity. See *zanyeno* in Frances Karttunen, *An Analytical Dictionary of Nahuatl* (Austin: University of Texas Press, 1983), p. 346.

2. According to Karttunen, *-tihu(i)* is a centrifugal purposive verbal compounding element, and as *yetiuh* it is expressed in the singular. See Karttunen (ibid.), p. 240. Also see Nancy D. Munn, "Transformation of Subjects into Objects in Wabiri and Pitjuntajara Myth," in *Australian Aboriginal Studies*, edited by Ronald M. Berndt (Nedlands: University of Western Australia Press, 1970), pp. 141–163, for another example of how death transforms human beings into the landscape.

3. See William T. Sanders, Jeffrey R. Parsons, and Robert S. Santley, *The Basin of Mexico: Biological Processes in the Evolution of a Civilization* (New York: Academic Press, 1979), pp. 81–85, and maps 1 and 24. A full-blown analysis, from my point of view, is in Philip P. Arnold, "The Aztec Ceremonial Landscape in the Valley of Mexico: Implications of Examining Religion and Environment" (M.A. thesis, Institute of Latin American Studies, University of London, 1986), pp. 15–19.

4. The tropics are defined as the region north and south of the earth's equator where the sun reaches zenith (casts no shadow at noon) during some part of the year. It extends from 23° north latitude to 23° south.

5. See maps, "Milpa Alta," E14 A49, Carta Geológica, and "Ciudad de México," E14 A39, Carta Topográfica (Mexico City: Instituto Nacional de Estadística, Geograffica e Informática, 1984 and 1986).

6. Johanna Broda, her students, and associates led Anthony Aveni and me to this site in January 1989. In the previous year, Edward Calnek had positively identified this site from a map, dated 1714, called "Titulos de Tola y Ixhuatepec," as being Quauhtepetl. On the summit and in the saddle between the east and west peaks, there was a large amount of cut stone probably used in the construction of ceremonial buildings. This stone was quarried at the base of the mountain and carried to the summit. From the top, one has a panoramic view of the northern part of the valley, including Teotihuacan, Texcoco, and perhaps even the Tula Valley (today the smog severely limits one's vision). To the south, all of Mexico City and the volcanoes are completely visible on a clear day. See the map "Cuautitlan," E14 A19, Carta Topográfica (Mexico City: Instituto Nacional de Estadística, Geografía e Informática, 1986).

7. See Johanna Broda, "Las fiestas Aztecas de los dioses de la luvia: una reconstruccíon según las fuentes del siglo XVI," in *Revista Española de antropología Americana* 6 (Madrid, 1971), p. 263.

8. The relationship between the pre-Columbian shrine at Guadalupe dedicated to Tonantzin ("our honored mother") and the shrine on Yohualtecatl is complex and the subject of ongoing debate.

9. Anthony Aveni, Johanna Broda, Edward Calnek, and I visited this site in January of 1988. There was a large amount of stone, which is currently used for penning animals and dividing small agricultural fields. We then postulated that the presence of so much cut stone was evidence of it having been a large ceremonial site. In addition we found a scattering of Late Aztec shards around a small mound, probably a ceremonial platform. According to Broda, there also appear what seem to be the remains of a road leading straight from the summit of the hill to the center of Mexico City. Unfortunately, there is no survey data available on this site, as it was not included in the basin survey of Sanders, et al., in *The Basin of Mexico*. We had to imagine the view of Mexico City from there, as the air pollution is too thick today. Still, we were able to see the larger volcanoes of Iztaccihuatl and Popocatepetl and the Panamerican building downtown poking above the smog. See map "Ciudad de Mexico," E14 A39, Carta Topográfica.

10. In January 1988, Broda, Aveni, Calnek, and I attempted to visit this site. Due to its sensitive location near the international airport, we were denied access by the military, who currently occupy this hill. Although it is listed as a large ceremonial site in Sanders, et al., *The Basin of Mexico*, I have not been able to get any more detailed information on the site. Also see Luis Gonzalez Aparicio's map in his *Plano reconstructivo de la region de Tenochtitlan* (Mexico City: Instituto Nacional de Antropología e Historia, 1973), which describes Tepetzinco as a place of baths used as a "Royal Retreat." His map also suggests very interesting alignments between these sites and ceremonial structures at Tlatelolco.

11. The corresponding Spanish text explains that Poyauhtlan "es un monte, que esta en los termjnos de Tlaxcalla, y alli cabe tepetzinco." See Fray Bernardino de Sahagún, *Florentine Codex: General History of the Things of New Spain*, 12 books, 13 parts, edited and translated by Arthur J. O. Anderson and Charles E. Dibble, Monographs of the School of American Research, number 14 (Salt Lake City: University of Utah Press, 1951–1982), book 2, p. 43, note 12.

12. See Fray Diego Durán, *Book of the Gods and Rites and the Ancient Calendar*, edited and translated by Fernando Horcasitas and Doris Heyden (Norman: University of Oklahoma Press, 1971), pp. 164 and 166. In the chapter "The God Tlaloc," he suggests that it was here that the lake drained. But this was a dangerous place. "Occasionally a tremendous whirlpool appears when the water is sucked down." But he also tells us that "[o]thers disagree, [saying] that it was a spring and that during the rainy season a great quantity of water burst forth, filling the entire City of Mexico and its canals with water, almost flooding all the towns which stood on the beaches and shores (of the lake), and occasionally the water rose as far as their homes." The flow of water at Pantitlan may have varied depending on the time of year.

13. The setting of these poles took place during the ritual of IV-Huei tozoztli ("great vigil"), which is most colorfully described by Durán (ibid.), pp. 156–171.

14. Today this site is not clearly identifiable. After the colonial government drained most of the lake in the eighteenth century, this area became habitable. Currently a barrio exists in this area called Pantitlan, which is home to hot baths, but the precise location of the pre-Columbian site is unknown. Gonzalez Aparicio, in *Plano reconstructivo de la region de Tenochtitlan*, tentatively located this site on his map.

15. See the map "Amecameca," E14 B41, Carta Topográfica (Mexico City: Instituto Nacional de Estadística, Geografía e Informática, 1986).

16. For example, see Pedro Armillas, "Gardens and Swamps," *Science* 174 (1976): 653–666; Micheal D. Coe, "The Chinampas of Mexico," *Scientific American* 211, no. 1 (1964): 90–98; J. P. Darch, "Drained Fields in the Americas: An Introduction," in *Drained Field Agriculture in Central and South America*, edited by J. P. Darch (Oxford: B.A.R. International Series 189, 1983), pp. 1–10; William M. Denevan, "Aboriginal Drained Field Cultivation," *Science* 169 (1970): 647–654; and Ian S. Farrington, "The Wet, the Dry and the Steep: Archaeological Imperatives and the Study of Agricultural Intensification," in *Prehistoric Intensive Agriculture in the Tropics*, edited by Ian S. Farrington (Oxford: B.A.R. International Series 232, 1985), pp. 1–10. For the political implications of *chinampa* agriculture, see Jeffrey R. Parsons "Political Implications of Pre-Hispanic Chinampa Agriculture in the Valley of Mexico," paper presented at the 45th International Congress of Americanists (Bogotá: 1–6 July 1985). Currently, *chinampa* agriculture is seeing something of a resurgence in central Mexico. See A. Gómez-Pompa, et al., "Experiences in Traditional Hydraulic Agriculture," in *Maya Subsistence: Studies in Memory of Dennis E. Puleston*, edited by K.V. Flannery (New York: Academic Press, 1982), pp. 327–342; D. E. Vasey, "Nitrogen Fixation and Flow in Experimental Island Bed Gardens: Implications for Archaeology," in *Prehistoric Agriculture in the Tropics*, edited by Ian S. Farrington (Oxford: B.A.R. International Series 232, 1985), pp. 233–246; William M. Denevan, "Hydraulic Agriculture in the American Tropics: Forms, Measures, and Recent Research," in *Maya Subsistence: Studies in the Memory of Dennis E. Puleston*, edited by Kent V. Flannery (New York: Academic Press, 1982), pp. 181–203; and Dennis E. Puleston, "Experiments in Prehistoric Raised Field Agriculture: Learning from the Past," *Journal of Belize Affairs* 5 (1977): 36–43, on the reconstruction of raised fields.

17. Cited by Anthony F. Aveni in "Mapping the Ritual Landscape: Debt Payment to Tlaloc During the Month of Atlcahualo," in *To Change Place: Aztec Ceremonial Landscapes*, edited by Davíd Carrasco (Niwot: University Press of Colorado, 1991), p. 69. See map, "Ciudad de Mexico."

18. The description of I-Atl cahualo does not make it explicit whether or not the ritual moved in a circular procession from site to site or radiated to each of the sites simultaneously from the center. This question is unanswerable; however, listing the sites in this manner suggests either a prioritizing relative to one another and/or a temporal arrangement of visitation of each of these seven sites.

19. See Aveni in "Mapping the Ritual Landscape," pp. 58–73. In particular, see his Table 6.1, "Tlacateuihtin (Human Banners) Sacrificed in Atlcahualo," p. 62.

20. See Gonzalez Aparicio's map in *Plano reconstructivo de la region de Tenochtitlan*, which integrates sight lines connecting ceremonial spaces. In particular, the relationship between the Templo Mayor and Quauhtepec seems to have acted as a point of orientation for the city layout. A second striking spatial feature of these sites is that

the ritual sequence moves in a clockwise direction. This is unusual given that most of the codices follow a counterclockwise direction (Anthony Aveni, personal communication).

21. See Anthony F. Aveni, Edward Calnek, and Horst Hartung, "Myth, Environment, and the Orientation of the Templo Mayor of Tenochtitlan," *American Antiquity* 53 (1988), pp. 287–304.

22. Indeed, in the descriptions of Quauhtepec and Yohualtecatl, the linguistic item *san ie no* (or *zanyeno*, "same place/time"), used in conjunction with *yetiuh* ("goes to be"), extends an understanding of correspondence to temporal and spatial dimensions. See Karttunen, *An Analytical Dictionary of Nahuatl*, p. 346.

23. See Johanna Broda, "Templo Mayor as Ritual Space," in *The Great Temple of Tenochtitlan: Center and Periphery in the Aztec World*, edited by Johanna Broda, Davíd Carrasco, and Eduardo Matos Moctezuma (Berkeley: University of California Press, 1987), p. 105.

24. I would like to thank Jeffrey Parsons of the University of Michigan for letting me examine and photocopy the site reports of his survey of the Zumpango region. These reports have yet to be published, but contain an abundance of information that should be followed up. Unfortunately, the survey undertaken was not particularly interested in documenting ceremonial complexes, but rather focused on population densities of each pre-Columbian era. As a result, the maps generated in Sanders, et al., *The Basin of Mexico*, and Jeffrey Parsons, Keith Kintigh, and Susan Gregg, *Archaeological Settlement Pattern Data from the Chalco, Xochimilco, Ixtapalapa, Texcoco, and Zumpango Regions, Mexico* (Museum of Anthropology Technical Reports, number 14, Research Reprints in Archaeology Contributions 9 (Ann Arbor: University of Michigan, 1983), have tended to neglect the seven or more sites recorded by the survey team. Only two sites in the Citlaltepec area recorded in Parsons were published in the tabulated data. Twenty years ago many of these sites were in excellent condition, and there is the possibility that more intensive surveys in this area could connect some of these places with VI-Etzalcualiztli. Names used in the ritual, such as Temilco, Tepexic, and Oztoc, appear to be descriptive and could possibly be linked to actual sites in the vicinity of San Juan Zitlaltepec. See map "Zumpango de Ocampo," E14 A19, Carta Topográfica (Mexico City: Instituto Nacional de Estadística, Geografía e Informática, 1987).

25. Tlamacazque literally means "they give it" and is used as the title of Tlaloc priests.

26. *Calmecac* means "whip house" or "house of penance," and was where young men were instructed in appropriate actions with respect to the gods.

27. This festival was the precursor to the contemporary Dia de las Muertos. See Hugo G. Nutini, *Todos Santos in Rural Tlaxcala: A Syncretic, Expressive, and Symbolic Analysis of the Cult of the Dead* (Princeton, NJ: Princeton University Press, 1988), p. 56; cited in Davíd Carrasco, *Religions of Mesoamerica: Cosmovision and Ceremonial Centers* (San Francisco: Harper & Row, Publishers, 1990), p. 143. Also see Jacques Galinier, "La Muerte," in *Pueblos de la Sierra Madre: Ethnografía de la Comminidad Otomí* (Mexico City: Instituto Nacional Indigenista, número 17, 1983), pp. 483–505, for a description of Day of the Dead among another contemporary Indian group.

28. According to Bray, the souls of those who had committed suicide, been struck by lightning, had drowned, or died of leprosy, rheumatism, or dropsy all went to Tlalocan after death. See Warwick Bray, *Everyday Life of the Aztecs* (New York: Dorset Press, 1987), pp. 71–72. Also see Bernard R. Ortiz de Montellano, "The Body, Ethics and Cosmos: Aztec Physiology," in *Imagination of Matter: Religion and Ecology in Mesoamerican Traditions*, edited by Davíd Carrasco (Oxford: B.A.R. International Series 515, 1989), pp. 191–209.

29. According to Bray, *Everyday Life of the Aztecs*, these bodies were laid in a tomb and their faces were smeared with liquid rubber and decorated on their foreheads with blue paper. An imitation lock of hair was made from paper and attached to the back of the neck and paper capes were wrapped around the shoulders. Wooden staves were placed in each of their hands. On the tomb was laid a dry bough that turned green when the soul had arrived in Tlalocan.

30. I am currently unable to identify the last three mountains mentioned with certainty. They do, however, refer to important deities, all of whom are associated with Tlaloc. Ehecatl is listed on Gonzalez Aparicio's map in *Plano reconstructivo de la region de Tenochtitlan*, but I have been unable to find additional evidence that this was the mountain honored in the ceremony.

31. José Luis Lorenzo, *Las zonas arqueológicas de los volcanoes Iztaccíhuatl y Popocatépetl* (Mexico City: Instituto Nacional de Antropología e Historia, 1957). Also see Stanislaw Iwaniszewski, "La arqueología de alta montaña en México y su estado actual," *Estudios de cultura Náhuatl* 18 (1986): 249–273, for an updated view of high mountain sites.

32. This female revelry is reminiscent of what Ann Grodzins Gold calls "Goat Play" among Rajasthani village women of India. It is joking, a rowdy behavior that undoes male hierarchies and death to celebrate female sexuality and fertility. See Ann Grodzins Gold, *Fruitful Journeys: The Ways of Rajasthani Pilgrims* (Berkeley: University of California Press, 1987), pp. 123–132.

33. It is interesting to note that during the ritual of VI-Etzalcualiztli various places are referred to as Tlalocan, including the altar at the Templo Mayor as well as other areas of ritual action.

34. Nutrients would come in the form of "green fertilizer," which would be taken from canals that defined the boundaries of the raised *chinampa* fields. The complexities of *chinampa* agriculture are manifold and are most fruitfully explored through reading the attempts over the last several years to reconstruct this type of agriculture. For example see Gómez-Pompa, et al., "Experiences in Traditional Hydraulic Agriculture"; Puleston, "Experiments in Prehistoric Raised Field Agriculture"; and Vasey, "Nitrogen Fixation and Flow." Edward Calnek has recently shown me aerial photographs of Mexico City taken around the time of WWII that clearly show traces of *chinampa* agriculture south of what is now the International Airport of Mexico City. See Edward Calnek, "Settlement Pattern and Chinampa Agriculture at Tenochtitlan," *American Antiquity* 38, no. 2 (1973): 190–195; and "Organización de los sistemas de abastecimiento urban de alimentos: el caso de Tenochtitlan," in *Las cudades de América Latina y sus áreas de influencia a través de la historia*, edited by Jorge E. Hardoy and Richard P. Schaedel (Buenos Aires: Ediciones SIAP, 1975), pp. 41–60. For an examination of pre-Colombian raised-field agriculture in Mexico, see Armillas, "Gardens and Swamps," and Coe, "The Chinampas of Mexico"; and Jeffrey Parsons, "Chinampa Agriculture and the Aztec

Urbanization in the Valley of Mexico," in *Prehistoric Intensive Agriculture in the Tropics*, edited by Ian S. Farrington (Oxford: B.A.R. International Series 232, 1985), pp. 49–96. From the point of view of ethnohistorical texts, see Edward E. Calnek, "The Localization of the Sixteenth Century Map Called the Maguey Plan," *American Antiquity* 38, no. 2 (1973): 190–195. For a different view of the significance of *chinampa* agriculture, see Inga Clendinnen, "The Cost of Courage in Aztec Society," *Past and Present* 107 (1985): 44–89. She ties the uncertain nature of this form of agriculture to "Flowery Wars" and a warrior's sacrificial cult.

35. The most significant of these dikes has been attributed to Netzahuacoyotl, the poet king of Texcoco during the early sixteenth century. There are several things that demonstrate that Netzahuacoyotl, in particular, was interested in water and its organization. Along with projects to regulate the seasonal cycles of the lake system, he constructed other important water works, sometimes referred to as "royal retreats" or "pleasure gardens," such as Acatetelco and the famous Tetzcotzinco. See Richard Townsend, "Pyramid and Sacred Mountain," in *Ethnoastronomy and Archaeoastronomy in the American Tropics*, edited by Anthony F. Aveni and Gary Urton (New York: *Annals of the New York Academy of Sciences*, volume 385, 1982), pp. 37–62, for an excellent overview of the site Tetzcotzinco and its cosmological significance. Also see maps "Texcoco," E14 A49, and "Chalco," E14 B31 (Mexico City: Instituto Nacional de Estadística, Geografía e Informática, 1985 and 1984).

36. This is another of the "royal retreats" of the Aztec nobility, which was located on the western shore of Lake Texcoco and also the source of fresh water for the city of Tenochtitlan.

37. According to Durán, *Book of the Gods and Rites*, pp. 167–168, the valley hydrology was a mysterious reality: "There is a remarkable thing about this lake [Texcoco]. Many times it becomes angry and turbulent in that place [Pantitlan]. There the water boils and froths; according to my conjectures regarding its cause, it seems to be that spring or vent in the lake." He goes on to relate an event where he and another friar were boating across a peaceful lake, "when suddenly, without any air or wind from any direction, there arose a hurricane and a movement so strange that we thought we would drown. When I asked the rowers who carried us . . . the reason . . . they answered that it was the air below which sought an exit."

38. According to Heyden and Horcasitas, Durán's account of the violent nature of water in the valley is substantiated by more contemporary events:

> Durán's speculations about the rise and fall of the waters of the Basin of Mexico remain unproved. The enigma of the workings of the volcanic clefts under the soil of Mexico City and of the movements of the subterranean waters have never been satisfactorily mapped. An example is the lake village of Mixquic, near Xochimilco. In 1955 its canals and ponds almost completely dried up. The villagers, distraught at the sight of parched cornfields and vegetable plots, prayed for the water to return. On May 3, the Feast of the Holy Cross, a sizable spout of water erupted near the village and has continued to grow. On May 3 of each year visitors to Mixquic can observe the Thanksgiving ceremonies of the villagers. (See translators' commentary in ibid., p. 166, note 8.)

39. Today not much survives of the aqueduct that ran from Chapultepec (now a city park) and Tenochtitlan. In the area of Texcoco, however, there still remain many

miles of pre-Columbian aqueducts, some of which are still in use locally. These aqueducts originate at Mount Tlaloc, in the eastern sierra, and end in the towns of Texcoco and Huexotla on the lake shore. A major water artery directed water from Mount Tlaloc to a small hill known as Tetzcotzinco (from Texcoco, spelled "Tetzcohco" by Karttunen in *An Analytical Dictionary of Nahuatl*, p. 237), meaning "honored place of Texcoco." This was the site of the gardens of Nezahualcoyotl, the famous poet-king of Texcoco, which boasted an enormous diversity of plants and animals taken from all over Mesoamerica. Water from Mount Tlaloc entered the hill at its eastern end and traversed around the hill via a road. In January 1989, I had the opportunity to visit this site with Anthony Aveni and his team. Currently there are pre-Columbian remains of temples, statues, and ceremonial plazas. On the summit there is a carved image of Tlaloc. At the base of the hill there is a large cave opening that local people say houses a strange animal. When some of our group asked it they could explore it, the guide could not understand why we wanted to put ourselves at such risk. See Jeffrey R. Parsons, *Prehistoric Settlement Patterns in the Texcoco Region, Mexico*, Memoirs of the Museum of Anthropology, no. 3 (Ann Arbor: University of Michigan, 1971), pp. 145–152. Water was first used by the king, then sent to the rest of the city, articulating in the landscape a hierarchy of authority and responsibility from Tlaloc to the king to the common people. See Richard Townsend, "Pyramid and Sacred Mountain," and *State and Cosmos in the Art of Tenochtitlan*, Studies in Pre-Columbian Art and Archaeology, no. 20 (Washington, DC: Dumbarton Oaks, 1979).

40. At the beginning of this section, Sahagún tells us that the phrase *atoyatl* comes from *atl*, "water," and *totoca*, "it runs along." How this becomes *atoyatl* is unaccounted for, however, in either Karttunen or Andrews, even though they mark the vowel length differently. See Karttunen, *An Analytical Dictionary of Nahuatl*, p. 14. The linguistic elements of the term "river" are not clear.

41. See Sahagún, *Florentine Codex*, book 11, pp. 247–248.

42. There are a few surviving examples of these glorious feather adornments in existence. The most significant resides in the National Museum of Archaeology and History in Mexico City. Other pieces include a shield in Vienna's Museum of Ethnology, and a piece found in a cave in Utah was crafted in central Mexico during the twelfth century. The last item is also interesting in that it directly connects Mesoamerican and North American cultural groups. See Thomas Canby, "The Anasazi Riddles in the Ruins," *National Geographic* 162, no. 5 (1982): 572–573.

43. According to Jane Rosenthal (personal communication), the formation of rain clouds on mountain peaks is referred to among the Tlaxcalans as rain "raising" or "emerging." Indeed, in paragraph 19 of I-Atl cahualo the verb *quetza* is used, which means "to stand up" or "to raise something," but in this context means "to rain." See Sahagún, *Florentine Codex*, book 2, p. 44.

44. See Rémi Siméon, *Diccionario de la lengua Nahuatl o Mexicana*, (Mexico City: Siglo Veintinuno editores, 1977), p. 390.

45. See Karttunen, *An Analytical Dictionary of Nahuatl*, p. 120.

46. During Cortes's march to Tenochtitlan, he passed this peak. At that time it was still active and sent smoke out from its top (hence the Nahuatl name). Cortes sent

a party of men to the top to investigate, but only a few actually saw the crater at the top. Native people went with the party and their reaction to the ascent is interesting.

> [Diego de Ordás] took with him two of our soldiers and certain Indian chiefs from Huexotzingo, and the chiefs that he took with him frightened him by saying that when one was half way up Popocatepetl . . . one could not endure the shaking of the ground and the flames and stones and ashes which were thrown out of the mountain, and that they would not dare to ascend further than where stood the cues of the Idols which are called the Teoles of Popocatepetl.

The wildness of the *tlaloque* was manifest also in the raging volcano and was considered dangerous to human life. See Bernal Diaz del Castillo, *The Discovery and Conquest of Mexico; 1517–1521*, translated by A. P. Maudslay (New York: Farrar, Straus, and Cudahy, 1956), pp. 158–159.

47. This sense of the term *tititl*, which is also the name of the following (seventeenth) month, is outlined by Dibble and Anderson, in Sahagún, *Florentine Codex*, book 2, page 155, note 1. The primary source, however, is Fray Juan de Torquemada's description of the ceremony in *Monarquía Indiana*, 3 vols. (Mexico City: Editorial Porrúa, 1969), vol. 2, p. 300.

48. The word for squash, *ayohtl*, is also a cognate with "turtle" and "watery thing."

49. This may be a larger version of what is now known as the rain stick sold to tourists throughout Mexico.

50. This contrasts with a mythically expressed binary opposition used by structuralism, as discussed in chapter 1.

51. It is quite obvious that Sahagún's primary informant for VI-Etzalcualiztli was much more intimately familiar with its priestly duties than the informants for the other festivals discussed. The viewpoint I will be expanding on may well be simply expressing different points of view within each of the celebrations. For example, it may be like examining I-Atl cahualo from a spectator/*macehualli* viewpoint and examining VI-Etzalcualiztli from a priest/*tlatoani* perspective. This plurality of viewpoints, if correct, simply enriches our more complete appreciation for the overall significance of Tlaloc rituals. According to Inga Clendinnen, *Aztecs, an Interpretation*, (Cambridge: Cambridge University Press, 1991), pp. 129–130, this constitutes the only source for priestly ritual life and must then be a firsthand account.

52. Ibid., p. 182.

53. As Lawrence E. Sullivan has pointed out in his *Icanchu's Drum: An Orientation to Meaning in South American Religions* (New York: Macmillan Publishing Co., 1988), p. 287, the sonic markers could signal at once their position in a transitional place (i.e., lake shore), as well as the activity of transformation that they were involved in.

54. In Book II of Sahagún, *Florentine Codex*, pp. 224–225, there is a "Song to Tlaloc." Speculation is that it is a fragment of one of the rituals that Sahagún recorded, but it is impossible to connect it to a single event. It is essentially a poem with images of death, sustenance, and glorious afterlife. See Arthur J. O. Anderson, "A Look into Tlalocan," in *Smoke and Mist: Mesoamerican Studies in Memory of Thelma D. Sullivan*, edited by J.

Kathryn Josserand and Karen Dakin (Oxford: B.A.R. International Series 402[i], 1988b), pp. 151–160, and Willard Gingerich, "Tlaloc, His Song," *Latin American Indian Literatures* 1 (1977): 79–88.

55. The ethnobotanists Robery Bye and Edelmira Linares, along with others, have initiated work on popular uses of plants and animals. The future of this area of correspondence between the flora and fauna of the Valley of Mexico and the ethnohistorical texts is very promising. Less attention has been focused on the symbolic and religious dimensions of this investigation, which could reveal, in the collaboration between historians of religion and ethnobotanists, a wealth of detail to fold into this analysis.

56. Reeds are also tied to the founding of the Templo Mayor, where Huitzilopochtli descended on a nopal cactus amid a reed field in the middle of the lake. In general, reeds seem to have signified a connection with ultimate sacred power. See Leonardo López Luján, *The Offerings of the Templo Mayor of Tenochtitlan*, translated by Bernard R. Ortiz de Montellano and Thelma Ortiz de Montellano (Niwot: University Press of Colorado, 1994).

57. The relationship between kingship, violence, divine authority, and fertility in Mesoamerica has been explored particularly among Mayanists. Perhaps it has to do with the nature of their sources, which consist primarily of stelae erected by ruling monarchies to depict their exploits in human and cosmological realms. Some of their findings could gainfully be used in examining central-Mexican materials as well. See Linda Schele and Mary Ellen Miller, *The Blood of Kings: Dynasty and Ritual in Maya Art* (New York: George Braziller, Inc., 1986), and Linda Schele and David Freidel, *A Forest of Kings: The Untold Story of the Ancient Maya* (New York: William Morrow and Co., Inc., 1990). For Polynesian materials, see Valerio Valeri, *Kingship and Sacrifice: Ritual and Society in Ancient Hawaii*, translated by Paula Wissing (Chicago: University of Chicago Press, 1985).

58. The corresponding Spanish gloss of VI-Etzalcualiztli identifies this use of *tototl* as being the turkey. An extensive description exists in Sahagún, *Florentine Codex*, book 11, pp. 53–54, in which Sahagún elaborates, in Nahuatl, on the merits of this bird. It was of great importance for the Aztecs, as it was for the Spanish.

59. See Doris Heyden, "Guajolote, guajolote, en realidad, ¿quién eres?" in *Códices y Documentos sobre México, Primer Simposio*, edited by Constanza Vega (Mexico City: Colección Científica, INAH, 1995), pp. 173–192. For an interesting discussion of Aztec social order and waterfowl, see Scott O'Mack, "Yacateuatli and Ehecatl-Quetzalcoatl: Earth-divers in Aztec Central Mexico," *Ethnohistory* 38, no. 1 (Winter 1991): 1–33.

60. See my "Paper Ties to Land: Indigenous and Colonial Material Orientations to the Valley of Mexico," *History of Religions* 35, no. 1 (August 1995): 27–60.

61. *Amatl* is Nahuatl for paper, which is composed of *atl*, "water," and *matl*, "hand" or "branch," and literally translated as "water hand" or "water branch." Elements of water and wood combine within the word to signify the importance of this tree.

62. See Alan R. Sandstrom and Pamela Effrein Sandstrom, *Traditional Papermaking and Paper Cult Figures of Mexico* (Norman: University of Oklahoma Press, 1986), pp. 11–

31. They reconstruct pre-Columbian paper-making practices and how it was used by combining ethnohistorical texts with their observations of current practices among the contemporary Nahuas.

63. At the Templo Mayor, in the altar area to Tlaloc, one can still see red and white stripes painted on the plastered walls, which connect blood with rain.

64. Broda discusses fertility with reference to the numerous ocean artifacts found at the Templo Mayor: "The offerings of marine animals thus seem to suggest that by the magic of analogy, the Aztecs wanted to conjure the presence of the sea at the Templo Mayor. The sea was a symbol of *absolute fertility embodied in water.*" Broda, "Templo Mayor as Ritual Space," p. 101.

65. *Tlapalli,* "something dyed or colored," metaphorically referred to blood and bloodletting. See Karttunen, *An Analytical Dictionary of Nahuatl,* p. 289.

66. See Alfredo López Austin, *The Human Body and Ideology: Concepts of the Ancient Nahuas,* 2 vols., translated by Thelma and Bernard Ortiz de Montellano (Salt Lake City: University of Utah Press, 1988), vol. 1, p. 350. For example, as in English, the Nahua refer to the "head," "trunk," and "foot" of a tree, thus linking human and faunal bodies in a meaningful correspondence. In addition, as with humans, four species of sacred trees were considered to be generators of particular influences upon the world.

67. Wood poles used to support banners on people's houses were called by two names. *Cuenmantli,* or "cultivated land," may be a reference to the digging stick used in the *chinampas* and signified a relationship between children and agriculture. Just as children issue from the human body, plant life sprouts from the earth of a Tlalocan body. On the other hand, poles were also called *matlaquauh,* which was a thin pole used to prop up the bird-net snares in the middle of the lake. Not only does this refer to water but also sets the whole discussion of the ritual within the larger context of eating and general food acquisition.

68. See Edward Seler, *Gesammelte Abhandlungen zur Amerikanschen Sprach-und Alterhumskunde,* 5 vols. (Graz, Austria: Akademische Druck-und Verlangsanstalt, 1960), vol. 2: pp. 849–853. He tells us that these cowlicks were seen as horns that may have symbolized the mountains.

69. Jane Rosenthal, personal communication.

70. Henry B. Nicholson, "Religion in Prehispanic Central Mexico," in *Handbook of Middle American Indians: Guide to the Ethnohistorical Sources,* vol. 11, edited by R. Wanchope (Austin: University of Texas Press, 1971), pp. 395–445.

71. According to Broda, in "Las fiestas Aztecas de los dioses," p. 263, Chicomecoatl, Xilonen, Cinteotl, and Ilamateuctli were intimately associated with the deities of rain and fertility. See the discussion of this connection in chapter 1 and earlier in this section of how this relationship is elaborated ritually during VI-Etzalcualiztli in the feasting and sacrifices to tender maize.

72. This text can be found in Angel María Garibay, *Teogonía e historia de los Mexicanos: Tres opúsculos del siglo XVI* (Mexico City: Editorial Porrúa, 1965). Also see Doris Heyden, "The Skin and Hair of Tlaltecuhtli," in *The Imagination of Matter: Religion*

and Ecology in Mesoamerican Traditions, edited by Davíd Carrasco (Oxford: B.A.R. International Series, 515, 1989), pp. 112–124.

73. For a look at pre-Columbian food, see Teresa Castelló Yturbide, ed., *Presencia de comida prehispanica* (Mexico City: Forento Cultural Banamex, A.C., 1987).

74. See Philip P. Arnold, "Eating Landscape: Human Sacrifice and Sustenance in Aztec Mexico," in *To Change Place: Aztec Ceremonial Landscapes,* edited by Davíd Carrasco (Niwot: University Press of Colorado, 1991), pp. 219–232. Also see Irving Goldman, *The Mouth of Heaven: An Introduction to Kwakiutl Religious Thought* (New York: John Wiley and Sons, 1975).

75. This quote is published by Broda in "Templo Mayor as Ritual Space," p. 107, from Tim Knab, *Words Great and Small: Sierra Nahuatl Narrative Discourse in Everyday Life* (unpublished manuscript, 1983).

76. Clendinnen, *Aztecs, an Interpretation,* p. 181. A useful point of comparison with Mesoamerican ritual is the place of cooking in Thai Buddhist cosmology, which links cosmogony to human procreation as a cooking process. See Frank E. Reynolds and Mani B. Reynolds's translation of *Three Worlds According to King Ruang: A Thai Buddhist Cosmology* (Berkeley: University of California Press, Berkeley Buddhist Studies Series, no. 4, 1982), p. 314, note 12. Rice "sustains life and religion" for Thai village Buddhists, and eating it is a cosmogonic act. See Stanley J. Tambiah, *Buddhism and the Spirit Cults in North-East Thailand* (Cambridge: Cambridge University Press, 1970), p. 353. Also see Penny van Esterik, "Interpreting a Cosmology: Guardian Spirits in Thai Buddhism," *Anthropos* 77 (1982): 1–15, and "Feeding Their Faith: Recipe Knowledge Among Thai Buddhist Women," *Food and Foodways* 1 (1986): 197–215, for links between cosmology, community religious organization and interactions, and recipe knowledge.

77. See Paul Mus, *India Seen from the East: Indian and Indigenous Cults in Champa,* translated by I. W. Mabbett, Monash Paper on Southeast Asia, no. 3 (Monash University, Australia: Centre of Southeast Asian Studies, 1975), p. 24.

Part Two

*Tlalocan and New Spain:
Hermeneutics of Occupation
in the Valley of Mexico*

5 The Interpretive Legacy of Conquest

This chapter begins with an examination of the life and work of Bernardino de Sahagún and its culmination as the *Florentine Codex*. Particularly important were his techniques of collecting information from Nahuatl informants, his editing of the data, and the cultural context in which he worked. All these factors come to bear on the type of ceremonial practices that can be most clearly attributed to the Aztecs. As outlined above, ritual activity dedicated to Tlaloc was most coherently expressed as a method of meaningfully relating to material conditions of existence in the Valley of Mexico. It is then necessary to relate these interpretive phases both to the interpretive legacy that the academy has inherited from colonialism and to the methodological consequences of practice. Finally, issues of how to read and authorize an interpretation of Mesoamerican and colonial worlds will be appraised as the activities of understanding that are intimately involved with current scholarship. The integration of these three phases of practice (Aztec, Sahagún, and current scholarship) does not pretend to render Aztec, Franciscan, or modern academic worlds transparent, but is discussed to acknowledge the limits of the interpretive enterprise with reference to the physical constraints of occupying a meaningful landscape.

In Mesoamerican studies, there is a constant concern over whose voice is being heard in the documents. Although recorded in Nahuatl, there is no question that the *Florentine Codex* was primarily the work of Sahagún. Therefore, it was a predominantly Spanish medieval/early modern monastic Christian world that organized what we currently know of Tlaloc and his cult. This chapter will proceed with a hermeneutics of suspicion in order to clarify the mechanisms by which Aztec religion can be rendered understandable. As a result, I intend to approach the problem of sources in a critical manner. What emerges is a larger picture of the distinct consequences of Aztec, Spanish, and contemporary hermeneutics of occupying the Americas.

Sahagún's life is known only through his work. His early life in Spain is shrouded in silence. It is remarkable that one such as Sahagún, who had such a tremendous effect on our modern understandings of Native America, is such an enigma.[1] Born about 1499 in Sahagún, Leon, his surname may have been Ribeira, perhaps a member of a *converso*, or recently converted, family of Jews.[2]

He had arrived in Mexico by 1529, only eight years after the fall of Tenochtitlan to Cortes. This was a time of intense European missionary activity fueled by a millennial vision of the New World. Sahagún belonged to a "second wave" of "preacher-ethnographers" whose initial focus was on linguistically capturing Nahuatl on the written page.[3] A mere ten years after his arrival, Sahagún was writing sermons and translating passages of the Bible into Nahuatl. Probably through the urgings of his provincial, Fray Francisco de Toral,[4] Sahagún began to focus on aspects of Aztec culture that did not address an immediate pastoral need. It seems that he took his cues from the ethnographic work of some of his contemporaries, including Fray Andres de Olmos, Fray Alonso de Molina, and Fray Torbio de Benavente Motolinía; all of whom had spent time at the Colegio de Tlatelolco at some point in the twenty-five years immediately following the Conquest. It was the combined linguist-ethnographer who emerged among these Franciscan intellectuals, who hoped to at once explore, expose, and eliminate Aztec religious understandings. To promote this enterprise, the inscription of the Aztec language and practice was utilized in making Aztec ritual life public (outside of its performative context) by committing their traditions to writing.

According to López Austin, Bernardino de Sahagún developed a retrievable questionnaire used to probe his informants.[5] It seems that not only was it Sahagún's intention to create a source for pre-Columbian culture, but also to create a repository of Nahuatl lexical items that could eventually be turned into a dictionary. In particular, Sahagún discusses the similarity of his project to the work of Ambrosio Calepino's Latin dictionary, which was built on the sayings of classical orations. His vision of a New Spain was one free from the impurities of the old. As López Austin says, paraphrasing Sahagún,

> [i]t was essential to collect and record the testimonials of the old life, to separate the young Indians as much from their fathers (and hence idolatry) as from the Spaniards (and hence corruption), to initiate them into a truly Christian life, and then, after suppressing everything idolatrous in the pre-Hispanic norms and practices, to re-implant these practices for the benefit of Christ. *The land that the infidel and the heretic had alienated from the church was being recovered in New Spain,* whose men had sufficient capacity—as Sahagún was demonstrating in his work—to initiate there the Republic of Christ. For this reason, he could compare the Nahuas to the Greeks and Romans.[6]

In some respects, the land of the New World was seen as compensation for the loss of the Holy Lands during the Crusades and, through the activities of linguistics and ethnographers, was being purified for the Church.

Sahagún's first work in what was eventually to be his *General History of the Things of New Spain* was focused on the intellectual pursuits of the Aztec. What is now Book VI, *Rhetoric and Moral Philosophy*, grew out of his early work with Native informants in Tlatelolco while he was training Nahuatl priests at the Colegio de Tlatelolco. According to Sullivan, these texts are very close to an authentic pre-Columbian past.[7] At Tlatelolco he sought out older, respected members of the community. It seems, however, that his most sustained contact was with members of the merchant class. According to

Clendinnen, the only ritual description that includes a specialist's perspective is that of the festival of VI-Etzalcualiztli, which presents the activity from a point of view expressed by the novice priests.[8] In the rest of the *General History*, the voice of the priests is absent, having been eliminated by their Old World rivals and replaced by Nahuatl men of the marketplace.

Once Sahagún had secured a workable outline, he went to Tepepulco, a small village east of the present city of Sahagún. It is perhaps significant that he met there with the local inhabitants. First he laid out his intentions and asked them who would be the most qualified respondents to his questions. They answered that they would have to discuss the matter and would give him an answer another day. Later, they came back and "made a solemn speech" indicating ten or twelve elders who would be capable of telling him what he wanted to know. Sahagún's informants were thus selected by the indigenous people of the area. Given the intensity of interaction between Europeans and Indians at the time, their motives could have either been to confound his ethnographic project,[9] or to genuinely give him the data he requested.[10] In either case, his informants would have presented themselves in such a way as to promote the life of their people in light of the Conquest—the most devastating and profound transformation of Nahuatl life and culture up until that point. With four native Nahuatl speakers, whom he had trained in Latin and Spanish at Tlatelolco, he began his work.

According to López Austin, there were four primary stages to Sahagún's work.[11] First, there is the schematic plan identified with the work at Tepepulco and now called the *Primeros Memoriales*.[12] Second, there is the extensive document that was broken into two parts called the *Madrid Codex of the Royal Academy of History* and the *Madrid Codex of the Royal Palace*.[13] These documents are linked to Sahagún's work at Tlatelolco. Although these could have originally been a smooth copy written in various hands, it was later split into a rough draft. Third, there is the *Florentine Codex*, whose Nahuatl column Sahagún must have considered definitive. The Spanish column, however, was not a translation of the Nahuatl but a gloss that actually can be used to supplement what is being said in Nahuatl. This was finalized at

Tenochtitlan, where the language was polished[14] and it was divided into paragraphs, chapters, and books. Fourth, among the pages of the Madrid codices there are passages known as "Memoriales con Escolios," in which Sahagún translates Nahuatl text in great detail. This was the foundation for his dictionary, which was never finished. The most important data-gathering moments in Sahagún's enterprise corresponded to his time at Tepepulco and Tlatelolco—his efforts at Tenochtitlan were directed more to fine-tuning his work. Little is known of the pre-Columbian cultural distinctions between these three places. As a consequence of Sahagún's work in these separate places, the distinctions between them were undoubtedly folded into the *Florentine*. For example, although Nahuatl was the common language, evidence of the Aztec religion, dramatized by the twin temple, is only attested to at Tlatelolco. Tepepulco, in particular, could have been a very different place and almost certainly had a different history. This illustrates Sahagún's assumption that ritual life was dictated by the center (i.e., Tenochtitlan) and that religion in the New World, like religion in the Old World, was essentially a single seamless phenomenon.

Toward the end of the sixteenth century, Spanish attitudes toward missionary work in Mexico were changing. Efforts to train Native priests, for example, were halted with the closing of the Colegio de Tlatelolco. While Sahagún was in the "second wave" of New Spain missionaries, who were optimistic about the possibilities of a New Jerusalem, they were being replaced by priests more concerned with their allegiances to the crown. In part, this had to do with conflicts that arose during the latter part of the sixteenth century between Catholic and Protestant countries. Illustrative of this conflict are the etchings of the exiled Dutchman Theodore de Bry, who committed to images the horrific stories of Spanish brutality in the New World.[15] In addition, due to Indian rebellions in Peru, the crown was becoming more nervous about ethnographic enterprises.[16] Proof that missionary work was proceeding further with the destruction of indigenous cultures and beliefs, rather than their preservation, had to be put forward in order to justify continued ethnographic inquiry. It became necessary to produce a Spanish version of Sahagún's work to legitimate this effort before the Inquisition. The

Florentine Codex was the resulting text, which was sent to Spain with Fray Rodrigo de Sequera as its advocate.

The process of interpretation that generated the *Florentine Codex* involved several mediums and required many creative movements. Sahagún utilized previous styles of writing to produce his ethnography. Several scholars over the last fifty years have been trying to unravel the resources and methodology in the construction of his work.

Encyclopedic works such as *Archaeology* of Flavius Josephus, *History of Animals* and *Parts of Animals* by Aristotle, works by Albert of Cologne, *Natural History* of Pliny,[17] and *On the Properties of Things* by Fray Bartholomew de Glanville,[18] served as inspirations for Sahagún's work. Starting with ancient Greek studies of animals, which were passed through Latin natural histories, these works arrived in the New World as medieval encyclopedias in which all beings were organized into a rigorous hierarchical order beginning with the Trinity and ending with minerals. This arrangement of the world encyclopedically betrayed a European worldview.

In addition, the reformist work of Fray Alonso de la Veracruz in New Spain would have been a likely influence on Sahagún. Veracruz took to heart the intellectual challenge of the archbishop of Valencia, Santo Tomás de Villanueva, "that in the New World all things should be done anew," when he arrived in Mexico in 1536.[19] Veracruz, who held a chair in philosophy at the Colegio de Santa Cruz in Tlatelolco, advocated a method of analysis that relied more on logic and empirical data and less on church authority. The scope of this revisionist view mapped out the hope of New Spain as full of new possibilities for understanding the world over and against the traditional and decadent scholarship of the Old World. In these commitments can be seen the beginnings of modern empiricism.

Many scholars have written and discussed the eschatological and humanist vision that took shape in sixteenth-century Mexico. In Valladolid, Spain, a debate took place between Juan Ginés de Sepulveda, an Aristotelian scholar, and the Dominican priest Bartolomé de las Casas, at the request of Charles V. These two, before the Council of Fourteen, were to debate the question of whether it was "lawful for the King to wage war on the Indians before preaching the faith to them in order to subject them to his rule, so that afterwards, they may more easily be instructed in the faith."[20] The major questions of this "great debate" centered on what was the true nature of the Indians and what were the appropriate methods for their conversion. Two philosophical/theological axes for the European occupation of New Spain were expressed by these two scholars. For Sepulveda, Indians were ordered beneath the Spaniards in the natural hierarchy of things. Their natural condition, therefore, was social slavery. Further, any resistance on their part could be taken as a reasonable basis for using force. On the other hand, las Casas, who had served as the Bishop of Chiapas, argued that Indians demonstrated all the civilized accomplishments of Europeans. Indeed, they met all the criteria for a civil society as defined by Aristotle. For las Casas, the Indians lived in a state of primitive Christianity that could be easily developed through persuasion. He stressed an Augustinian theology that was more in line with Thomism yet contrary to Franciscan thought.[21] When dealing with Native Americans, he argued, one must acknowledge them as full, yet underdeveloped, human beings. In his study of New World diabolism, Cervantes characterizes the Franciscan understanding as "nominalist," which, in contrast to Thomist reflection, enhanced the prestige of the Devil to be on a par with that of God. By linking Aztec religiousness, as well as material existence, with the activity of the Devil, Franciscans were able to generate an evangelical fervor that reified a dichotomy between material and spiritual life, thus transforming the Christian theological tradition.[22] The Franciscan attack on Thomas Aquinas was to become particularly significant in the New World.

There is an irony expressed in both the positions of Sepulveda and Las Casas. While these scholars appear to be on opposite sides, the consequences of their interpretations had similar results. Neither cared for Native American cultures or their survival. Indeed, as Todorov has pointed out, it was Sepulveda, in his strong statements regarding the Otherness of Native Americans, who signaled the beginning of anthropology.[23] Las Casas, the defender of the Indians, eroded differences between all humankind with his appeal to Christian love. His vision was of a unified world that transcended cultural constraints.[24]

For Phelan, Sepulveda and las Casas represent two of the three main philosophical/theological axes for the conquest of New Spain. Unlike the two expressed at Valladolid, the third was uniquely Franciscan. The work of Fray Geronimo de Mendieta (1525–1604) stressed the mystical interpretation of conquest. His apocalyptical, Messianic, and prophetic mysticism was rooted in the life of St. Francis and the Spiritual movement of the Franciscan order.[25] Mendieta saw the movement of Europeans into the New World as the unfolding of an eschatological event. He described the Discovery in apocalyptic terms, as did las Casas.[26] The key figure for Mendieta was Cortes— whom he saw as Moses. The twelve missionaries who arrived after the fall of Tenochtitlan heralded the coming of a divine prototype in the process of revitalizing the world. He thought of the Indian Church as the pre-Constantinian community of the primitive Christian community that lacked the defects of the European personality. It was during this period that Charles V gave considerable freedom to the friars by allowing them to create new forms of religious communities, including the "open" chapel where large groups of Native Americans would participate in an outdoor mass. His ideas were geared to isolate this nascent millennial kingdom of the New World from the contamination of the old. In this way he drew upon other utopian writers of his time, including More and Cervantes.

With Philip II, the sixteenth-century millennial vision of occupying the New World of the Franciscans became obsolete. Although Sahagún preceded Mendieta, he nonetheless drew on some components of the utopian vision. His temperament was more pragmatic in emphasis, yet it seems that he too wanted to insulate Native people from the ravages of European civilization.[27] In some ways Sahagún exhibited an interpretive stance that grew out of his Franciscan heritage and yet also challenged the underlying assumptions of the brotherhood through his rigorous method of the empirical collection of data. It appears that he saw his contribution to the development of New Jerusalem in working out the linguistic and ethnographic details of its occupation of New Spain.

Sahagún's world was organized by his monastic order. Central to the organization of the Franciscan movement was the life of St. Francis.[28] The Franciscan brotherhood, with St. Francis's exemplary life as its beacon, had a large impact on those working in New Spain. St. Francis's life's mission was to make his way back to the Father by the imitation of the Son. In this quest he put particular emphasis on transcending the "spirit-matter" dichotomy. His example was one that overcame this seeming opposition, "making him a sublime example of both the spirituality of matter and the materialization of spirit."[29] Between the time of St. Francis and the beginning of the fifteenth century, the concept of Franciscan mission had changed very little. They understood that God had sent Francis and his order to renew the life of Christ and the apostles. Their eschatology compelled them toward the imitation of Christ—particularly his passion. Their missionary task was to summon all people, Christian and non-Christian, to repent and prepare themselves for the end of history and the final judgment.[30] As Franciscans moved into the New World, however, their traditional emphasis on erasing a dichotomy between spirit and matter was transformed. Their "nominalist" attack on Thomist theology and emphasis on the workings of the Devil in the New World were interpretive positions that theologically justified the colonial enterprise. One of its consequences seemed to have been a shift away from imitating the life of St. Francis.

Evangelism was tied to Francis's understanding of the Gospels and his own quest for perfection. Through his *imitatio crucis*, Francis strove to emulate Christ first through an evangelical perfection and second through poverty.[31] Revelation was not only present in history but also in the natural world. Poverty became the means by which access was gained to a revealed world. The brotherhood was a community that was based on an understanding of the primitive Christian community. At least at first, unlike other monastic houses, the minor friars lived itinerate lives. Evangelical perfection and poverty were consistently expressed as key elements of the Franciscan world.

In the twelfth century, an emphasis on poverty as a religious example, however, was a consequence of the emerging power of mercantilism, or a monetary economic system. The social context into which the Franciscans were born in the twelfth century was of great importance to the Franciscan movement in the New World and also to Sahagún's work in the sixteenth century. In the late twelfth and early thirteenth centuries, European religion was going through a crisis. Heretical movements were emerging, particularly in urban areas, that were challenging the traditional authority of the Church.[32] St. Francis and his followers came very close to being identified with the Waldensians, as well as other groups condemned as heretical by Rome.[33] Their ideological proximity to one another indicated that there was a religious reaction taking shape against the social shift into an emerging profit economy. Voluntary poverty became a key element in renewed forms of religious life during St. Francis's time. Ironically, however, it was the monastic orders that paved the way for an emerging profit economy to flourish. This led to a reified categorical distinction between nature and culture.

According to Little, during St. Francis's life, medieval Europe's old economic relations were giving way to new ones.[34] In pre-Christian Europe, social organization was based on a gift economy that was a practice of negotiating material life based on a reciprocity between beings (e.g., fertility and ancestor cults) and was analogous to the Tlaloc cult. A gift economy was being replaced by a centralized profit economy in which abstract representations of value (i.e., money) determined how people oriented themselves to the material world. Understandings of wealth shifted from a gift to a profit economy, chiefly due to the church's bureaucratic power. Money was more and more the symbolic center of this emerging economy. Its value was guaranteed by the powerful institutions it supported.[35] The new profit economy raised problems involving impersonalism and economic and moral uncertainty.

Previously, the village was the prototypical integrated social system. Symptomatic of this shift, then, was the agricultural revolution in which, to increase production there were initiated new types of deep-ploughing methods, which transformed the countryside. As agricultural products entered a profit economy in the mid-eleventh century, the resultant effect on the land was deforestation, the creation and growth of cities, and, with that, a rising urban population. This led to even further deforestation of the land, and the depopulation of the village. The mobile wealth of a monied economy drove people from the country to the city. The urban world of Europe came into its own due to a shift in values reoriented toward a profit economy.

St. Francis was a religious product of a new understanding of occupying the material world. Instead of conforming to his merchant class, whose ranks were growing in numbers and influence during this time, he became God's "juggler," or God's fool, who by appealing to carnivalesque folk culture created a religious order highly critical of the emerging urban reality. He shouted from the streets and in the open air. For St. Francis religion was street theater. St. Francis was responding to the shift from gift to profit economies by utilizing folk culture. In the process, however, folk life was transformed away from what I am calling an indigenous religious existence.[36] In the medieval city, identity was tied to the exchange of powerful symbols (profit economy) and not to the exchange of materialities (gift economy), as in the barter system of the rural fair. Negotiating new forms of wealth, which were simultaneously organized by the church and scorned by many of its influential members, created new forms of piety that understood the world in fundamentally distinct ways.

Some light can now be shed on Franciscan notions of evangelism and poverty. The life of St. Francis was a reaction to a monied world. His revelatory stance toward the world attempted to overcome the symbolic abstractions by engaging directly in what he deemed a "natural" world. His natural world always stood in opposition to, and was therefore defined by, an urban reality. Poverty only has meaning within a particular economic context, and in the Franciscan case this was the monetary context. "Nature" was a sphere of life that, for the most part, remained outside human life. It was the enrapture of gaining access to the Otherness of "nature" that led to revelation. In the case of evangelical perfection, the Otherness of a human object was approached as the Same.[37] The early Franciscans emphatically rejected a profit economy that was tied to the Church by promoting a zealous confidence in the significance of nature outside of human habitation. Evangelical perfection was a reaction against human symbolic appropriations of matter. At the same time, the Franciscans exhibited an extreme confidence in what the natural world revealed. Likewise, the Aztecs were conceived as being natural or primitive Christians who exhibited, simultaneously, a point of access to God through the fashioning of the utopian understanding of the New Jerusalem and a potential threat to this apocalyptic vision by their veneration of Satan, God's nemesis.[38]

In contrast, for the Aztecs themselves there was no "nature" conceptually separate from themselves. There was no word for or concept of nature, and it was not an important ideological construct. There were various evaluations of matter, however, which, using Little's categories, were engaged at the level of the gift rather than the profit economy. The Aztec empire flourished through a flow of tribute rather than money, or some other wholly symbolic representation of matter. Ritual expressed a material reciprocity that covered all levels of the human occupation of Mexico. European religious identity was, to a significant degree, a reaction to a novel economic understanding of matter inherited from the Middle Ages.

In the time that followed, indigenous material understandings often survived in Europe as "folk" or "pagan" traditions. The sixteenth and seventeenth centuries saw a renewed interest in subduing these cults in Europe. There are accounts of personal cosmologies,[39] folk festival life,[40] and local devotions.[41] Access to accounts of indigenous varieties of religious devotion are quite varied. Some come from Inquisitional documents,[42] histories of pilgrimage sites,[43] various kinds of scientific and dramatic writings,[44] and ethnographical analysis.[45] While Spain seemed to form a distinct reaction to these popular religious devotions, this seems due, in some measure, to a renewed self-confidence in Christendom after the reconquest of 1492.[46] Another type of analysis presents itself when religious and ethnic identity are tied to material realities.[47] After 1492, Spain was forging an imperial identity that redefined the significance of the material world.[48] Spanish efforts toward material domination were closely tied to religious identity. The Franciscan-utopian vision of evangelical perfection and monied poverty secured a place for European expansion, which was universal in scope yet connected to nowhere in particular. What emerged was a tremendous effort to utilize materials from all parts of the world to be used exclusively for the liberation from a material existence. As we will see, this spiritualism was opposed to an indigenous religious strategy, on *both* sides of the Atlantic, that saw the meaning of the material world, and human life, as being intimately involved with bodily existence.

Although Sahagún, like many humanists of his time, worked diligently for the survival of Indian populations, ironically he drew on the hermeneutics of world domination just as had the conquerors who preceded him. The colonial enterprise required an ethic of occupying lands, in a meaningful way, that were not traditionally one's own. As we will see, the colonial ethic was distinct from the indigenous understanding that propelled the Aztecs.

Most of the studies that hope to illuminate aspects of an Aztec world must use Sahagún's work. On one level, the investigator must proceed with some confidence in the accuracy of Sahagún's method of collecting data. At another level, less addressed in the literature, these texts used for Mesoamerican studies express a deep cultural bias and therefore cannot give us an accurate and authentic picture of Aztec realities.[49] The large numbers of Indian converts to Christianity during the first years of contact has led some scholars to conclude that Mexico was not only physically conquered but spiritually conquered as well.[50] More recently, however, scholars have been using the writings of Sahagún to dramatize a rhetoric of contact in which indigenous ideas come to be expressed in the context of a European worldview.[51] For those intrigued with a pre-Columbian worldview, the task is how to overcome the distance between cultures and bridge the conditions of history. One way to accomplish this is to examine these writings as dialogues between indigenous and colonial peoples. A consequence of this approach for Mesoamerican studies is that there are no clearly distinguishable voices to separate. The Nahualized Christianity (or Nahualized ethnography) that emerges from these documents undermines a strict separation of Native and European influences. The methodological strategy offered here, therefore, is to understand cultural formation as a process in which various places are meaningfully negotiated by distinctive cultural worldviews.[52]

The friars had to constantly defend their Indian charges from other colonial forces that sought to exploit them. Monks were sometimes pressured by secular priests within the Church who generally represented the exploitative views of the colonists. Ironically, however, while they objected to the abuses of conquest and colonization in theory, their efforts supported colonialism. The New World was seen as a land of children waiting to be gathered unto God. Dialogue between these cultures flourished in Mexico during a fragile forty-year period (1536–1579). This was the time of the Franciscan Colegio de Tlatelolco, which opened in 1536 to train young Indian nobles in theology and the liberal arts. Among other critical documents that were generated was the New World's first book, a Nahuatl catechism, printed in 1539.[53]

In his missionary writings, Sahagún tried to create a way of presenting Christianity to a Nahua audience. This is analogous to his ethnographic attempts of presenting the Nahua people to a European audience.[54] He was committed to the activity of translating cultural ideas at the particular level of language. While he held to the millennial Franciscan view, he expressed a more practical temperament. His primary objective was to create a mode of discourse of Christian concepts in Nahuatl. As a result, Aztec views necessarily influenced his doctrinal writings as he attempted to forge an indigenous Christian language.

For Burkhart, it was of utmost importance that the Franciscans find some way of expressing key Christian concepts in Nahuatl—such as "sin" (*pecado*, from the Latin *peccatum*). Sahagún chose the Nahuatl word *tlatlacolli*, which literally means "something damaged," as a synonym for sin.[55] Burkhart suggests that damage may have served as a unifying moral principle for Aztec life (as did the medieval Christian sense of sin), and that that was the reason it was chosen. "To behave immorally is to disrupt order, to promote decay over cohesion, randomness over continuity. Entropy is the essence of immorality."[56] Morality expressed itself, for the Aztecs, as living morally in the face of chaos (the "slippery earth"). Sin, on the other hand, may conceptually overlap with an idea of damage, but they are not synonymous. While sin is tied intrinsically to human existence for Christians, this is not a necessary attribute of *tlatlacolli*. Damage was a consequence of *activity* deemed inappropriate for continued existence and therefore contrary to life. Choosing this term to represent Christian ideas ironically served to promote and perpetuate Native categories with Church sanction.[57] In its Native usage, sin was a way of acting in the world and not a state of being. There are accounts in which Nahua people concluded, for example, that to overcome misfortune or sickness it was appropriate to make offerings to the Devil rather than to God.

Even though a dialogical understanding of the Nahua worldview is preserved in colonial documents, the context of the dialogue was limited. To textualize dialogue is to overdetermine its outcome—the outcome of the conversation is already assumed. The dialogue that is recorded in doctrinal writings stands in marked contrast to a dialogue that takes risks involving one's identity and the meaning of the world due to an openness to other cultural forms.[58] Sixteenth-century monks already knew what the world meant, and in their self-confidence they attempted to reconfigure Native categories to fit their vision. Fundamentally, there was no curiosity regarding the Otherness of Aztec existence or of Tlalocan.

Sahagún's unique response to his situation was to apply confessional techniques to his fieldwork. He thereby created the "confessor-informant."

> His method required that confession-like practices be applied systematically outside their sacramental context and that the informants be imbued with the ideological framework of self-examination that permits the self to be both subject (narrator) and object (the subject matter of the narration) at once.[59]

Sahagún's questions required informants to examine themselves as both inside and outside their community, thereby making them willing and able to relay those reflections to the investigator. Sahagún had to rely on an interpretation of confessional data, which rearranged the traditional modes of discourse. Simultaneously, Sahagún was collecting data and destroying Aztec culture. Just as the informant was required to disengage himself from his community, likewise Sahagún (as well as other contemporary ethnographers) was put in the position of being a passive observer, being present and inside but never *acting* like an insider. Klor de Alva links this asymmetrical relationship explicitly to a European technique of domination that reconfigured an understanding of Self as simultaneously introspective and also open to public scrutiny. This mode of domination, however, had consequences for both the indigenous informant, whose world constituted the object of scrutiny, and the colonial-investigator, whose world was indefinitely suspended, thus eliminating the subject.[60]

There is a tragic irony embedded in doing ethnography, according to Fabian.[61] While experience of another culture in the field is necessarily participatory in nature, this experience is transformed through writing into primary data. Through various machinations, an experience of "coevalness" is transformed to ethnography. Literary devices, such as the "ethnographic present" and uses of the third person, function to artificially distance the subject and object who were once colleagues in the field. There are direct consequences of this activity. For Fabian, ethnography, as a means of knowing the Others, perpetuates a colonial project that reinforces their "primitive" status at both temporal and spatial distance from the civilized world.[62] Another consequence of this construal of knowledge, however, is directly tied to the investigator. Clearly, the sociopolitical effects for indigenous people were devastating. But the investigator's forced disengagement from the world results in an analogous loss of meaningful relationships. Likewise, in the case of Sahagún, any objectification of his world would require that it (or they) become unrelated to his life.

Embedded in the field experience at the level of practice, however, are deep and significant spheres of interaction. In actuality, Sahagún's *Florentine Codex* exhibits a practical mastery of relationships in approximating knowledge of the "map" of the Aztec world. According to Bourdieu, a science of practice is the means by which human beings meaningfully negotiate their way through relationships.[63] The colonial enterprise, in its most optimistic light, fosters meaning by a reciprocity between cultures in dialogue. Knowledge, as Fabian and Burkhart have pointed out, is always in the process of exchange, and yet ethnographies such as Sahagún's deliberately misconstrue the activity of interaction, as if the reader can peer unhindered into an Aztec reality. This elimination of practice, or autobiography,[64] disintegrates the sustaining relationships between Self and Other, subject and object. Practice is replaced by the text, and with this substitution comes an overconfidence in expressing culture as an objective reality that is essentially the same everywhere.

Other aspects of Sahagún's work required a deep hermeneutical analysis. At the same time he was being affected by Aztec cultural expressions, he strove to find modes of articulating indigenous realities in his own terms. Detailed drawings in the *Florentine*, as well as other texts, underscore his strenuous efforts to translate Aztec lifeways. Sahagún's ethnography at Tepepulco was also based on information gathered through an engagement with pre-Columbian pictorial documents. These drawings served as the basis of interaction between ethnographer and informant. As he says, "All the things we discussed they gave to me by means of paintings, for that was the writing they had used, the grammarians saying them in their language and writing the statement beneath the painting."[65]

Interpreting pictorial representations dramatizes the difficulties that were presented to Sahagún and to his project. First, Nahua information was not a transparent reality to him. For him to accomplish his task required that there be difficult periods of negotiation between him and his informants in which cultural modes of expression be bridged to promote understanding. Second, the process of writing these cultural negotiations down would have required an enormous investment of hermeneutical labor. Sahagún's genius lay in the tenacity with which he engaged in this process of translating pictorial and oral experiences into written information: effectively a transition from Aztec to European culture. In the passage above we can see some of the difficulties that Sahagún may have faced in committing a performative medium (pre-Columbian images) to writing. He goes on to say that these people were illiterate and communicated solely by means of these images "in such a way that they knew and had memory of the things their ancestors had done and had left to their annals, more than a thousand years before the arrival of the Spanish in this land."[66] Clearly, Sahagún had his work cut out for him. The transformation of Aztec life from pictorial documents to Latinized script was analogous to the transformation from ritual activity to "the book." This transformation was one that signaled the beginning of ethnography, as we will explore, and had particular consequences for European occupation of the Americas.

It is often pointed out that most of the pre-Columbian documents were burned within the first decade of the Conquest. Some have survived, which now stand as primary source material for current Mesoamericanists.[67] The nature of the documents that Sahagún had access to is a subject of debate. It seems likely, however, that there were indigenous documents that Sahagún appropriated in various ways. While the primary objective in the *Florentine Codex* was to commit Nahua culture to writing, Sahagún also captured elements in drawings.[68] Clearly, drawings in the *Florentine* were not meant to record a pre-Columbian style. However, an analysis of these images reveals more evidence of Sahagún's working hypotheses.

According to Baird, the use of illusionistic space in the *Florentine* depictions betrays a particular lineage in the Franciscan tradition.[69] Uses of three-dimensional space were one of the hallmarks of European Renaissance art and can be traced to the fourteenth-century Florentine architect Filippo Brunelleschi. Baird traces this "linear" perspective to new emphasis in the mathematical ordering of space. While the *Florentine* illustrations are less strict in their application of a mathematical perspective, on the whole they were inspired by the Renaissance tradition. Western interest in geometric ordering of the natural world was closely linked with the Franciscans of the thirteenth century, particularly Roger Bacon, John Pecham, and Robert Grosseteste.[70] Bacon, in his *Opus Majus,* dedicated to the pope, states his aims on geometrical space clearly.[71] Geometrical ordering of space was not tied to revelation of the physical world, per se, but instead would reveal the structural dimensions of God's master plan of the universe. Baird argues that the use of illusionistic space functioned as a Christian theological construct in the *Florentine.* As she says, "[t]he use of framed, illusionistic, perspectival spaces in which to present indigenous customs, religion, and life breaks with the indigenous past and links it instead with the European present."[72] For example,

5.1 and 5.2. Gold-working scenes, redrawn from the *Florentine Codex*, Sahagún (1951).

the gold-working scenes in Book IX of the *Florentine* depict Aztec cities in the drawings that seem to more accurately represent the walled city of Jerusalem rather than Tenochtitlan. These images reveal, at once, the hope of the reconquest of Jerusalem, as well as the promise of the New World as revealing the New Jerusalem, within the structured space of the Franciscan tradition.

In translating understandings of landscape from indigenous to colonial contexts, Sahagún drew on inspirations from deep within his Franciscan and European traditions. What comes to us in the *Florentine* through these drawings is not only an attempt at representing Aztec life and custom but, more significantly, the transformation of an Aztec cosmology into a Franciscan vision of revelation. Conversely, pre-Columbian representations of landscape adhered directly to their medium. Depth was negotiated in the context of their *use* in divinatory contexts and not, strictly speaking, to their physical construction (as in illusionistic space). In the *Florentine*, there is the opposite movement of meaning. Depictions of landscape could, in and of themselves, unfold mysteries of God's plan, and the observer participated in this drama through the eyes, rather than through the activity of interpretation itself. The interpretive labor that lies behind the construction of images in the *Florentine* is formidable; *yet silent.*

Aztec representations of the landscape addressed the material attributes of their lives through their being ritually engaged. For the Franciscans, structural dimensions of a transcendent reality were revealed through the correct rendering of the landscape. In the first case, meaningful articulation of space originated from an immediate environment. In the second, meaningful articulation of space originated from another place (transformation into a New Jerusalem)—or no place (utopia) in particular.

"PRIMACY" AND THE IRONY OF INTERPRETATION

A pedestrian understanding of what constitutes a primary source could be that it is a text that somehow stands close to its point of origin. Implied, therefore, is that these texts occupy a privileged status because they more accurately and authoritatively describe the world from which they were engendered. The primary text stands the closest of any texts to the authentic nature of the world they portray. Secondary sources, conversely, are more "interpretive" in character, meaning that they are generally seen as more corrupted by other, "contaminating" influences that appropriate the text for their own reasons. The distinction between primary and secondary sources is seen, therefore, as a distinction based on a proximity of text to the thing and/or the intellectual world to which it refers. Implied in the "primacy" of the primary text is the gradation of authority based on its relative position to a more pure utterance. Ironically, as will be discussed, there is no way of attaining entrance to pre-Columbian primary texts. A few are present, but meaningfully remote.

Controversy over a textual record is one of the more engaging aspects of Mesoamerican scholarship.[73] There are currently sixteen primary sources in existence.[74] These are defined by their being produced previous to European contact. Although these books, sometimes called picture or story books, are uniformly considered the most authentic representations of a Mesoamerican worldview, there is sustained debate as to their specific meaning. This is partly due to their method of construction, partly due to their function and application, and partly due to the nature of the interpretive enterprise.

Mesoamerican primary sources are not easily categorized into a single form of human expression. Generally, these documents traverse conventional boundaries of art (and cartoon), astronomy (or more accurately, perhaps, astrology), geography, and writing, to name only a few. In content, these texts cover areas from mythical exploits of ancestors, to kingly propaganda and cosmological temporal cycles, which were all associated with the activities of deities. Their ability to categorically defy interpretive boundaries is one reason for there being a plurality of readings. Intrinsic to the pre-Columbian production of texts was the arbitrary character of meaning as generated between text and interpreter. Given such a diversity of images and the fluidity of their formal points of reference, it could be said that a plurality of interpretations is intrinsic to these texts. There is a closer proximity, however, between these texts and the cosmologies they depict than between the texts and the interpreter.

In contrast, alphabetic writing, which was introduced with the coming of the Spanish, stressed more and more the proximity of text to interpreter, and therefore the ambiguity of the world to which the text refers. For example, Saussure's first principle is the arbitrary nature of the sign.[75] This is the bedrock upon which he builds his general linguistics. While he is primarily interested in the relationship of an aural sign to an idea, the interpersonal and intrapersonal emphasis of his theory requires that there be no necessary linguistic relationship to the world. Linguistic concepts, such as "table," "mesa," "Tisch," etc., are not necessarily tied to their objects.

Conversely, Ricoeur maintains that, at a semiotic level (that is, at the level of the activity of making meaning) there is an "ontological condition of reference."[76] In a given dialogue, language must indicate a reality beyond itself and the terms of its own construction. This view is born out in Nahuatl. *Tlacualoyan* means "table" in conventional usage.[77] Literally, it means "place where one eats it," referring to the activity of sitting at a table rather than directly to the table as an object.[78] Nahuatl nouns often express things as sites of activity. Emphasis in the Nahuatl is consistently placed on an appropriate activity at a particular location. Thus the perspective of language changes from Saussure's semantic emphasis to Ricouer's semiotic emphasis. Meaningful existence in the world requires that a necessary relationship exist between the symbol and the world to which it refers. To exclude the arbitrary nature of this performative relationship means either that one strains to have no connection with existence at all, or that one has an omniscient view of the world in all its plural representations.

Mesoamerican texts had to be performed in order to be understood. For example, on the first eight plates of the *Codex Borgia* there is depicted the *tonalpohualli*, which was the divinatory calendar used to map the significance of events. This calendar consists of fifteen figures that successively represent days, which are arranged into twenty 13-day "weeks," making the *tonalpohualli* "year" 260 days long. According to Seler, each group of five 13-day weeks was dedicated to a cardinal direction.[79] A deity involved in penitential activity would

5.3. Page 5 of the *tonalpohualli*, redrawn from the *Códice Borgia*.

oversee the first days of the five weeks dedicated to a particular direction, then on to the second, third, fourth, etc. For example, the
days corresponding to the east, which fell on the first days of the 5-
day interval, were alligator (*cipactli*),[80] reed (*acatl*), serpent (*coatl*),
movement (*olin*), and water (*atl*). On the top and overseeing these
days are a penitent seated inside a temple and, on the bottom of the
page, the priest Quetzalcoatl. This example dramatizes how the *Borgia*
situates time and space with reference to particular deities and their
actions. Each day is also associated with a specific character embodied
by their names.

The *tonalpohualli* was used to divine the character of humans born
on a particular day, or what the most appropriate course of action to be

pursued should be on a given day. While the *Borgia* clearly marks the forces that influence each of the days, a simple reading of the text was not enough to get all the information. Rather, the *Borgia* had to be *performed* by people whose abilities would allow them to "read" signs other than those strictly associated with the document. These readings were associated with the functioning of their bodies and the events of their surroundings.

Tedlock gives a contemporary example of divinatory activity. Among the Maya of Momostenango, Guatemala, diviners (*curanderos*) also use the 260-day calendar, which roughly corresponds to the human gestation period. Knowledge of the human condition is gathered by people who have an ability to "read" the lightning in their blood. Usually these people are called in their sleep through their dreams. Lightning moves in the blood, tissue, and muscle of the body, and is associated with the movement of sheet lightning in the four corners of the world. While offerings are given to the earth at specific shrines, the diviners feel the lightning in their blood in order to understand a message. In this way, a correspondence is established between the body and the cosmos that allows a given reality, intrinsic to the cosmos, to be known. Following the pulses of the blood in the curandero's body corresponds to the mapping of shrines in the landscape. Water from particular lakes of the high sierra is brought back to these shrines just as the circulation of blood is encouraged to divine knowledge. "As one priest-shaman explained it, 'These shrines are like a book where everything—all births, marriages, deaths, successes, and failures—is written down.'"[81] Divinatory knowledge thus requires that human events, like all others, be meaningfully located in the landscape.[82]

Likewise, the significant factor of Aztec knowledge was not so much encoded in a textual artifact itself but in the manner in which it was "read." This was essentially a phenomenological concept of representation, and it expressed an emphasis on the conditions of material existence. Soon after their arrival, however, the Spanish employed Native artists to generate depictions of their material surroundings. The subject of these "post-Columbian" drawings, as with pre-Columbian drawings, was in the valley geography. Always with an eye toward exploitation of their newly acquired subject lands, the Spanish required that artists depict a literal view of the environment in the illusionistic Renaissance tradition described above. The result was a pictorial tradition distinctly different than that of pre-Columbian texts.[83] Spanish maps depicted a material world as a sensual reality objectified and outside of one's "participatory universe."[84] In pre-Columbian texts, landscape was an interactive reality within an intrinsically meaningful space upon which human life was materially based. In post-Columbian depictions, the relational quality of the landscape was discarded for a near-photographic image of objects as discrete, and therefore transparent, autonomous realities. A landscape of living relations was transformed into abstract space through its being rendered in texts.

Robertson has described the Aztecs' locative sense in pre-Columbian writing as using "signs of nature," which were then transformed by the Conquest into "cartoonish" depictions by Spanish colonial interests into "images of nature."[85] A pre-Columbian concept of an interactive landscape, in which each element stands in relationship to all other elements as a living organism, was stylistically transformed through conquest into "Nature." Previous to this time, it was inconceivable for the Aztecs to have understood the world as an entity that stood apart from human activity. Through the colonial experience, however, landscape was transformed into an abstraction (cartography and geography) in which insulated entities in the physical world could be catalogued on paper. This movement was analogous to the economic shift in Europe from gift to profit economies. The shift simultaneously expressed an overconfidence in a European interpretation of "Nature" as well as their creative disengagement with the world.

While Mesoamerican primary sources stand most proximate to the cultures that generated them, the lives of these texts have been erased. Without the appropriate performative linkages, primary sources are uninhabitable. The interpretation of primary Mesoamerican sources requires "readers" who enlist the attributes of their own bodies in order to reveal their meaning. Since the Conquest, the authority invested in the lives of divinatory experts to reveal meaning through these texts has been limited. Instead, expert knowledge and interpretation of these documents have been reformatted. No longer is it the priest who interacts with an image of the cosmos revealing at once his or her intimate connection to the world and community, but rather it is the scholar, whose primary expertise is in an ability to disengage him- or herself from their cultural vestments in the pursuit of collecting various data and arranging the data in a coherent order. The movement of these various hermeneutical enterprises flows in opposite directions. In the case of the Aztecs, a link with the text is formed through bodily, or interior, knowledge in order to draw upon the necessary connections that exist between the text and the cosmos to which it refers. Conversely, scholarship derives its interpretive authority by pulling apart the text from its points of reference and then reifying the connection between the text and its scholar-reader. For the ethnohistorian, a Mesoamerican world presents itself as a set of transparent images. Ironically, in Mesoamerican studies, the denial of a scholar's task as being an *active and creative* interpreter, replaced with that of an *objective and authoritative* interpreter, obfuscates the hermeneutical activity of any connection to the cosmos through pre-Columbian texts.

It is ironic that while these texts are more proximate to the Mesoamerican world that produced them, and in this sense seen as more authoritative than those that were generated later, they can never be fully comprehensible from our current hermeneutical vantage point. This is not to say, however, that they are not worth the trouble of interpreting. Indeed, even a brief overview of the history of Mesoamerican scholarship, beginning with the efforts of the first generation of priests in the Valley of Mexico, reveals that there was a constant and corporate effort (perhaps even a need) to meaningfully locate these depictions of pre-Columbian cosmology within a modern understanding.[86] While the texts have remained the same, the "primary readers" have changed.

Among some Mesoamericanists, due to a persistent uneasiness with the interpretability of primary sources,[87] a larger reliance has generally been placed on secondary sources, and particularly on Sahagún. This is because Sahagún's work is closer to a modern worldview. This demonstrates Sahagún's importance in bridging a distance between distinct cultural worlds. The irony of "primacy" is that it is not primary texts that constitute our greatest opportunity for understanding Aztec realities, but a nuanced reading of secondary materials such as the *Florentine Codex*, which embody a moment of contact that could therefore reveal our place in it.

NOTES

1. According to Munro S. Edmonson, "Introduction," in *Sixteenth Century Mexico: The Work of Sahagún*, edited by Munro S. Edmonson, School of American Research (Albuquerque: University of New Mexico Press, 1974), pp. 1–15, various aspects of Sahagún's early life could be clarified if access to Franciscan archives could be gained. I assume that although some have tried this tactic, they remain off-limits to curious outsiders. Also see the background work of Luis Nicolau D'Olwer (*Fray Bernardino de Sahagún; 1499–1590*, translated by Mauricio Mixco [Salt Lake City: University of Utah Press, 1987]), upon which much of Edmonson's work is based.

2. This is a very interesting facet of Sahagún's background that could be more completely explored by looking at it in the general context of the *converso* phenomenon in Spain at the time. For example, it would be very interesting to examine the degree to which Sahagún's Jewish past fueled his fervor not only to convert Native Americans but also to understand them and perhaps even appreciate them. Other rumored *conversos* were Columbus and Bartolomé de las Casas. See Benjamin R. Gampel, *The Last Jews on Iberian Soil: Navarrese Jewry; 1479/1498* (Berkeley: University of California Press, 1989), and Deirdre Green, *Gold in the Crucible: Teresa of Avila and the Western Mystical Tradition* (Longmead, Shaftsbury, Dorset, England: Element Books, Ltd, 1989). In a more general manner, the contributions of Jewish Spain have been looked at by Joseph F. O'Callaghan in *A History of Medieval Spain* (Ithaca: Cornell University Press, 1975) and Julio Valdeón, José M.ª Salrach, y Javier Zabalo, *Historia de España*, volume 4, *Feudalismo y consolidación de los pueblos Hispánicos (siglos XI–XV)*, series edited by Manuel Tuñón de Lara (Barcelona: Editorial Labor S.A., 1983).

3. According to J. Jorge Klor de Alva ("Sahagún and the Birth of Modern Ethnography: Representing, Confessing, and Inscribing the Native Other," in *The Work of Bernardino de Sahagún: Pioneer Ethnographer of Sixteenth-Century Aztec Mexico*, edited by J. Jorge Klor de Alva, Henry B. Nicholson, and Eloise Quiñones Keber [Austin: University of Texas Press, 1988], pp. 31–52), the primary method of Christianization in New Spain among these early evangelicals was through linguistic work that was used to create Bibles and sermons in indigenous languages. This tactic of conversion from the fruits of close scrutiny of a people was a particular favorite of the Franciscans in the fifteenth and sixteenth centuries. Also see J. Jorge Klor de Alva, "Religious Organization and Colonial Epistemology," in *To Change Place: Aztec Ceremonial Landscapes*, edited by Davíd Carrasco (Niwot: University Press of Colorado, 1991), pp. 233–245, for a detailed analysis of postconquest phases. A similar approach is also in operation today, although more ecumenical in design. The Summer Institute of

Linguistics has trained generations of people for fieldwork to translate the Bible into Native languages. Ironically, much of the best work in contemporary Nahuatl, for example, is generated by this program.

4. See Fray Bernardino de Sahagún, *Florentine Codex: General History of the Things of New Spain*, 12 books, 13 parts, edited and translated by Arthur J. O. Anderson and Charles E. Dibble, Monographs of the School of American Research, number 14 (Salt Lake City: University of Utah Press, 1951–1982), "Introductory Volume," pp. 53–54, where the editors attribute the genesis of his work to the vision of Toral. Also see Klor de Alva, "Sahagún and the Birth of Modern Ethnography," p. 34.

5. Alfredo López Austin, "The Research Method of Fray Bernardino de Sahagún: The Questionnaires," in *Sixteenth-Century Mexico: The Work of Sahagún*, edited by Munro S. Edmonson, School of American Research (Albuquerque: University of New Mexico Press, 1974), pp. 111–173.

6. In this passage, López Austin is paraphrasing from passages in Fray Bernardino de Sahagún's, *Historia de las Indias de Nueva España*, 2 vols., edited by Angel María Garibay (Mexico City: Editorial Porrúa, 1967). See López Austin, "The Research Method of Fray Bernardino de Sahagún," pp. 114–115 (emphasis added).

7. See Thelma Sullivan, "The Rhetorical Orations, or Huehuetlatolli, Collected by Sahagún," in *Sixteenth Century Mexico: The Work of Sahagún*, edited by Munro S. Edmonson, School of American Research (Albuquerque: University of New Mexico Press, 1974), pp. 79–109.

8. Inga Clendinnen, *Aztecs, an Interpretation* (Cambridge: Cambridge University Press, 1991), pp. 130–132.

9. The world of ethnography has come under sharp criticism in regard to its accuracy in representing the Other's culture. Pierre Bourdieu (*Outline of a Theory of Practice*, translated by Richard Nice [Cambridge: Cambridge University Press, 1977]), among others, has implicated the ethnographer in the process of colonialism. His solution has been to move the referents of writing away from a purely formal analysis of the text toward an ethnography of practice. The activity of working in the field is then seen as a reciprocal interaction between ethnographer and subject. In particular, for Bourdieu, the political and material dimensions of fieldwork come to the fore. In the case of Sahagún, given the turmoil of the times, it is not difficult to imagine that the selection of elders to answer his questions, from the Native side, would be done keeping in mind the consequences of such an exchange in knowledge for the Indians. For an analysis of the consequences of ethnography, also see Johannes Fabian, *Time and the Other: How Anthropology Makes Its Object* (New York: Columbia University Press, 1983).

10. On the other hand, desperation due to illness and poverty may have been seen by the Nahua as a signal to grant fully Sahagún's requests. In this it would be helpful to know his reasons for choosing Tepepulco. For example, was he already known to this community? Or had he achieved some standing with these local inhabitants that would have put him in a position to make such a request? See Arthur J. O. Anderson, "Sahagún's Informants on the Nature of Tlalocan," in *The Work of Bernardino de Sahagún: Pioneer Ethnographer of Sixteenth-Century Aztec Mexico*, edited by J. Jorge Klor de Alva, Henry B. Nicholson, and Eloise Quiñones Keber (Austin: University of Texas Press, 1988), pp. 151–161.

11. López Austin, "The Research Method of Fray Bernardino de Sahagún," pp. 117–118.

12. See Sahagún, *Primeros Memoriales*, edited by Francisco del Paso y Troncoso, vol. 6 (Madrid: Fototipia de Hauser y Menet, 1905).

13. Facsimile editions of both of these works exist under the names *Códice Matritense de la Real Academia de la Historia*, vol. 8, edited by Francisco del Paso y Troncoso (Madrid: Fototipia de Hauser y Menet, 1907); and *Códice Matritense del Real Palacio*, vol. 7, edited by Francisco del Paso y Troncos (Madrid: Fototipia de Hauser y Menet, 1905).

14. My comparison of the passages of the ceremony I-Atl cahualo in the *Códice Matritense*, the facsimile of the *Florentine Codex* (Fray Bernardino de Sahagún, *El Códice Florentino de Sahagún*, 3 vols. [Mexico City: Secretaría de Gobernación, 1979]), and the English translation of the *Florentine Codex* suggest that, at least when discussing the ceremonies considered here, the differences between the Nahuatl columns is very slight.

15. The works of Theodor de Bry include *Discovery of the New World; 1594–95*, facsimile of engravings, text by Gerolamo Benzoni (Amsterdam: van Hoeve, 1979), and *Conquistadors, Aztecs and Incas; 1596*, facsimile of engravings (Amsterdam: van Hoeve, 1980), and are very interesting in the present context. Even with sketches of various travels, as in the case of the travel accounts of Girolamo Benzoni (*History of the New World*, translated by Rear Admiral W. H. Smyth [London: The Hakluyt Society, volume 21, 1857]), he chose to depict the Natives as tonsured classical pagans whose bodies were set in stark contrast to the civilized Europeans. Due to the enormous success of his images on the Age of Discovery, de Bry's work has survived. His themes generally tend to vilify the Spanish, particularly in his depictions of the "Black Legend," in which the Catholic Spanish are seen murdering scores of innocent New World pagans.

Bernadette Bucher, in *Icon and Conquest: A Structural Analysis of the Illustrations of de Bry's Great Voyages*, translated by Basia Miller Gulati (Chicago: University of Chicago Press, 1981), gives a structural account of de Bry's work. She focuses closely on the various images of bodily mutilation and cannibalism to conclude on their effectiveness in legitimizing the colonization of the Americas, while at the same time vilifying particular European groups. In addition, several juxtapositions in these engravings between young and old, civilized and Native, etc., seem to have been deliberately employed by the de Bry family. The popularity of the images at once signal their importance as interpretive devices for people in Europe trying to conceptualize the Americas and demonstrate the concerns and opinions of certain people at the time. For an analysis of the consequences of the emerging vision of the New World from several points of view, also see Fredi Chiappelli, ed., *First Images of America: The Impact of the New World on the Old*, 2 vols. (Berkeley: University of California Press, 1976).

16. See Edmonson, "Introduction," p. 9.

17. Angel María Garibay, *Historia de la literatura Náhuatl*, 2 vols. (Mexico City: Editorial Porruá, 1953–1954), vol. 2, pp. 57–71.

18. Donald Robertson, "The Sixteenth Century Mexican Encyclopedia of Fray Bernardino de Sahagún," *Cuadernos de historia mundial* 9, no. 3 (1966): 617–628.

19. See Klor de Alva's provocative analysis of the ties between Sahagún and Veracruz in "Sahagún and the Birth of Modern Ethnography," p. 36.

20. Lewis Hanke, *Aristotle and the American Indians* (Bloomington: Indiana University Press, 1959), p. 38, and cited in Davíd Carrasco, *Religions of Mesoamerica: Cosmovision and Ceremonial Centers* (San Francisco: Harper & Row, Publishers, 1990), p. 7. Since its drafting in 1514, the *requerimiento* was read in Latin to Indians before they were engaged in battle. For standard histories of colonial Mexico, see Charles Gibson, *The Aztecs Under Spanish Rule: A History of the Indians of the Valley of Mexico; 1519–1810* (Stanford, CA: Stanford University Press, 1964), and R. C. Padden, *The Hummingbird and the Hawk: Conquest and Sovereignty in the Valley of Mexico; 1503–1541* (New York: Harper & Row, Publishers, 1967).

21. See Fernando Cervantes, *The Devil in the New World: The Impact of Diabolism in New Spain* (New Haven, CT: Yale University Press, 1994), p. 33.

22. Ibid., pp. 18–19: "[A] central and essential feature of the devil in Christian thought is his complete subordination to the will of God . . . Hermas, Polycarp and Plutarch taught that the devil had no power over the human soul . . . that evil was not an independent principle was to be reinforced by the Alexandrans, especially Clement and Origen [, and would] prepare the ground for St. Augustine's classic definition which denied evil all ontological existence . . . If evil had no substance, no actual existence, no intrinsic reality, if nothing was by nature evil, then a principle of evil—an evil being independent of God—was an absurdity . . . It would seem that this conviction about the impotence of Satan against God and his Church was badly shaken in the early modern period."

23. See Tzvetan Todorov, "Equality and Inequality," and "Enslavement, Colonialism, and Communication," in *The Conquest of America*, translated by Richard Howard (New York: Harper Torchbooks, 1984), pp. 146–181.

24. See Bartolomé de las Casas, *The Only Way*, translated by Helen Rand Parish and Francis P. Sullivan (Mahwah, NJ: Paulist Press, 1992), for a full treatment of his world vision.

25. See John Leddy Phelan, *The Millennial Kingdom of the Franciscans in the New World: A Study of the Writings of Geronimo de Mendieta (1525–1604)*, University of California Publications in History, vol. 42 (Berkeley: University of California Press, 1956), pp. 14–20. The most influential of what would later be called the Spiritual Franciscans was Joachim of Fiore. For a full treatment of Joachim in the context of western intellectual history, see Bernard McGinn, *The Calabrian Abbot: Joachim of Fiore in the History of Western Thought* (New York: Macmillan Publishing Co., 1985). In addition, see Bernard McGinn, ed., *Apocalyptic Spirituality: Treatises and Letters of Lactantium, Adso of Montier-en-der, Joachim of Fiore, the Franciscan Spirituals, Savonarola* (New York: Paulist Press, 1979). This contains a collection of the significant writings of Joachim of Fiore as well as other Spiritual Franciscans.

26. This was not unusual for the period. The only remaining copy of Columbus's first voyage, which was abstracted by Bartolomé de las Casas, *The Diary of Christopher Columbus's First Voyage to America; 1492–1493*, transcribed and translated by Oliver Dunn and James E. Kelly Jr. (Norman: University of Oklahoma Press, 1989), describes the taking of the "Indies" as not just enhancing Spain's prestige in the

spice trade, but primarily extending Christendom. Las Casas was captivated by Columbus's vision of the New World and created his own edited version of his diary. For an examination of Columbus's own millennial vision, see Pauline Moffitt Watts, "Prophecy and Discovery: On the Spiritual Origins of Christopher Columbus's 'Enterprise of the Indies,' " *The American Historical Review* 90 (1985): 73–102.

27. John Keber's, "Sahagún and Hermeneutics: A Christian Ethnographer's Understanding of Aztec Culture," in *The Work of Bernardino de Sahagún: Pioneer Ethnographer of Sixteenth-Century Aztec Mexico*, edited by J. Jorge Klor de Alva, Henry B. Nicholson, and Eloise Quiñones Keber (Austin: University of Texas Press, 1988), pp. 53–63, concludes that Sahagún, through his ethnographic approach to Aztec culture, argued for their having a distinctive moral tradition in order to counter the Sepulveda arm of the debate that they were completely outside Christian values, which would therefore have justified their subjugation and exploitation.

28. See Kajetan Esser O. F. M., *Origins of the Franciscan Order*, translated by Aedan Daly O. F. M. and Dr. Irina Lynch (Chicago: Franciscan Herald Press, 1970), p. 18, and Raymond Bucher O. F. M., "Francis of Assisi," in *The Encyclopedia of Religion*, edited by Mircea Eliade, vol. 5 (New York: Macmillan Publishing, 1986), p. 409, for the importance of Francis's biography to the Franciscan movement.

29. Bucher, "Francis of Assisi."

30. See E. Randolph Daniel, *The Franciscan Concept of Mission in the High Middle Ages* (Lexington: University Press of Kentucky, 1975), pp. 12–13.

31. Duane V. Lapsanski, *Evangelical Perfection: An Historical Examination of the Concept in the Early Franciscan Sources* (New York: Franciscan Institute Publications, St. Bonaventure University, 1977), pp. 1–5.

32. According to R. I. Moore in *The Origins of European Dissent* (Oxford: Basil Blackwell, Ltd., 1985), p. 40, heresy in the middle to late Middle Ages was generally tied to a turn toward the scriptures. There were two main groups that challenged the church: 1) the literati, whose private visions had priority over the church's, and 2) the *rustici, idiotae et infacundi,* who were uneducated men with some knowledge of the scriptures who thought the priests were incapable. Both of these types of heretics should be regarded as conservative and as reacting to the changing conditions of society. The Franciscans could have easily been seen as belonging to either of these groups.

33. The biography of Waldes of Lyon has several striking parallels to the story of St. Francis, and yet while the former was tied to a heretical movement, the latter was integrated into the Church almost from the beginning. Both shared a hatred for money (for Francis it was "filthy lucre" and linked to excrement) and had similar backgrounds in the urban industrial society. See Lester K. Little, *Origins of the Franciscan Order of Medieval Europe* (Ithaca: Cornell University Press, 1978), pp. 146–152. In his "Forward" to *Origins of the Franciscan Order*, Esser maintains, however, that Francis had in mind from the beginning that he and his followers would not be set against the workings of the world Church, but rather be committed to its purification. While he talked like a heretic, he understood himself as being at the center of the Church.

34. Little, ibid., pp. 3–18.

35. Little, in *Origins of the Franciscan Order*, pp. 5–6, maintains that in what has been referred to as the Dark Ages the reconversion of treasure into another form of treasure was typical of the "gift economy." Gifts, contrary to profit, were not calculated according to set values until the eleventh century, which were dictated by the Church. For example monks campaigned vehemently against the pagan German practice of burying gold and other riches with the dead. The last known German burial of this kind happened in the 1160s, which corresponds with the date of the first minted coins.

36. See Mikhail Bahktin's discussion of St. Francis in *Rabelais and His World*, translated by Hèléne Iswolsky (Bloomington: University of Indiana Press, 1984), p. 57. Also see his discussion of the degradation of folk culture in "Rabelais and the History of Laughter," ibid.

37. See Todorov, *The Conquest of America*, pp. 185–201.

38. For example, Anthony Pagden, in *The Fall of Natural Man: The American Indian and the Origins of Comparative Ethnology* (Cambridge: Cambridge University Press, 1982), examines the conceptual shift of "natural man" in light of contact with the New World.

39. See Carlo Ginzburg, *The Cheeze and the Worms: The Cosmos of a Sixteenth-Century Miller*, translated by John and Anne Tedeschi (New York: Penguin Books, 1982).

40. See Carlo Ginzburg, *The Night Battles: Witchcraft & Agrarian Cults in the Sixteenth and Seventeenth Centuries*, translated by John and Anne Tedeschi (Baltimore: Johns Hopkins University Press, 1983), for a description of agrarian cults of the Friuli people of northern Italy, which, according to him, became incorrectly labeled by Inquisitional authorities as witch covens. Instead, he sees these cults as having strong shamanic ties. Emmanuel Le Roy Ladurie, *Carnival in Romans*, translated by Mary Feeney (New York: George Braziller, Inc., 1979b), gives a stirring account of Carnival in Romans of southern France during the sixteenth century.

41. See William A. Christian Jr., *Local Religion in Sixteenth-Century Spain* (Princeton, NJ: Princeton University Press, 1981), about the local cults of Spanish indigenous groups. In the end it was the Inquisition that would insist on legitimating these cults, thereby judging their authenticity or not.

42. Ibid., and Ginzburg, *The Night Battles*, for example.

43. See William A. Christian Jr., *Apparitions in Late Medieval and Renaissance Spain* (Princeton, NJ: Princeton University Press, 1981). For a look at the modern significance of pilgrimage, see Mary Lee Nolan and Sidney Nolan, *Christian Pilgrimage in Modern Western Europe* (Chapel Hill: University of North Carolina Press, 1989). For the origins of pilgrimage and its ties to the circulation of body parts of the "glorious dead," see Peter Brown, *The Cult of Saints: Its Rise and Function in Latin Christianity* (Chicago: University of Chicago Press, 1981).

44. See Ioan P. Couliano, *Eros and Magic in the Renaissance*, translated by Margaret Cook (Chicago: University of Chicago Press, 1987), for an examination of the place of the imaginative sciences of the Renaissance, which linked the workings of a world of phenomena to the inner life of the humors. Also see the extraordinary work of

Mikhail Bakhtin, *Rabelais and His World*, on the effect of folk culture on the work of Rabelais. His analysis of this author sets him in the context of village life in which an arrangement of matter is adjudicated with reference to the open and gigantic body, and its associated openings. Bakhtin ties a literary convention to folk festivals such as the feast of fools, carnival, and the marketplace. For a full treatment of the history of play in the medieval European tradition, see Johan Huizinga, *Homo Ludens:A Study of the Play-Element in Culture* (Boston: Beacon Press, 1950).

45. See Timothy Mitchell, *Passional Culture: Emotion, Religion, and Society in Southern Spain* (Philadelphia: University of Pennsylvania Press, 1990), for a treatment of contemporary society in Andalusia. His thesis is that in this geographical region, religious devotion has a marked pitch of devotion that is unique in Spain. This is historically significant in that perhaps as many as 80 percent of the New World settlers originated from this part of Spain. Also see Julio Caro Baroja, *The World of the Witches*, translated by O.N.V. Glendinning (Chicago: University of Chicago Press, 1965), for an attempt at "reading back" from a contemporary context.

46. For historical overviews leading up to the reconquest, see Valdeón, et al., *Feudalismo y consolidación*, and O'Callaghan in *A History of Medieval Spain*.

47.Oftentimes an economic analysis, which brings together structural sociological and historical approaches, is tied to the "Anales school." For a working example, see Emmanuel Le Roy Ladurie, *The Territory of the Historian*, translated by Ben and Siân Reynolds (Chicago: University of Chicago Press, 1979). Also see Fernand Braudel, *The Mediterranean and the Mediterranean World in the Age of Phillip II*, 2 vols., translated by Siân Reynolds (London: Harper & Row, 1972), for a geographical analysis of cultural movements around the Mediterranean. Also see Huguette Chaunu and Pierre Chaunu, *Seville et l'Atlantique de 1504 à 1650*, 8 vols. (Paris: A. Colin, 1955–1957), for a history of economic relationships between the port of Seville and the Atlantic geography.

48. See John Mohawk, "Discovering Columbus: The Way Here," *Northeast Indian Quarterly* 7, no. 3 (1990): 37–46, for a treatment of the structural/historical attributes that lay behind Columbus's voyage.

49. See Louise M. Burkhart, *The Slippery Earth: Nahua Christian Moral Dialogue in Sixteenth Century Mexico* (Tucson: University of Arizona Press, 1989), p. 5.

50. See Robert Richard, *The Spiritual Conquest of Mexico*, translated by Lesley Byrd Simpson (Berkeley: University of California Press, 1966).

51. See Klor de Alva, "Sahagún and the Birth of Modern Ethnography"; J. Jorge Klor de Alva, "European Spirit and Mesoamerican Matter: Sahagún and the 'Crisis of Representation' in Sixteenth-Century Ethnography," in *The Imagination of Matter: Religion and Ecology in Mesoamerican Traditions*, edited by Davíd Carrasco (Oxford: B.A.R. International Series 515, 1989), pp. 17–29; and Louise M. Burkhart, "Aztecs in Limbo: The Harrowing of Hell in Nahua-Christian Literature," paper presented at the 47th International Congress of Americanists (Tulane University, New Orleans, 11 July 1991).

52. Analogous to the negotiation of meaning between Native American and European views is the negotiation of spaces between a Mesoamericanist and his/her object of study. Given this reality of our documents, how is it best to overcome the historical and cultural distances between twentieth- and sixteenth-century worlds?

53. See Burkhart, *The Slippery Earth*, p. 20. It was at the Colegio that the first American press was established. See John Frederick Schwaller, "A Catalogue of pre-1840 Nahuatl Works Held by the Lilly Library," *Indiana University Bookman* 11 (1973): 69–88. Also see Lynn Glaser, *America on Paper: The First Hundred Years* (Philadelphia: Associated Antiquaries, 1989).

54. See Burkhart, "Aztecs in Limbo." Also see Louise Burkhart, "Doctrinal Aspects of Sahagún's *Colloquios*," in *The Work of Bernardino de Sahagún: Pioneer Ethnographer of Sixteenth-Century Aztec Mexico*, edited by J. Jorge Klor de Alva, Henry B. Nicholson, and Eloise Quiñones Keber (Austin: University of Texas Press, 1988), pp. 65–82.

55. According to Frances Karttunen in *An Analytical Dictionary of Nahuatl* (Austin: University of Texas Press, 1983), p. 263, this should be written *tlahtlacōlli*.

56. Burkhart, *The Slippery Earth*, p. 29.

57. Other interesting Native categories that translated back into Christian ideas were good and evil, translated similarly to the sin/damage pair as order and chaos. The "semidualist" religious tone of Christianity was not a feature of the Nahua. Even more distinct from Aztec conceptions was the linking of evil to matter (as in materialism); however, a certain engagement with matter could result in a chaotic condition for the Aztecs.

58. In *Plurality and Ambiguity: Hermeneutics, Religion, Hope* (New York: Harper & Row, Publishers, 1987), David Tracy discusses the risks of a dialogical method of religiousness. Plurality is a reality that addresses adjudicating the distance between Self and Other and always requires the transformation of individual and world.

59. From Klor de Alva, "Sahagún and the Birth of Modern Ethnography," p. 39. He goes on to say that Franz Boas, among other modern ethnographers, also led the framing of information gathering in analogous ways.

60. Ashis Nandy describes a similar transformation as a consequence of the colonization of India in his *The Intimate Enemy: Loss and Recovery of Self Under Colonialism* (Delhi: Oxford University Press, 1983).

61. See Fabian, *Time and the Other*.

62. Ibid., p. 31. Fabian discusses this as a "denial of coevalness" that disrupts communication. "By that I mean a *persistent and systematic tendency to place the referent(s) of anthropology in a Time other than the present of the producer of anthropological discourse.*"

63. See Bourdieu, *Outline of a Theory of Practice*, particularly chapter 1, "The Objective Limits of Objectivism."

64. The reinsertion of autobiography into ethnography is one of the ways that Fabian, in *Time and the Other*, suggests a more authentic, and less exploitive, connection can be attained with the Other. Autobiography has been used recently as another mode of doing ethnography, as in Paul Stoller and Cheryl Olkes, *In Sorcery's Shadow: A Memoir of Apprenticeship Among the Songhay of Niger* (Chicago: University of Chicago Press, 1987); Ann Grodzins Gold, *Fruitful Journeys: The Ways of Rajasthani Pilgrims* (Berkeley: University of California Press, 1987); and Michael Jackson, *Barawa and the Ways Birds Fly in the Sky: An Ethnographic Novel* (Washington, DC: Smithsonian Institu-

tion Press, 1986). In addition, a biographical method of analysis has been used by Clifford Geertz, *Works and Lives: The Anthropologist as Author* (Stanford, CA: Stanford University Press, 1988), and Wendy Doniger O'Flaherty, *Other People's Myths: The Cave of Echoes* (New York: Macmillan Publishing Co., 1988). The difficulties of this type of approach in Mesoamerican studies are more extreme given the distance from the material alluded to above. However, Inga Clendinnen, *Aztecs, an Interpretation*, pp. 4–6, has recently made the attempt at "getting inside the experience of being Aztec."

65. Sahagún, *Florentine Codex*, book 1, pp. 105–106.

66. Ibid., book 2, p. 165.

67. According to Davíd Carrasco in *Quetzalcoatl and the Irony of Empire: Myths and Prophecies in the Aztec Tradition* (Chicago: University of Chicago Press, 1982), pp. 24–28, and in *Religions of Mesoamerica*, pp. 11–19, based on the work of a number of ethnohistorians, there are currently sixteen of these pre-Columbian "picture books" in existence. There are, however, known to be many more held within individual Native communities and these texts seem to be closely guarded by traditional people. Generally, texts that are kept by village Nahua still exist at the center of a community ritual life, and therefore at the center of their indigenous identities.

68. The *Florentine Codex* is the last version produced of the *General History of the Things of New Spain*. It contained a Spanish gloss to accompany the Nahuatl, as well as including drawings. For an update on the work on Sahagún since the mid 1970s, see Henry B. Nicholson, "Recent Sahaguntine Studies: A Review," in *The Work of Bernardino de Sahagún: Pioneer Ethnographer of Sixteenth-Century Mexico*, edited by J. Jorge Klor de Alva, Henry B. Nicholson, and Eloise Quiñones Keber (Austin: University of Texas Press, 1988), pp. 13–30. For a bibliography of Sahagún's extant work, see Eloise Quiñones Keber, "The Sahaguntine Corpus: A Bibliographic Index of Extant Documents," in *The Work of Bernardino de Sahagún*, ibid. above, pp. 341–345. From this point forward, I will refer to Sahagún's *General History* as either one of the two surviving documents: the *Codex Matritense* or the *Florentine Codex*.

69. See Ellen Taylor Baird, "Sahagún's *Primeros Memoriales* and *Codex Florentino*: European Elements in the Illustrations," in *Smoke and Mist: Mesoamerican Studies in Memory of Thelma D. Sullivan*, edited by J. Kathryn Josserand and Karen Dakin (Oxford: B.A.R. International Series 402[i], 1988), pp. 15–40, and "The Illusion of Space and the Perception of History in Sahagún's *Codex Florentino*," a paper presented at the 47th International Congress of Americanists (Tulane University, New Orleans, 11 July 1991).

70. For an extensive study of the history of linear perspective, see Samuel T. Edgerton, Jr., *The Renaissance Rediscovery of Linear Perspective* (New York, Basic Books, Inc., 1975).

71. As quoted in Baird (1991, n. 69 above), p. 6, from Edgerton's citation of Bacon's *Opus majus* (ibid., pp. 17–18), the full passage reads:

Now I wish to present the . . . [purpose] . . . which concerns geometrical forms as regards lines, angles, and figures both of solids and surfaces. For it is impossible for the spiritual sense to be known without a knowledge of the literal sense. But the literal sense cannot be known, unless a man knows the significations of the terms and the properties of the things signified . . . Oh, how the ineffable beauty of the divine wisdom would shine and infinite benefit would overflow, if these matters relating to geometry, which are contained in Scripture, should be placed before our eyes in their physical forms! . . . I count nothing more fitting for a man diligent in the study of God's wisdom than the exhibition of geometrical forms of this kind before his eyes . . . without doubt the whole truth of things in the world lies in the literal sense, as has been said, and especially of things relating to geometry, because we can understand nothing fully unless its form is presented before our eyes and therefore in the Scripture of God the whole knowledge of things to be defined by geometrical forms is contained and far better than mere philosophy could express it.

72. Baird, "The Illusion of Space," p. 8.

73. For example, see Gordon Brotherston, *Image of the New World: The American Continent Portrayed in Native Texts* (London: Thames and Hudson, 1978).

74. See Carrasco, *Quetzalcoatl and the Irony of Empire*, p. 24.

75. Ferdinand de Saussure, *Course in General Linguistics* (Chicago: University of Chicago Press, 1966), pp. 67–70.

76. Paul Ricoeur, *Interpretation Theory: Discourse and the Surplus of Meaning* (Fort Worth: Texas Christian University Press, 1976), p. 21. Also see Bourdieu's critique of Saussure as an intellectualist/structuralist construction of language that can only conceive of language as "execution" and never practice. Bourdieu, *Outline of a Theory of Practice*, p. 24.

77. Karttunen, *An Analytical Dictionary of Nahuatl*, p. 257.

78. This interpretation is supported by Alonso de Molina, *Vocabulario en Lengua Castellana y Mexicana y Mexicana y Castellana* (Mexico City: Editorial Porruá, 1977), p. 85r, as he translates this word as "mesa, donde comemos."

79. *Códice Borgia*, facsimile, commentary by Eduard Seler, 3 vols. (Mexico: Fondo de Cultura Económica, 1963). These weeks would be dedicated to directions following the path of the sun. Beginning in the east, they would then go to the north, west, and south.

80. This word is only found in Réne Siméon, *Diccionario de la lengua Nahuatl o Mexicana* (Mexico City: Siglo Veintiuno editores, 1977), p. 111, who describes it as a shark, or a fish that is extremely ravenous.

81. Barbara Tedlock, *Time and the Highland Maya* (Albuquerque: University of New Mexico Press, 1982), p. 80.

82. Also see Joseph W. Bastien, *Mountain of the Condor: Metaphor and Ritual in an Andean Ayllu* (Prospect Heights, IL: Waveland Press, Inc., 1978), and "Qollahuaya-Andean Body Concepts: A Topographical-Hydraulic Model of Physiology," *American Anthropology* 87 (1985): 595–611, for examples of divination among the Aymara of Bolivia. The human body directly corresponds to the mountain body, where knowledge is acquired through offerings at earth shrines and messages that come to people through the pulsing of various fluids through their bodies.

83. See Edward Calnek, "The Localization of the Sixteenth Century Map Called the Maguey Plan," *American Antiquity* 38, no. 8 (1973): 190–195, for an analysis of the "maguey plan" and for a comprehensive treatment of a pre-Columbian map and how it relates to geographical features.

84. The use of the term "participatory universe" comes originally from F. Helitzer, "The Princeton Galaxy," *Intellectual Digest* 3, no. 10 (1973): 25–32, and expresses interstellar dynamics in astronomy. However, Johannes Wilbert, in "Eschatology in a Participatory Universe and Destinies of the Soul Among Warao Indians of Venezuela," in *Death and Afterlife in Pre-Columbian America*, edited by Elizabeth P. Benson (Washington, DC: Dumbarton Oaks, 1975), pp. 163–189, adapts the term to apply to travel of the soul in the afterlife among the Warao Indians. My sense of this phrase is the understanding that orientation within a dynamic space is an activity. Phenomenological reality is not stationary, but is made up of an ongoing process of interactions between various types of living beings.

85. Donald Robertson, *Mexican Manuscript Painting of the Early Colonial Period: The Metropolitan Schools* (New Haven, CT: Yale University Press, 1959), pp. 185–186. A treatment of the transformation of the depiction of space is found in Carrasco, *Quetzalcoatl and the Irony of Empire*, p. 18.

86. See Brotherston, *Image of the New World,* as a detailed example of the utilization of Native American texts to dramatize a history and cultural continuity.

87. There are very important exceptions to this feature of Mesoamerican studies. For example, art historians have tended to prefer, particularly in recent scholarship, to focus interpretations on various iconographic attributes and trace those attributes thematically in an assortment of mediums and contexts. See, for example, Cecelia F. Klein, "Who Was Tlaloc?" *Journal of Latin American Lore* 6, no. 2 (1980): 155–204, whose treatment of the history of Tlaloc follows his manifestations through an assortment of archaeological and graphic contexts. Another study in this vein is Esther Pasztory, "The Aztec Tlaloc: God of Antiquity," in *Smoke and Mist, Mesoamerican Studies in Memory of Thelma D. Sullivan*, edited by J. Kathryn Josserand and Karen Dakin (Oxford: B.A.R. International Series 402[i], 1988), pp. 289–327, and her examination of the consequences of Tlaloc iconography throughout Mesoamerican history. There is also the esteemed tradition, which was initiated with the monumental work of Eduard Seler, in which primary documents are painstakingly analyzed in minute detail. For examples of Seler's work, see *Gesammelte Abhandlungen zur Amerikanschen Sprach-und Alterhumskunde*, 5 vols. (Graz, Austria: Akademische Druck-und Verlangsanstalt, 1960–61), and *Códice Borgia*. Boone's interpretation of the *Codex Magliabechiano, The Book of Life of the Ancient Mexicans* (2 vols., edited and interpreted by Elizabeth Boone [Berkeley: University of California Press, 1983]) is a fine contemporary example of this type of scholarship. A recent notable effort to grapple with these thorny issues of interpreting various sorts of Mesoamerican texts is Elizabeth Boone and Walter Mignolo, eds., *Writing Without Words: Alternative Literacies in Mesoamerica and the Andes* (Durham, NC: Duke University Press, 1994).

6 The (No)Place of Sahagún

Initially, the zeal to forge a utopian world from what was seen as the raw materials of the New World (which included its "primitive" inhabitants) initiated the production of texts. In light of the previous discussion of the Aztec ritual occupation of land, the question emerges as to what kind of landscape does the text engender? What kind of performance originates from occupying a utopian world? These are questions that can be asked of sixteenth-century Mexico but are no less urgent for our present context. My intention is to critically evaluate aspects of utopia in the New World, not only with reference to Mesoamerican texts (as in the previous chapter), but with reference to how it came to terms with a living landscape (i.e., Tlalocan) that existed previous to European occupation. An examination of Sahagún's interpretive location in the Valley of Mexico is then also a self-conscious appraisal of scholarly activity. This serves to heighten the disjunction between those involved in textual understanding (including Sahagún and other contemporary scholars) and those involved in ritual articulation (including the Aztecs and other indigenous people) in the process of occupying the Americas. Using Sahagún's work to reflect larger issues, my intention is to dramatize the disjunction between locative and utopian worldviews as a precondition for understanding Aztec religion and radically other than colonial or modern understandings. Looking at the "referential practice" of these worldviews gives us some position by which to adjudicate the distance between the Aztecs and the Europeans.

Evidence of a radical disjunction between Native Americans and Europeans is borne out of the devastation of conquest. According to recent demographic studies, approximately 80 percent of the nearly 20 million people of Mesoamerica died within the first sixty years of European occupation.[1] Although many died as a result of European diseases rather than cold-blooded extermination, Crosby has shown that the consequences of the biological shock of new illnesses on Native people in the Americas was no less imperialistic than outright warfare.[2] This enormous loss of life in the years immediately following 1492 came to be known as the "Black Legend," a myth of Spanish brutality that was largely the creation of Bartolomé de las Casas, and then utilized by Protestant countries in northern Europe to fuel anti-Catholic sentiments and justify European commercial expansion in other parts of the Americas.[3] Although the justifications for conquering the Americas may have differed in various European countries, the consequences of European occupation throughout the Americas were consistent in generating a tremendous loss of life, culture, and land and resulted in the shrinking of indigenous communities up to the present day.[4] While the Aztecs are renowned for human sacrifice, as discussed below, these practices pale in comparison with the European extermination of humans.

The Conquest is, at once, proof of the radical Otherness of Europeans in the Americas and an impediment to fostering a locative understanding of religion. To explore religion as tied to the human occupation of a meaningful landscape seems closer to approximating Aztec religion (if not most Native American religions). Yet in applying this definition of religion to the colonial Spanish (or other "American religions"), it is apparent that Sahagún, as well as others of his time, would not have seen landscape as the primary point of orientation for their religion. Rather, the transcendent realm, or heavenly world of God, was more important than material life. European optimism about the utopian possibilities of the New World simultaneously limited the colonial understanding of the Americas as an important *religious* point of orientation, while at the same time justifying what Stannard calls "the American holocaust." This suggests that locating Sahagún, along with much of what is called "American religion," requires that the scholar of religion be self-consciously involved in the legacy of the Conquest. By comparing the religion of Sahagún with that of the Aztecs with reference to their material occupation of the New World, perhaps a fuller understanding of the impact of Native American religion can be brought to bear on the American experience.

Twentieth-century interest in Sahagún's work has generated a subcategory of Mesoamerican studies that is sometimes referred to as Sahaguntine studies. Due to the obscure character of his life and agenda, scholarly examination of Sahagún dovetails with the present issue of how to "locate" the author. While some of the particulars of Sahagún's life and intellectual tradition were fleshed-out in the previous chapter, we now turn more fully to those aspects of his material situation that articulate his place and practice in sixteenth-century Mexico.

Sometimes called the "father of modern ethnography," Sahagún and his work, both in terms of methodology and ethnographic detail, represent a conceptual shift in the organization of knowledge of the empirical Other.[5] It seems evident that Sahagún had an agenda when constructing the *Florentine Codex*. His purpose was to carefully record the details of Aztec religious life so that they could be systematically identified and destroyed. He makes this agenda abundantly clear throughout the codex.[6] These apologetics begin all of his writings, and they clearly frame an appropriate reading of the *Florentine*. In this light, however, the question becomes: How can Sahagún be at once the father of ethnography and its enemy?

Several scholars have been working on the conceptual and cosmological underpinnings of Sahagún's work, as examined earlier. These studies have proven to be profoundly revealing in tracing the methods of interpretation that he initiated with the *Florentine*. It is not my intention to necessarily add to these efforts, but rather to take

[219]

them in another direction. In the context of the current analysis of the Tlaloc cult as an indigenous hermeneutic of occupying Mexico, questions arise regarding the consequences of Sahagún's hermeneutical activity for a colonial occupation of the valley. Can his ethnographic project, reconceived as a hermeneutics of occupying the Valley of Mexico, illuminate interpretive dimensions of colonialism when set in relationship with pre-Columbian evidence? Furthermore, do Sahagún's writings shed additional light on current conceptions and problems of doing ethnography, archaeology, and history of religion? Does his interaction with the Aztec civilization, through writing, tell us something about the origins and meaning of the modern world and the occupation of the New World? The implications of these questions will be addressed in the final chapter, but first we must assess the place of Sahagún within the context of his writing about the Tlaloc cult.

An examination of the ritual descriptions in the facsimile of the *Florentine* reveals a marked distinction between the Spanish and Nahuatl columns.[7] As Anderson has noted, any translation of the Nahuatl must also take into account the Spanish side of the page.[8] The striking feature of the *Florentine* is that while the Spanish side physically parallels the Nahuatl, it is actually a running commentary, or gloss, of the action, and not a translation. Thus there is a shift from Nahuatl to Spanish voices, but Sahagún's interpretation in Spanish is authorized by the Nahuatl side. Both Spanish and Nahuatl voices are contained in the document, but the voices are not in dialogue with one another. If there is some interaction between Aztec and European worlds, it should be characterized as seepage rather than dialogue.[9] Also, there is an interplay of authority between the Nahuatl and Spanish versions. The confines of the text do not allow us to participate in the activity of interaction, but only to participate in the canonization of the colonial project. The *Florentine* demonstrates that dialogue may or may not have taken place previous to the text's creation. Dialogue, as it is conceived by Tracy, is the hermeneutical activity of standing and negotiating the distance between various meaningful speakers.[10] While dialogue, in this sense, is undoubtedly present between Sahagún, informant, and reader, this interaction itself goes unrecorded within the *Florentine*.

In a similar way, there is a striking absence of Sahagún's presence in the text. Even though he is the acknowledged author of this work, his absence is conspicuous in the descriptive aspects of the text. This contrasts with the work of Durán, for example, who also describes these same rituals in Spanish but in a more abbreviated and value-laden manner.[11] Durán is not timid about characterizing Aztec rituals as demonic, and he is less interested in writing an objective report of Aztec traditions. Likewise, he is untroubled about replacing Native perspectives for his own Spanish renderings of the rituals. The difference between Sahagún and Durán can, to some degree, be accounted for historically by distinctions between Franciscan and Dominican orders in Mexico.[12] Unlike the Dominicans, the Franciscans in the New World embraced an ethnographic-linguistic approach to their missionary activities; they wished to discover and utilize elements of indigenous worldviews that would correspond to Christian ones. This broke with the conventional wisdom of missionary activity in the Old World.[13] But Sahagún went beyond the methodological rigor of his time. His decision to record Aztec life in Nahuatl proved to be an enormous undertaking. As he writes,

> Another thing about the language which will also annoy those who may understand it, is that for one thing there are many synonymous names, and one way of speaking and one sentence is said in many ways. It became a challenge to know and write down all the words for each thing and all the ways of saying one sentence, and not only in this book but in the whole work.[14]

Without question, Sahagún worked hard to accurately represent the Aztecs. He drew on elements from his background to create new ways of recording their world. Given all this effort, however, one cannot help but wonder why his labor wasn't included in his final product. Sahagún's ethnographic style did not include his own creative labors—why? Instead he opted for a presentation of the Aztecs *as if their world were transparent to him,* and therefore crafts a fictive relationship for the reader.[15] Analogous to his graphic use of illusionistic space, a presentation of Aztec life as if it were a transparent reality expressed the fiction that Sahagún did not have, and did not need to have, an interaction with the Aztecs. One of the messages conveyed is that what needs to be known is bounded by the document. Ironically, while Sahagún committed his life and energy to the "practice" of working with the Aztecs, the activity of writing about their festivals does not include him. Yet this absence of Sahagún and the transparency of the Aztecs is a fiction that is promoted by the material consequences of book production, and which in turn materially authorized colonial existence. Sahagún was the editor—he framed much of what we currently know of pre-Columbian life.[16]

The consequences of his writing style are that there seems to be no connection between Native and European realities. Furthermore, in their seeming transparency, indigenous understandings can be misleadingly judged, seemingly on their own merits, or on the merits of others, apart from historical and cultural frameworks. As Fabian has pointed out, the consequences of writing about people conceptually distant from one's own world can lead to exploitative policies between powerful and weak nations.[17] Sahagún's conceptual (not practical) absenteeism also results in his not being there. It expresses a certainty about what the world is (in particular, the New World) and what it is for. The successful elimination of other interpretations is achieved through his methodology combined with the medium of writing. While we have a dazzling array of cultural formulations in the *Florentine,* Sahagún chose not to regard them. He is an author involved in a monumental interpretive task, yet he cannot be present in the representations of that task.

Sahagún was a colonial inhabitant of Mexico. As with the Aztecs, his life was materially sustained by indigenous foods that were nurtured through the efforts of Native people. From an Aztec perspective, he was constituted and sustained by Tlalocan. Ideologically, however, Sahagún was oriented toward the book (both the sacred books of Christendom and his own ethnographic work) even though he was materially sustained indigenously. It was the book that simultaneously promoted a Franciscan utopian vision and authorized colonial occupation of it. The split between religious and bodily realities is therefore reified in the text. His identity was drawn exclusively, and defined ideologically, from features of the Old World (Jerusalem). Sahagún's work reveals a discontinuity of occupying Mexico between locative and utopian religious perspectives that resulted from colonialism. Conceptually, he was not present, drawing instead on interpretive models outside his own bodily experience. Substantively, he was present, but his understanding was undermined by his relegating it to an imperfect, or "fallen," physical involvement. It is precisely this discontinuity of existence and meaning that, for my purposes, defines colonialism.

Currently in Mesoamerican studies, the predominate tact when utilizing the *Florentine Codex*, however, has been to ignore Sahagún's voice as much as possible. Ethnohistorians have attempted to isolate the Franciscan voice and Aztec voices in an attempt to determine exactly what was true Aztec culture. By various strategies of textual analysis, scholars have claimed to be able to distinguish regional variations of pre-Columbian culture. Also, they have reconstructed Sahagún's questions that were put to the local elders. The reasons for this kind of close examination of the text is what Carrasco calls a "hermeneutics of suspicion,"[18] wherein the authority of the text has to be subverted in its interpretation to more clearly apprehend the cultural elements embedded in it. Through the author's reformatting of the data, these realities, it is supposed, have been silenced.

A thorough hermeneutics of suspicion would also allow contemporary scholars to question what would constitute an authoritative rendering of voices in the text, no matter whose they might be. Just as primary documents are at such a distance from a contemporary interpretive location, secondary sources are just as distant and not transparent to interpretation. From this perspective, Sahagún's work is just as remote from us as the Aztec and Nahuatl primary sources. But the reasons why both primary and secondary documents are remote are in opposition to one another. Primary texts (those created by pre-Columbian people themselves) are directly uninterpretable because they need to be read with reference to the material realities of ultimate significance (i.e., Tlalocan, in this case). These texts, and we could include archaeological evidence here, are interpretively remote because a scholarly rendering of their meaning necessarily eliminates those performative and material conditions that had rendered them intelligible. Instead, they are read through a disjunctive colonial lens. Secondary sources, however, are remote because they seemingly present the pre-Columbian world as transparent to the reader, without the need to traverse the material disjunction that is characterized by the shift from Tlalocan to colonial worlds.

The interpretive gridlock of textual exegesis gives way to an appeal for an interpretive third term, which has an ongoing material substance and which can arbitrate between indigenous and colonial contexts. That third term is *landscape,* or Tlalocan. The religious implications of both an indigenous and colonial occupation of Tlalocan are clarified, because Tlalocan requires the ongoing assessment of the material and substantive qualities of existence. To some degree this is made possible by way of a phenomenological perspective in the history of religion.

It seems clear that creativity initiated and sustained Sahagún's work. Likewise, it is a similar creativity that promotes Mesoamerican scholarship.[19] But there is a dire necessity to take stock of the consequences of ones creative impulses, particularly when the work involves a sustained conversation about the Other. I will examine the methodological implications of this issue in the final chapter. With reference to Sahaguntine and Mesoamerican studies, however, the issue is: What will appropriately anchor a creative hermeneutics of occupation? While acknowledging the ongoing creativity of interpretation, in all its attempts, what aspect of this process could interject self-consciousness?

A beginning would be in acknowledging the significance of the material dimensions of one's interpretive location in such a way as to have that serve as an arena for cultural contact. For the Aztecs, it was the material necessity of the Tlaloc cult that focused the creative energies involved in the process of articulating and forming their cosmovision. While the creative energies of Sahagún's project were also an articulation of a European cosmovision, which resulted in cultural formation (some might argue for a uniquely Mexican identity),[20] the difficulty remains in finding the arena for interaction. To put the problem forth in terms of the Tlaloc cult: What is the place of Sahagún? Where does he belong? This becomes the critical question when considering that he is absent from his work, as discussed above. With his involvement absent from the text, his stated aims for creating the *Florentine* (to uproot and exterminate Aztec religion) determine the ways in which the reader of his work interprets Aztec traditions. The utopian (no)place of Sahagún and his book is ubiquitous. Moreover, the tension between his simultaneous absence and omnipresence has required that Mesoamerican scholars must seek to discover his "true" identity apart from his interpretive activity.

Thus the difficulty of interpreting the *Florentine* is due, in large measure, to Sahagún's inhabiting an abstract space: space without material points of orientation. Writing was his mode of interaction with the Aztecs and Tlalocan. The *Florentine*, in his Franciscan tradition, was his means of divining the essential meanings of the world. The materiality of life in this world had to be rendered transparent (which, as for Bacon, implied a violent disruption) through his ethnographic work in order to to imagine the full promise of a utopian (i.e., placeless) vision actualized through conquest. Likewise, a plurality of religious practices had to be erased and purified. Writing was the appropriate medium for this project and was the basis of a colonial occupation of the New World. It enabled Europeans to meaningfully inhabit any place as abstract space. For Eliade, it allowed Europeans to occupy "unfounded," insignificant space. The various meanings of landscape were overdetermined by the text. As a colonial inhabitant of New Spain, Sahagún's (no)place obfuscates Aztec realities. With reference to the *Florentine*, the colonial occupation of Tlalocan stands in stark contrast to the indigenous one. Through this process of indigenization, accounting for the material conditions of his own life and thought, Sahagún's work thus serves as a vehicle for promoting understanding between these worlds.

Conquest, therefore, is not an impediment to understanding the Aztecs but rather constitutes the basis for interpreting all pre-Columbian realities. Focusing on the disjunction between Aztec and European modes of occupying Tlalocan is an interpretive strategy for negotiating the distance between these worldviews. The disruption to the Aztecs through conquest was the condition that resulted in the creation of the textual sources in Mesoamerican studies. Studies of the Native people of the sixteenth century are not objective documents that give contemporary scholars an unhindered view of pre-Columbian worlds. An obvious point of critical importance regards the reliability or authority of books like the *Florentine*. But how are contemporary scholars to judge their reliability? What criteria can be utilized to make these judgments? These questions become more problematic when considering that textual production put in context (i.e., the beginning of ethnography in the Americas) is also a point of origin for contemporary understandings of scholarly work. Consideration of a hermeneutics of occupation in which texts like the *Florentine* play a significant role, but not in determining all the angles of interpretability, orients the scholar in such a way as to adjudicate the hermeneutical gap self-consciously.

An examination of Sahagún's location in the New World, with reference to the Aztecs, is an examination of the limits of his ability to adequately represent them in writing. As with other ethnographies, the *Florentine Codex* does not offer us the unobstructed, unhindered, and transparent view of Aztec religious life that was previously assumed. Sahagún's intentions to destroy Aztec ceremonial practices, which also justified his (and European) occupation of the New World, can be seen as just one of several limitations on his, and therefore our, understanding of the Aztecs.

Knowing Sahagún had a limited location, however, does not mean that he was not engaged in an important interpretive activity that has consequences today for our understanding the Aztecs. An acknowledgment of Sahagún's creativity in reformatting the pre-Columbian Aztec performative world into the world of books also suggests that the friar had some part in their contemporary creation. Using Charles Long's typology, Sahagún actively *signified* the meaning of Aztec culture, and was thus involved in their second creation.[21] For Long, the first creation of a culture is where a meaningful orientation to the world is worked-out by a given community for itself. This, by virtue of its intimate connection to the material world, kin, language, etc., is unavailable to anyone outside that context (e.g., that world into which one is born). Particularly during the colonial era, a second creative process came more aggressively into play. In the New World ethos, as the Others' first creation was being erased, they were being re-created in their second creation by being signified. Writing played an important role in this movement from first to second creations.

When relating the process of signification to Sahagún's work, however, one needs to consider the kind of place he hoped to engender. The New World of colonial Mexico had no intention of extending or developing a first creation. As O'Gorman indicated, the Americas were primarily an invention rather than a discovery.[22] The second creation of the Aztecs, however, was formed in a textual utopian world, a disoriented (no)place, that by its nature, could not directly involve the reader in the performative modes of occupying land that were Aztec.

This study uses Sahagún as one of its primary sources for understanding Aztec rituals and therefore is also involved in the Aztecs' second creation. Some have seen this writing about the empirical other (i.e., ethnography) as part of a hegemonic process of colonialism that, like the military conquest of the Americas, eclipses Native American cultural traditions. But, if like the sacred, the Aztecs are unavailable in their first creation, then an important first step in a self-conscious, self-critical interpretation would be the acknowledgment that we are primarily involved in a secondary creative process. Writers such as the present author need to find some way to be responsible to their creations—or, to use Smith's language, to be rigorously self-conscious about their creative impulses.[23]

Part of the strategy in this work has been to make an appeal to landscape as the third term that can stand to mediate between various understandings. The Aztecs, Sahagún, and the contemporary scholar need to be able to ground cultural contact around some *thing*. It is of little use to assume that the scholar can answer questions about others by citing various opaque sources. For my purposes, land has likewise served as the touchstone. As difficult and overdetermined as land may be on one side, and as religiously obscure on the other, an Aztec meaning of land (Tlalocan) serves as the Other('s) place to orient our secondary creative activities.

Sahagún and the contemporary Mesoamericanist are bound together in the common task of writing. This performative relationship
indicates that placelessness is the central conundrum of scholarly
interpretations. As during the colonial period, writing articulates a
disorientation to meaningfully occupying the Americas. If interpretations refer only to writers and their books, then no significant pressure can be exerted on the worldview dominated by the book. The
result of these considerations shifts the focus of an investigation of
Aztec religion away from the fiction of revealing their world as *they*
understood it to one of creating an interpretation of their world in
such a way as to heighten a contemporary *self*-consciousness about *our*
world. The task of writing about the Aztec is thus reconceived as a
creative approximation of a radically other way of inhabiting the world.
The Aztecs then speak to, and critique, specific cultural assumptions,
such as the meaning of land. Questions regarding the choice and assemblage of data are responsive to an author's cultural constitution.
Questions such as, what is it that needs to be known? or, how do the
Aztec ceremonies reveal another modality of being human? are not
only personal fascinations but reflections of the parallel ways in which
distinct cultural groups have inhabited the Americas. In the final chapter, I turn to the consequences of my "approximate" understanding and
rendering of the Aztec Tlaloc cult. These consequences seem to me to be
significant and profound not only in terms of Mesoamerican scholarship, but also for contemporary understandings of landscape that, as
demonstrated above, are hermeneutically associated with colonial culture.

NOTES

1. David E. Stannard, *American Holocaust: The Conquest of the New World* (New York:
Oxford University Press, 1992).

2. Alfred W. Crosby, *Ecological Imperialism, The Biological Expansion of Europe, 900–1900*
(Cambridge: Cambridge University Press, 1986). Europeans sometimes consciously utilized disease as a way to subdue Native people of the Americas and gain access to
their lands and resources. The creation of these diseases, which also had devastating effects on Old World populations, seem to have originated out of a cultural
understandings of the "proper" human relationship to plants, animals, water, etc.

Although not directly addressed by Crosby, a more thorough examination of the *cultural* roots of disease would be very interesting.

3. Theodor de Bry drew heavily on the stories of Bartolomé de las Casas and others to create his fanciful images of the New World. See his *Discovery of the New World (1594–95)*, engravings, text by Gerolamo Benzoni (Amsterdam: van Hoeve, 1979), and *Conquistadors, Aztecs and Incas (1596)*, engravings (Amsterdam: van Hoeve, 1980); and *Discovering the New World: Based on the Works of Theodore de Bry*, edited by Michael Alexander (New York: Harper & Row, 1976). De Bry was Dutch but was forced to flee his country to Frankfort in 1570 after his family fortune was confiscated by Spanish interests. His work then promoted a sense of anti-Catholic feeling that was supplied partly by las Casas and his *The Devastation of the Indies* (translated by Herma Briffault [Baltimore: The Johns Hopkins University Press, 1992]). See Bernadette Bucher, *Icon and Conquest: A Structural Analysis of the Illustrations of de Bry's Great Voyages*, translated from the French by Basia Miller Gulati (Chicago: University of Chicago Press, 1981), and Fredi Chiappelli, ed., *First Images of America: The Impact of the New World on the Old*, vols. I and II (Berkeley: University of California Press, 1976).

4. The variable status of indigenous people of Mexico and the United States/Canada is an important but neglected subject of study. There are very large differences between Mexican and U.S. involvements in a Native past, which, in turn, have consequences for Native Americans who currently reside in those countries. Acknowledging the differences will have to be enough for now, but I maintain that in their frequent contacts with Europeans (and European Americans) the outcome for Native Americas has consistently been loss of life and land.

5. Although this title is a controversial one, it has been currently argued that it appropriately situates Sahagún in the ethnographic tradition. See Klor de Alva, "Sahagún and the Birth of Modern Ethnography: Representing, Confessing, and Inscribing the Native Other," in *The Work of Bernardino de Sahagún: Pioneer Ethnographer of Sixteenth-Century Aztec Mexico*, edited by J. Jorge Klor de Alva, Henry B. Nicholson, and Eloise Quiñones Keber (Austin: University of Texas Press, 1988), pp. 31–52.

6. Prologues for all twelve books of the *Florentine* are published in the Dibble and Anderson translation of Fray Bernardino de Sahagún, *Florentine Codex: General History of the Things of New Spain*, 13 parts, edited and translated by Arthur J. O. Anderson and Charles E. Dibble, Monographs of the School of American Research, no. 14 (Salt Lake City: University of Utah Press, 1951–1982), "Introductory Volume."

7. Fray Bernardino de Sahagún, *El Códice Florentino de Sahagún*, 3 vols. (Mexico City: Secretaría de Gobernación, 1979).

8. Arthur J. O. Anderson, "Sahagún and His Times," in *Sixteenth Century Mexico: The Work of Sahagún*, edited by Munro S. Edmonson, School of American Research (Albuquerque: University of New Mexico Press, 1974), pp. 17–25. Also see the "Introductory Volume" of the *Florentine* by Dibble and Anderson, in Sahagún, *Florentine Codex*.

9. I am using the term "dialogical" following Paul Ricoeur's *Interpretation Theory: Discourse and the Surplus of Meaning* (Fort Worth: Texas Christian University Press, 1976) and David Tracy's *Dialogue with the Other: The Inter-Religious Dialogue*, Louvain Theological and Pastoral Monographs (Louvain and Grand Rapids, MI: Peeters

Press and William B. Eerdmans Publishing Co., 1990). Louise M. Burkhart, in *The Slippery Earth: Nahua Christian Moral Dialogue in Sixteenth Century Mexico* (Tucson: University of Arizona Press, 1989), seems to align her notion of dialogue along the lines of my use of "seepage." I make this point to clarify a distinction between theological and linguistic conceptions of the term "dialogical."

10. To my mind, the use of "dialogue" by theologians such as Tracy and Ricoeur is unfortunate. While their intention is to create a living context within which to center an engagement with sacred texts, the consequence is that conversation is determined by a written formulation of the world. For example, it would skew the nature of the Tlaloc cult as a hermeneutic of practice to describe it as "dialogical." Assigning it this designation could set the limits of activity too closely around a particular species of intellectual activity.

11. Fray Diego Durán, *Book of the Gods and Rites and the Ancient Calendar*, edited and translated by Fernando Horcasitas and Doris Heyden (Norman: University of Oklahoma Press, 1971), pp. 412–414, 430–433, 441–443, and 461–462.

12. The story of ideological clashes between rival orders in sixteenth-century Mexico, principally including the Franciscans, Augustinians, and Dominicans, is a fascinating aspect of what lay behind the generation of various types of colonial documents. Interactions with Native groups can be seen as also participating in a larger discourse between monastic orders. In terms of the valley region, however, the Franciscans seem to have held control. Louise M. Burkhart, *The Slippery Earth*, p. 17.

13. According to Arthur J. O. Anderson, "Sahagún and His Times," p. 20, strategies of winning souls, which had been effective in the Old World through an appropriation of Native religious sites, names, and ritual days, did not fit with the Franciscan social and political ideals in the New World. Their stance in defense of Indians pitted them against imperial Spanish policy.

14. He is referring to his work in Fray Bernardino de Sahagún's *Historia de las Indias de Nueva España*, 2 vols., edited by Angel María Garibay (Mexico City: Editorial Porrúa, 1967), vol. 2, p. 256. This passage was cited and translated by Alfredo López Austin, "The Research Method of Fray Bernardino de Sahagún: The Questionnaires," in *Sixteenth-Century Mexico: The Work of Sahagún*, edited by Munro S. Edmonson, School of American Research (Albuquerque: University of New Mexico Press, 1974), p. 122.

15. See Long's analysis of resistance to this tendency to render the Other as transparent with opaque theologies of color in "Freedom, Otherness, and Religion: Theologies Opaque," in Charles H. Long, *Significations: Signs, Symbols, and Images in the Interpretation of Religion* (Philadelphia: Fortress Press, 1986), pp. 185–199. In particular, see his discussion and quotation of Vine Deloria Jr., on p. 192:

> Our foremost plight is our transparency. People can just tell by looking at us what we want, what should be done to help us, how we feel, and what a "real" Indian is really like. Indian life, as it relates to the real world, is a continuous attempt not to disappoint people who know us.

From Vine Deloria Jr., *Custer Died for Your Sins* (New York: Avon Books, 1970), p. 1.

16. It is still a mystery as to exactly why Sahagún decided to highlight the things he did in the *Florentine*. For example, more emphasis on myths of creation (such as found in the *Leyenda de los soles*) would have furthered his missionary program, but are not included. It could be that it has been the unsatisfactory status, from the viewpoint of a curious and engaged reader, of an absent author and transparent object that propels Sahagúntine and Mesoamerican studies.

17. This is tied to his understanding of what he calls "absentee colonialism." Johannes Fabian, *Time and the Other: How Anthropology Makes Its Object* (New York: Columbia University Press, 1983), p. 69.

18. Davíd Carrasco, *Quetzalcoatl and the Irony of Empire: Myths and Prophecies in the Aztec Tradition* (Chicago: University of Chicago Press, 1982), pp. 11–12. Carrasco is drawing on Paul Wheatley's use of the phrase. Paul Wheatley, "City as Symbol," inaugural lecture delivered at the University College, London, on 10 November 1967, unpublished manuscript.

19. This is essentially Geertz's argument in Clifford Geertz, *Works and Lives: The Anthropologist as Author* (Stanford, CA: Stanford University Press, 1988). His work has been most powerfully dramatized by Clendinnen's approach to Aztec material (Inga Clendinnen, *Aztecs, an Interpretation* [Cambridge: Cambridge University Press, 1991]).

20. Edmundo O'Gorman, *The Invention of America: An Inquiry into the Historical Nature of the New World and the Meaning of Its History* (Bloomington: Indiana University Press, 1961).

21. Long, *Significations: Signs, Symbols, and Images,* "Introduction."

22. O'Gorman, *The Invention of America.*

23. As J. Z. Smith has said, "[T]he student of religion, and most particularly the historian of religion, must be relentlessly self-conscious. Indeed, this self-consciousness constitutes his primary expertise, his foremost object of study." Jonathan Z. Smith, *Imagining Religion: From Babylon to Jonestown* (Chicago: University of Chicago Press, 1982), p. xi.

7 Violence, Sacrifice, and Utopia

In this study, religion has been partially defined as a process of reflecting on one's interpretive location and how that process has been largely connected with a legacy of ways in which material life has been meaningfully construed. While there are wide discontinuities between colonial (the legacy of our contemporary world) and indigenous modes of occupying land, both constitute an authentic basis for religious reflection.

Another aspect of this study has been that the work of the history of religion scholar is intrinsically comparative. An analysis of the meaning of other cultural expressions (for Aztec and colonial Spanish alike) is simultaneously a self-conscious interrogation of one's own understandings. To claim knowledge of another religion, therefore, requires that their worlds be interjected into the dynamics of the interpreter's cultural location. The comparative work of the history of religion is essentially to find meaning in another religious context that necessarily pressures the scholar's own worldviews.

In this chapter, we will explore the consequences of the foregoing discussion by self-consciously moving toward the implications of a hermeneutics of occupation. While one could take a confessional stance (i.e., what Tlalocan means to me), I prefer to self-consciously adjudicate a cultural location upon which an Aztec hermeneutic of occupation can act as a critique. The very act of locating one's interpretive labors in our contemporary context is a critical exercise. As discussed in previous chapters, the scholarly activity (i.e., writing) has an intrinsic utopian, or placeless, emphasis. The activity of writing is comprised of a fictive organization of life as essentially dislocated, omniscient, etc. Thus scholarly labors are generally inattentive to their own interpretive location.

As with Sahagún, writing about others is a violent activity of reduction and assimilation and one in which this work is also necessarily involved. Confining the various meanings of the Valley of Mexico to a text, as will be discussed, is a violent erasure of an ongoing performative interplay of beings. For this violence to have meaning, however, this final chapter will attempt to bring the consequences of understanding Tlalocan into our contemporary world. To do this we must locate the violent character of interpretive activity by using the case of sixteenth-century Mexico.

THE VIOLENCE OF UTOPIA

Since their appearance in the European imagination, the Aztecs have been synonymous with human sacrifice and cannibalism. The emphasis on sacrifice as the center of their religious practices has been deeply troubling to many people and, since the sixteenth century, this brutality has been used to justify colonial occupation of the New World. Yet, while professing a religion of love, the Spanish, as well as other European people, have been much more aggressively violent than the Aztecs. Even today, however, European violence against other people is generally regarded as being less troubling, or more explainable, than that of the Aztecs.

To initiate an exploration of the distinctive Aztec and Spanish practices of human violence, I will invoke Todorov's analysis of the movement from pre-Columbian to Spanish colonialism as being one from sacrificial to massacre cultures.[1] The meaning of human life, in the sacrificial culture of the Aztecs, was determined by its being expended in the rejuvenation of the cosmos. As we have seen, the

7.1. Images of Spanish conquistadores killing children, redrawn from de Bry (1980).

consumption of life in ritual sacrifice was an elaboration of the processes of eating and feeding. The location of one's appearance in a reciprocal cosmos determined the character of one's involvement within a consumptive cycle of things and beings. At any one moment, everyone was either eating or being eaten and this accounted for much of the ritual activity to Tlaloc. Todorov, however, was puzzled by the Aztecs' enthusiastic embrace of sacrificial violence. Our current sensibilities regarding the sanctity of human life, in large measure, push the Aztec understandings of the necessity of violence in an eating landscape as far away as possible from acceptable cultural expressions. To some degree, a popular interpretation of the Otherness of Aztec religious practices is due to the centrality of human sacrifice.

But Todorov is equally puzzled by the relish with which some Spanish conquistadors destroyed indigenous people in Mexico. It is in his attempts to understand colonial violence that he makes his most important contribution to Mesoamerican studies. For example, as horrific as the Aztec sacrifice of children appears to contemporary understandings, their "debt payments" seemed to be made with compassion and as a way of giving back life to the land. For Europeans, the extermination of Native children was even more brutal. De Bry's images, taken from Bartolomé de las Casas's *Devastation of the Indies*, retells the story of how Spanish conquistadors would tear open the bodies of childbearing women and destroy their babies. They would also slam small children against walls and sometimes throw them to their war dogs. What is most disturbing, however, is that this was done by the Spanish with a cool detachment.

Although taken from the western United States, an incident during the Sand Creek massacre in 1864, which was led by the reverend Colonel John Chivington, also highlights the contempt with which Native American children were held by Europeans. As cavalrymen nearly exterminated this Cheyenne village, a boy was spotted who was trying to flee.

> There was one little child, probably three years old, just big enough to walk through the sand. The Indians had gone ahead, and this little child was behind following after them. The little fellow was

perfectly naked, traveling on the sand. I saw one man get off his horse, at a distance of about seventy-five yards, and draw up his rifle and fire—he missed the child. Another man came up and said, "Let me try the son of a bitch; I can hit him." He got down off his horse, kneeled down and fired at the little child, but he missed him. A third man came up and made a similar remark, and fired, and the little fellow dropped.[2]

Throughout modern American history the overwhelming desire has been to attain gold and riches. In itself, however, a profit motive can account for neither las Casa's "Black Legend" nor the Sand Creek Massacre. It was the impact of the symbolism of money that had a powerful effect on the imaginations of Europeans during the Age of Discovery. This new symbolism forged a unique reformulation of a human engagement with the world and fostered a new kind of human violence—massacre.

The undying quest for gold in the New World colonial period was only meaningful with reference to the Old World. Economically, one's prestige, gauged by fame and fortune, could never be bound to indigenous referents (i.e., to Tlalocan) but only to the degree of influence one could wield within the world-dominating institutions (i.e., Christendom, or the kingdoms of Europe). The economic organization of the New World was necessarily colonial and utopian, and could never have the locative character of the Aztecs'.

This still does not completely account for the enthusiasm with which whole cultures, often described as paradises, would be destroyed by the Spanish. For Todorov, the answer is that indigenous people simply did not have human status. Monetary systems determined the relative worth of the material world as it pertained to human consumption, and this included the worth of New World inhabitants. The movement, therefore, was toward the abstraction of human life from its material context, or in the dislocation of human existence from the relationships oriented around a gift economy. Likewise, indigenous people of the New World were seen as another species of objects (i.e., they were objectified) and were therefore an impediment to this emerging ideology of commodification. Like gold, the Native people of the Americas were seen as either another commodity or an obstruction to the promises of Christendom.

[237]

Their objectification as commodities had violent consequences for the Aztecs and other Native peoples as well. Although both the Spanish and Aztecs meaningfully occupied the New World around consumptive models, they were radically distinct from one another. For the Aztecs, human sacrifice was a necessary precondition for living in an eating landscape, and this epitomized their locative orientation to the Valley of Mexico. For the Spanish (and other European cultures), the massacre of humans was necessary to promote a utopian ideology, materially expressed through the acquisition of gold, which posited that the world was primarily for human beings in their quest to sanctify the world. Conquest was a necessary first step in imposing this utopian vision. The development of a culture of massacre is one of modernity's defining features.

Ethnography, or the scholarly objectification of empirical others, was generated by the conquest of the New World. For Sahagún and other missionaries in Mexico during his time, ethnography was utilized as an instrument of control. By codifying Aztec existence in writing, they could effectively render a pre-Columbian world transparent. These efforts went on in tandem with the more direct militaristic erasure of Native cultures. Writing about the Other became a means of fixing indigenous worlds, as if apart from a reader's world, to take on the appearance of a separate, or objective, reality. The fluid Aztec understanding of the ongoing interplay of beings in the valley (of floral, faunal, and divine origin), whose meaningful orientation in the world was embedded in their practice, became fixed in texts.

Although ethnography, to some extent, was Sahagún's innovation (at least in the sophistication of his methodology), it was also rooted in his tradition's quest for God. This was a God who was *otiosus*, remote or hidden from the material world. Through the media of art, writing, and music, one's being in the world could be transcended in order to clearly apprehend God's plan. While for Bacon mathematics could overcome the world of plural forms to reveal divine structure, ethnography for Sahagún could wipe away the diversity of indigenous expressions to reveal a primitive and pure Christianity. The world of Sahagún, unlike the Nahua with whom he interacted, had to be rendered as a transparent reality. To achieve a fundamental relationship with God required the elimination of the world's plurality. Variety had to be reduced, silenced, and erased for the apprehension of God and truth.

It has been said that like the Spanish the Aztecs were an imperial power who authorized their presence in the Valley of Mexico by appropriating Tlaloc (the dominate pan-Mesoamerican indigenous cult) into their central religious conceptions. Their strategy of occupying the valley was founded on a cultic practice that they adopted as their own. Tlaloc, the ancient deity of the Mesoamerican landscape, was placed on a parity with their tribal god, Huitzilopochtli, at the Templo Mayor. While the Aztec hermeneutic of occupation took the form of ritual devotion, however, Sahagún's authorization of the Spanish presence took the form of *authorship*. Writing about the Other became the means by which to effectively reformat a relationship with the landscape into terms more fitting with the realization of a New Jerusalem.

Violence was implied, though unstated, in the imposition of a utopian vision on the world. In the invention of America, utopia presented the possibility that humans could attain the full potential of their divine origins in a movement toward transcending the limits of material existence. Simultaneously, however, in order to create the New World it required the total annihilation of what was present in Tlalocan. Ironically, while missionaries lauded the status of human beings as preeminate in the world, as demonstrated in the Valladolid debate, this status was only materially achieved by the subjugation and massacre of Native cultures. Like the violence of objectifying Aztec religion in books, or speaking for them as if in their voice, the utopian vision of the New World objectified material life as if human beings were the only beings that mattered. A colonial hermeneutic of occupation, therefore, overdetermined the meaning of land, and the contour of a landscape of the New World was created previous to its physical discovery.

In pre-Columbian Mexico various types of matter, such as earth, water, plants, and animals, were sites for the discovery of a human orientation in the cosmos. Through rituals to Tlaloc, correspondences between material and bodily existences were brought to the forefront.

Human flesh and bone became earth and rock; blood and tears became water and rain; stages of plant life became hair; animals became coterminous with the total fact of human life. Tlaloc devotions were choreographed events designed to negotiate an understanding of a meaningful place in the valley with reference to a diversity of living beings. Contrary to Sahagún and a colonial hermeneutic, these practices were embedded in the phenomenon of the Otherness life's plurality. Like the Franciscan God, Tlaloc was a hidden reality. Unlike the Franciscan God, however, the way to interact with a Tlalocan landscape was by addressing the density of material existence, rather than by its erasure.

Orientation to the eating landscape of Tlalocan elicited a practice of ritual sacrifice to reciprocate for life taken. During the rituals examined above, a child sacrifice was understood as a payment of debt. A colonial hermeneutic of occupation, however, moved toward the perfection and sanctification of existence. It therefore severed the relationship of human beings from a living landscape (i.e., Tlalocan). Through rendering land as a transparent object, the possibilities of meaning gained from material life in the New World were rigorously cut off. Locative and utopian modes of occupying land, as viewed in relationship to violence, moved in opposite directions.

Many scholars have examined the place of writing, and its history, among other people and cultures as legitimizing a colonial project.[3] However, indigenous people have also taken writing into their own hands, thereby authorizing their own histories that, according to them, have been eliminated from view.[4] From the viewpoint of the performative dimensions of occupation, I would like to address some of the consequences of ethnographic labors for the modern world. If Sahagún's work has served as a benchmark for ethnography, as Klor de Alva and others have maintained, how is a colonial hermeneutic of occupying land currently manifesting itself in scholarship? What is the interpretive legacy of colonizing the Americas? Some of the contours of this big question may be indicated by referring to the Tlaloc cult in particular and Mesoamerican and Native American studies in general. In that the work of the history of religion is inherently comparative, this move will serve as a final one. When we ask a question of meaning for others, we are simultaneously subjecting those interpretations to our own interpretive legacy. Given the present interpretation of the Aztecs and colonial Spanish, which is necessarily a secondary imaginative creation, I would be remiss if I did not ask: What pressure does this exert on current modern understandings of the religious significance of land?

THE MATERIALITY OF RELIGION

This work stresses the need for a definition of religion as being organized by, and involved with, material life. This is not to reemphasize the more utopian, canonical understanding of matter—that is, one in which God is *otiosus* and revelation is finished—as with colonial ethnographers. Instead, I am suggesting a definition of religion as one open to the revelatory possibilities of material existence, which is expressed in a locative and performative interpretive position. Materialism, an ideology (or theology) of matter, is a species of the colonial project in that the meaning of the world is overdetermined. Materialism is then the means by which colonial occupation of the New World was made possible and lives today in the methodologies of cultural ecology and consumerism. The assumption of materialism is that the material world is for human consumption, which, religiously speaking, is proper for the perfection of a world in which a sacred reality is absent.

Conversely, *materiality* is a modest (i.e., not essentialist) phenomenological position in which religion is negotiated as a constant process of orientation within living processes. This is a phenomenology of the obvious and unlike a phenomenology of history of religion's past, which stressed religious mystical or spiritual dimensions. The methodological consequences of this definition are that an understanding of the world and the Aztecs alike have to be self-consciously appraised in regard to shared points of reference, or to a "referential practice." Land is one of those preeminent points of reference on which Aztec worldviews, and other indigenous understandings, can have some consequences for contemporary understandings.

The modern view of human life is intimately related with a colonial hermeneutic of occupation. As dramatized by Sahagún, indigenous performative orientations to land have to be stripped away, or reassembled, in such a way as to perfect and aggrandize humanity. In my estimation, and particularly in the United States, the phenomenal world is seen as more voraciously in the service of paradise—or utopia—than during colonial times. Likewise, Native populations are generally still seen as either being in the service of this movement toward a transcendent ideal or as being a detriment to its realization. The modern world has eliminated the colonial vision of the millennial kingdom. Instead, land and its "natural resources" are now seen as being completely in the service of human existence, but without any hopeful realization of uniting with God, as was the case for the colonists. Consumerism, like materialism, confidently *scapes* the land in ways that already assume its meaning. Likewise, these modern cultural attributes insist on a definition of religion as interior to the human imagination (i.e., religion as belief) in marked distinction from a locative and indigenous worldview.

For both the modern and colonial worlds, a book-centered hermeneutic predominates. As with ethnographies about the Aztecs, writing renders the plurality of worldly forms transparent and frozen in abstract space. Authorship is the vehicle for overdetermining the meaning of the world. It is the medium through which meaningful occupation of the New World was predicated, and it therefore implies a rigorous maintenance by contemporary scholarship. Although the times have changed, the medium by which the modern world conceives of its connection to the phenomenal world has not. Occupation of modern landscapes is authorized by abstract symbolic realities. Performative dimensions of meaningful life are reciprocated solely between human beings. The movement from indigenous to colonial strategies of occupation is accompanied by a shift in referents of activity from phenomenological to anthropocentric. It may well be that an objectification and abstraction of the world creates unnoticed, yet overwhelming, strains on contemporary human communities. For example, Eliade's "terror of history" may be also seen as a consequence of a colonial hermeneutic of occupying land.[5]

[242]

For phenomenologists, *epoché* is a methodological strategy by which personal judgments, or prejudices, are "bracketed" or constrained, in order that phenomena can work to create new understandings of existence.[6] *Epoché* is a sense of anticipation, or suspense, regarding one's interpretive enterprise.[7] For some, however, *epoché* is intrinsic to human existence. For van der Leeuw, *epoché* has distinct moments. The powerful conditions of existence make themselves known to human beings through *epoché*, and therefore the contingent status of one's interpretation on reciprocal relationships is acknowledged.[8] This approximates my use of Hanks's term "referential practice."

For Merleau-Ponty, however, the methodological and ontological dimensions of knowing the world constitute the basis of perception. His phenomenology is initiated as a study of essences that assigns to the world an a priori status before reflection begins. Although the material world is his object, it is superseded by problems and possibilities of perception. Essential to phenomenal existence is an acknowledgment of prejudice, or an acknowledgment of our *conditional confidence* in the interpretation of our relationships with the world.[9] Interpretive prejudice is our window into reality because it offers us a point of origin in which to act on our understandings through our bodies. Prejudice, through an ongoing and active commitment to engage the Otherness of the world, offers human beings, through various means, an ability to meaningfully inhabit reality.[10]

Aztec rituals to Tlaloc were a way of meaningfully occupying a living landscape. Tlaloc was, and still is among many Nahua people, a coherent bodily reality upon which life, including human life, was contingent. Rituals to Tlaloc were articulations of the Aztec relationship with a living landscape. Bodily existence was negotiated with reference to other bodily realities, and these distinct existences were ritually linked together. While sharing many features of the structuralist schematization, best represented by the work of Lévi-Strauss's studies of myth, this cosmos was seen as less fixed, as it would be in a text, due to its performative dimensions. While the structuralist tends to view symbolic systems along the lines of the grammarian's rules, a more appropriate view to performance as language would be in its ability to illuminate dimensions in the practice of life that is embedded in a meaningful landscape.[11]

The primary condition of prejudice that the phenomenologists at once embed in their methodology, and seek to conditionalize, ceases to be a concern when all interpretation is approached as a type of performance. If, for example, the landscape is a living being (Tlaloc, Pachamama, or Mother Earth) and one's life is organized around this understanding of material existence, *epoché* is the most appropriate and natural response to the world. *Epoché* loses its status as a "method" by which to set aside one's determination of life. Rather than its being an abstract methodology, interpretive restraint is the only process by which living beings or empirical others can interact. *The performance of epoché* is less a technique and more an attribute of processes by which one who stands in an intimate and necessary relationship to the Other feels the urgency to promote that connection. The overdetermined condition of modern material existence, which phenomenology seeks to overcome, is undone by defining religion as an orientation to the meaning of material existence.

Some Native American scholars have recently emphasized the need to focus on contact between European and indigenous people as a way of organizing American Indian studies.[12] For these scholars, the rubric of "contact" functions to clarify dimensions of interaction between cultural groups. The focus on contact shifts the object of study from written representations of indigenous people by authors outside these communities to the manifold strategies developed through conquest and that grew out of colonialism. Several interpretive issues come to light when reflecting on this shift. First, the object of investigation is no longer a human community but the forces that constitute a particular worldview as demonstrated through a series of events. With Native Americans no longer being the object of study, their agency to interact with and affect Europeans is restored. Second, this shift assumes that all interpretive viewpoints, including those scholars who may claim the omniscience of Sahagún, are embedded in a particular historical and cultural location. It is the claim of ecological determinists, for example, to know the meaning of a particular landscape without knowing their part in its constitution. This presupposition has its historical roots in the European intellectual tradition.[13] With contact as its object, Native American studies can explore the various impulses that led up to key events in the invention of "America." Third, there is no privileged location from which to know another group of people or their history. And fourth, there are always consequences for interpretative activity, but its privileged position can be neutralized by subjecting that position to the scrutiny of other voices. The critique of "contact" takes the form of self-conscious appraisal of those influences that went into the fabrication of an interpretation. By refocusing the object of ethnographic analysis away from human beings, which assumes that another life can be rendered transparent, to these issues of contact, a host of other dimensions can be brought to light.

The Tlaloc cult demonstrates that substantive dimensions of human existence are embedded in an ongoing contact with the phenomenal world. Indigenous practices are not sentimental or spiritual. In an indigenous context, meaningful orientation to a living landscape constantly acknowledges, by ritual means, contact between living beings. With the Aztec cult of Tlaloc as a guide, the contact between diverse human groups necessarily activates a modest phenomenology. Contact between people is oriented around material conditions of existence. Interpretive strategies are organized around an interaction with material life, the consequences of which are that they organize human interaction.

The often brutal contact between colonial and indigenous people is not only an ongoing facet of what constituted the Americas, but was also a defining feature of its creation. These relationships, however, were defined by alternative visions of the value of matter. The primary interpretive feature of contact is how a culture conceives of its relationship to the world. In turn, this hermeneutical practice extends to the contact with other living beings. Charles Long has been the most vocal historian of religions to articulate the need for religious studies to ground itself in the various human engagements with matter. For example, his work on cargo cults has emphasized a need to conceptualize an authentic way of dealing with the colonial past.[14] Significantly, some Native American scholars have likewise insisted on an evaluation of human history that is tied to economic realities (i.e., human relationships with matter through time) instead of political or ideological ones.[15] This methodology is born out of a need to develop a performative strategy with which to redefine evaluations of material relationships other than in economic terms and, also, to conform to a developing indigenous methodology in the academic study of religion. A performative view of contact with the world allows the scholar to enter into various types of relationships constitutive of their existence. This is achieved by orienting one's reflection with reference to the meanings of specific material and shared, aspects of human existence.

Today, as during the colonial age, contact with indigenous interpretations of material existence often takes place in court. Recent examples in North America have revolved around the reburial issues and land disputes. In a recent article on the moral and legal dimensions of the reburial issue, Deloria asks, "Are American Indians human beings?"[16] Although initiated with the Sepulveda/las Casas debate, the legal system has never been able to resolve this issue. According to Deloria, Indian ancestors are categorically nonhuman because they are legally defined as "natural resources" (and essentially the same as a utopian understanding of land) and therefore justified primarily as objects for scientific exploitation. Contact between indigenous and modern interpretations of material life are centered around fundamental relationships with bones. The question of whether Native Americans are human beings or not hinges on the question: What do bones mean? Are bones living beings that connect current human beings to their ancestral, and therefore cosmological, past? Or are they important only insofar as they can reveal histories of disease vectors for human beings? By their being categorically redefined as "natural resources," as opposed to "human remains," the legal system has revealed a structural attribute of modern life in which even human material remains (of those who have not been accounted for through written histories) are deemed useful only for ethnographic/ scientific purposes. The phenomenology of bones gives way to anthrocentrism and degrades all human beings to the status of resources.

The status of Indian lands in the United States is more directly tied to the subject at hand. As with the Aztecs, land is of primary importance to Native American identity and survival in North America. Deloria discusses four possible definitions of land as being sacred.[17] First, they are places where some significant historical event has occurred in the life of a community. Second, they are places that have a deeper significance in the sacred history of a people, such as the places of emergence. Third, they are places "of overwhelming Holiness where Higher Powers, on their own initiative, have revealed themselves to human beings." This expresses a range of modalities of sacred contact with humans rather than, strictly speaking, a topology. Ceremonies at these sites take the form of thanksgiving, according to Deloria, and have been seen in legal courts as being central to the life and identity of all people. He goes on to say, however, that these rituals involve a process of continuous revelation and provide the people with the necessary information to enable them to maintain a balance in their relationships with the earth and other forms of life. Because there are higher spiritual powers who are in communication with human beings, there has to be a fourth category of sacred lands: Human beings must always be ready to receive new revelations at new locations. If this possibility did not exist, all deities and spirits would be dead.[18]

Ritual practices in an inherently meaningful landscape always include the possibility of new orientations. A view of sacred spaces that determines them as artifacts of history is not an interpretation grounded in a hermeneutic of practice, but in an orientation toward texts. According to Deloria, due to the federal courts' insistence on defining places as sacred solely on the basis of their always having been central to a tribe implies that, for our federal policymakers, God is dead; an event of the inaccessible past. But *deus otiosus* has long been a feature of the utopian vision. Moreover, in the modern world the landscape as a container of sacred realities can only be a sentimental attachment for human groups historically connected with a place, and this is therefore not a vital one. In our modern context, there is only the first type of sacred place, as described by Deloria, with the others all being reduced in scope to legal definitions. Seen as an institution whose interpretive stance is based in a colonial hermeneutic of occupation, the law's role in adjudicating the practice of interacting with the landscape is clarified by grounding an analysis in the materiality of religion, rather than materialism. With contact negotiated as lived space, and taken seriously, this illuminates a variety of modes of material existence.

The modern vision of place has been illustrated by approximating Sahagún's rendering of Aztec realities. Both prioritize a value of a landscape in human terms. In this sense, the interpretive legacy since Sahagún is not Spanish but European. Because there are myriad layers of labors with respect to the Aztecs from all sorts of European and European-American agendas, groups other than the Spanish have invested interpretive capital in Tlalocan. For Sahagún, the resources of the valley consisted primarily in their possible transformation into a New Jerusalem through the converting efforts of the friars. Likewise, in the modern worldview a landscape is judged, like Indian bones, on the basis of its value as a "natural resource" for human "consumption." The Otherness of land is erased in exchange for an end that has already been predetermined. The overdetermined position of a colonial hermeneutic of occupation can be uncovered by adopting a performance-centered approach within the rubric of contact. Performance, in this sense, is a strategy of articulating a human orientation with reference to other living material realities. This approach is one that engages all parties living and dead, human and nonhuman, in a living relationship. A hermeneutic focused on performance realigns a scholarly relationship with the object of study in such a way as to account for the interpretive consequences of the work. This becomes particularly critical for those of us who write about those who do not write themselves. The violence of scholarly reduction and assimilation of other worlds is undone, to some degree, with the rigorous application of a modest phenomenology used to critically examine the features of the creation of cultural understandings with which one is always involved.

An appropriate hermeneutic for examining the significance of the Aztec Tlaloc cult cannot be satisfied purely with a reappraisal of ethnohistorical texts. The irony of the sources, which is built into their production and existence, is that a creative engagement with the rituals they describe is debilitated. Seriously engaging the referent of a Mesoamerican fertility cult involves that one reflect on the material influences that promote life. A more successful tact is a self-conscious engagement with matter combined with a close reading of these sources. This allows one to subject assumed understandings of life with reference both to Native American interpretations of a landscape and to one's life as it is being lived, and thus to risk bringing the contemporary world into contact with Tlalocan.

NOTES

1. Tzvetan Todorov, *The Conquest of America*, translated by Richard Howard (New York: Harper Torchbooks, 1984), pp. 143–145.

2. From the testimony of Major Scott J. Anthony, First Colorado Cavalry, before the United States Congress, House of Representatives: "Massacre of Cheyenne Indians," in *Report on the Conduct of the War* (38th Congress, Second Session, 1865), p. 27. Cited in David E. Stannard, *American Holocaust: The Conquest of the New World* (New York: Oxford University Press, 1992), p. xi, n. 6.

3. For example see Johannes Fabian, *Time and the Other: How Anthropology Makes Its Object* (New York: Columbia University Press, 1983); Michel de Certeau, *Heterologies: Discourse on the Other*, translated by Brian Massumi, Theory and History of Literature series, vol. 17 (Minneapolis: University of Minnesota Press, 1986); Stephen J. Gould, *The Mismeasure of Man* (New York: W.W. Norton & Co., 1981); Jean and John Comaroff, *Of Revelation and Revolution: Christianity, Colonialism, and Consciousness in South Africa*, vol. 1 (Chicago: University of Chicago Press, 1990); and James Clifford and George E. Marcus, eds., *Writing Culture: The Poetics and Politics of Ethnography* (Berkeley: University of California Press, 1986).

4. For example, see *Traditional Teachings* (Cornwall Island, Ontario: North American Indian Travelling College, 1984). This book is a compilation of teachings as told by Iroquois elders in the Seneca and Mohawk communities in order to correct misleading and skewed information recorded by outside ethnographers. For a Haudenosaunee, or Iroquois, example of what I am calling a hermeneutic of occupation, see *Thanksgiving Address, Greetings to the Natural World; Ohén:ton Karihwatéhkwen, Words Before All Else*, Six Nations Indian Museum and The Tracking Project, 1993. Also see Gonzalo Castillo-Cárdenas, *Liberation Theology from Below: The Life and Thought of Manuel Quintín Lame* (Maryknoll, NY: Orbis Books, 1987). Castillo-Cárdenas interprets the life and struggles of Manuel Quintín Lame, a Páez Indian of Colombia whose writings served as a way of highlighting an indigenous history within the context of white-Native relations. For a more in-depth analysis of the consequences of indigenous histories as told by Manuel Quintín Lame and others, see Joanne Rappaport, *The Politics of Memory: Native Historical Interpretation in the Colombian Andes* (Cambridge: Cambridge University Press, 1990).

5. Mircea Eliade, *Myth of the Eternal Return, or, Cosmos and History*, translated by Willard R. Trask (Princeton, NJ: Bollingen Series, Princeton University Press, 1954), pp. 139–162.

6. Gerardus van der Leeuw, *Religion in Essence and Manifestation*, translated by J. E. Turner, edited by Hans H. Penner (Princeton, NJ: Princeton University Press, 1986), pp. 674–675.

7. "The term *epoché* is a technical expression employed in current phenomenology by Husserl and other philosophers. It implies that no judgment is expressed concerning the objective world, which is thus placed 'between brackets,' as it were. All phenomena, therefore, are considered solely as they are presented to the mind, without any further aspects such as their real existence, or their value, being taken into account; in this way the observer restricts himself to pure description systematically pursued, *himself adopting the attitude of complete intellectual suspense*, or of abstention from all judgment, regarding these controversial topics." Ibid., p. 646, note 1 (emphasis added).

8. Ibid., p. 672.

9. M. Merleau-Ponty, *Phenomenology of Perception* (London: Routeledge and Kegan Paul, 1962), pp. 5–6.

10. Yuasa is, perhaps, more rigorous in investigating processes of methodological cultivation largely based in various Japanese Buddhist schools of praxis. He is more willing to explore other points of origin to initiate habitation of the world as he explores various technics employed in rituals than is Merleau-Ponty, who seems content to ground his inquiry in a post-Cartesian experience of dualism. Yuasa Yasuo, *The Body: Toward an Eastern Mind-Body Theory*, edited by Thomas P. Kasulis, translated by Nagatomo Shigenori and Thomas P. Kasulis (Albany: State University of New York Press, 1987).

11. For Sahlins, this is the poverty of structuralism that stems from the Saussurean tradition. In his view, pairs of oppositions lead to an empty "yin-yang structuralism, without a Book of Changes." In Marshall Sahlins, *Islands of History* (Chicago: University of Chicago Press, 1985), p. xvi. There is no clear referent for grounding the structural cosmology outside of the text in which these systems are recorded.

12. See Ward Churchill and M. Annette Jaimes, "American Indian Studies: A Positive Alternative," *The Bloomsbury Review* (September/October 1988): 27.

13. See Michel Foucault, *The Order of Things: An Archaeology of the Human Sciences* (New York: Random House, Inc., 1970).

14. See Charles Long, "Cargo Cults as Cultural Historical Phenomena," in *Significations: Signs, Symbols, and Images in the Interpretation of Religion* (Philadelphia: Fortress Press, 1986), pp. 114–127, which takes its inspiration from Kenelm Burridge, *Mambu: A Study of Melanesian Cargo Movements and Their Social and Ideological Background* (New York: Harper Torchbooks, 1960). Also see Charles H. Long, "New Space, New Time: Disjunctions and Context for New World Religions," *Criterion* 24, no. 1 (1985): 2–7.

15. As one writer has put it in *Basic Call to Consciousness*, edited by Akwesasne Notes (Mohawk Nation, Rooseveltown, NY: Akwesasne Notes, 1978), p. 49,

[250]

The Creation is a true, material phenomenon, and the Creation manifests itself to us through reality. The spiritual universe, then, is manifest to Man as the Creation, the Creation supports life. We believe that man is real, a part of the Creation, and that his duty is to support Life in conjunction with the other beings.

16. Native American remains are currently being housed in museums, universities, and other federal and state agencies in the United States. Several tribes are challenging the claims of these institutions to these artifacts in the courts. This debate, for Deloria and others, highlights colonial and indigenous distinctions regarding the importance of the dead. Vine Deloria Jr., "A Simple Question of Humanity, the Moral Dimensions of the Reburial Issue," *Native American Rights Fund Legal Review* 14, no. 4 (1989): 1.

17. Vine Deloria Jr., "Sacred Lands and Religious Freedom," *Native American Rights Fund Legal Review* 16, no. 2 (1991): 1–6.

18. Ibid., p. 5.

References

Anderson, Arthur J. O. "Sahagún in His Times." In *Sixteenth Century Mexico: The Work of Sahagún*. Edited by Munro S. Edmonson. Albuquerque: School of American Research and University of New Mexico Press, 1974, pp. 17–25.

———. "Sahagún's Informants on the Nature of Tlalocan." In *The Work of Bernardino de Sahagún: Pioneer Ethnographer of Sixteenth-Century Aztec Mexico*. Edited by J. Jorge Klor de Alva, Henry B. Nicholson, and Eloise Quiñones Keber. Austin: University of Texas Press, 1988, pp. 151–161.

———. "A Look into Tlalocan." In *Smoke and Mist: Mesoamerican Studies in Memory of Thelma D. Sullivan*. Edited by J. Kathryn Josserand and Karen Dakin. Oxford: B.A.R. International Series 402(i), 1988, pp. 151–160.

Andrews, J. Richard. *Introduction to Classical Nahuatl*. Textbook and workbook. Austin: University of Texas Press, 1975.

Aparicio, Luis Gonzalez. *Plano reconstructivo de la region de Tenochtitlan*. Mexico City: Instituto Nacional de Antropología e Historia, 1973.

Armillas, Pedro. "Gardens and Swamps." *Science* 174 (1976): 653–661.

Arnold, Dean E. *Ceramic Theory and Cultural Process*. Cambridge: Cambridge University Press, 1985.

Arnold, Philip P. "The Aztec Ceremonial Landscape in the Valley of Mexico: Implications of Examining Religion and Environment." M.A. thesis in archaeology submitted to the Institute of Latin American Studies, University of London, 5 September 1986.

———. "Eating Landscape: Human Sacrifice and Sustenance in Aztec Mexico." In *To Change Place: Aztec Ceremonial Landscapes*. Edited by Davíd Carrasco. Niwot: University Press of Colorado, 1991, pp. 219–232.

———. *The Matter of Understanding: Ritual Ecology and the Aztec Tlalocan Landscape*. Ph.D. dissertation, University of Chicago, 1992.

———. "Paper Ties to Land: Indigenous and Colonial Material Orientations to the Valley of Mexico." *History of Religions* 35, no. 1 (August 1995): 27–60.

———. "Parallel Consumptive Cosmologies." In *Mesoamerica's Classic Heritage: Teotihuacán to the Aztecs*. Edited by Davíd Carrasco, Lindsay Jones, and Scott Sessions. Mesoamerican Worlds Series. Niwot: University Press of Colorado, 1999.

Aveni, Anthony F. "Concepts of Positional Astronomy Employed in Ancient Mesoamerican Architecture." In *Native American Astronomy*. Edited by Anthony F. Aveni. Austin: University of Texas Press, 1977, pp. 3–19.
———. *Sky Watchers of Ancient Mexico*. Austin: University of Texas Press, 1980.
———. "The Role of Astronomical Orientation in the Delineation of World View: A Center and Periphery Model." In *Imagination of Matter: Religion and Ecology in Mesoamerican Tradition*. Edited by Davíd Carrasco. Oxford: B.A.R. International Series 515, 1989, pp. 85–102.
———. "Mapping the Ritual Landscape: Debt Payment to Tlaloc During the Month of Atlcahualo." In *To Change Place: Aztec Ceremonial Landscapes*. Edited by Davíd Carrasco. Niwot: University Press of Colorado, 1991, pp. 58–73.
———, ed. *The Sky in Mayan Literature*. New York: Oxford University Press, 1992.
Aveni, Anthony F., and Sharon Gibbs. "On the Orientation of Ceremonial Centers in Central Mexico." *American Antiquity* 41 (1976): 510–517.
Aveni, Anthony F., Horst Hartung, and B. Buckingham. "The Pecked Cross Symbol in Ancient Mesoamerica." *Science* 202 (1978): 267–279.
Aveni, Anthony F., and Horst Hartung. "New Observations of the Pecked Cross Petroglyph." *Lateinamericka Studien* 10 (1982): 25–41.
Aveni, Anthony F., Edward Calnek, and Horst Hartung. "Myth, Environment and the Orientation of the Templo Mayor of Tenochtitlan." *American Antiquity* 53 (1988): 287–309.
Aveni, Anthony F., and Gordon Brotherston, eds. *Calendars in Mesoamerica and Peru: Native American Computations of Time*. Oxford: B.A.R. International Series 174, 1983.
Baird, Ellen Taylor. "Sahagún's *Primeros Memoriales* and *Codex Florentino*: European Elements in the Illustrations." In *Smoke and Mist: Mesoamerican Studies in Memory of Thelma D. Sullivan*. Edited by J. Kathryn Josserand and Karen Dakin. Oxford: B.A.R. International Series 402(i), 1988, pp. 15–40.
———. "The Illusion of Space and the Perception of History in Sahagún's *Codex Florentino*." Paper presented at the 47th International Congress of Americanists, Tulane University, New Orleans, 11 July 1991.
———. *The Drawings of Sahagún's Memoriales: Structure and Style*. Norman: University of Oklahoma Press, 1993.
Bahktin, Mikhail. *Rabelais and His World*. Translated by Hélène Iswolsky. Bloomington: University of Indiana Press, 1984.
Barreiro, José. *The Indian Chronicles*. Houston: Arte Público Press, 1993.
Basic Call to Consciousness. Edited by Akwesasne Notes. Mohawk Nation, Rooseveltown, NY: Akwesasne Notes, 1978.
Basso, Keith H. *Wisdom Sits in Places: Landscape and Language Among the Western Apache*. Albuquerque: University of New Mexico Press, 1996.
Bastien, Joseph W. *Mountain of the Condor: Metaphor and Ritual in an Andean Ayllu*. Prospect Heights, IL: Waveland Press, Inc., 1978.

———. "Qollahuaya-Andean Body Concepts: A Topographical-Hydraulic Model of Physiology." *American Anthropology* 87 (1985): 595–611.

Bateson, Gregory. *Steps to an Ecology of Mind.* New York: Ballantine Books, 1972.

Baudot, Georges. *Utopia and History in Mexico: The First Chronicles of Mexican Civilization, 1520–1569.* Translated by Bernard R. Ortiz de Montellano and Telma Ortiz de Montellano. Niwot, CO: University Press of Colorado, 1995.

Bell, Catherine. "Discourse and Dichotomies: The Structure of Ritual Theory." *Religion* 17 (1987): 95–118.

———. *Ritual Theory Ritual Practice.* New York: Oxford University Press, 1992.

Bender, Barbara, ed. *Landscape: Politics and Perspectives.* Oxford: Berg Publishers, 1993.

Benzoni, Girolamo. *History of the New World.* Translated by Rear Admiral W. H. Smyth. London: The Hakluyt Society, vol. 21, 1857.

Blanton, Richard R. *Prehistoric Settlement Patterns of the Ixtapalapa Peninsula Region.* Occasional Papers in Anthropology, no. 6. University Park: Department of Anthropology, Pennsylvania State University, 1972.

Boone, Elizabeth, ed. *The Aztec Templo Mayor: A Symposium at Dumbarton Oaks, 8th and 9th October 1983.* Washington, DC: Dumbarton Oaks, 1987.

———. "Migration Histories as Ritual Performance." In *To Change Place: Aztec Ceremonial Landscapes.* Edited by Davíd Carrasco. Niwot: University Press of Colorado, 1991, pp. 121–151.

Boone, Elizabeth, and Walter Mignolo, eds. *Writing Without Words: Alternative Literacies in Mesoamerica and the Andes.* Durham, NC: Duke University Press, 1994.

Bourdieu, Pierre. *Outline of a Theory of Practice.* Translated by Richard Nice. Cambridge: Cambridge University Press, 1977.

Braudel, Fernand. *The Mediterranean and the Mediterranean World in the Age of Phillip II.* 2 vols. Translated by Siân Reynolds. London: Harper & Row, Publishers, 1972.

Bray, Warwick. "Landscape with Figures: Settlement Patterns, Locational Models, and Politics in Mesoamerica." In *Prehistoric Settlement Patterns: Essays in Honor of Gordon R. Wiley.* Edited by Evan L. Vogt and Robert M. Leventhal. Cambridge, MA: Harvard University Press, 1983, pp. 167–193.

———. *Everyday Life of the Aztecs.* New York: Dorset Press, 1987.

Briggs, Charles L. *Competence in Performance: The Creativity of Tradition in Mexicano Verbal Art.* Philadelphia: University of Pennsylvania Press, 1988.

Broda, Johanna. "Las fiestas Aztecas de los dioses de la lluvia: Una reconstruccíon según las fuentes del siglo XVI." *Revista Española de antropología Americana* 6 (1971): 245–327.

———. "El culto Mexica de los cerros y del agua." *Multidiscipline* 3, no. 7 (1982): 45–56.

———. "Astronomy, *Cosmovisión*, and Ideology in Pre-Hispanic Mesoamerica." In *Ethnoastronomy and Archaeoastronomy in the American Tropics.* Edited by

Anthony F. Aveni and Gary Urton. New York: *Annals of the New York Academy of Sciences* 385, 1982, pp. 81–110.

———. "Ciclos agrícolas en el culto: Una problema de la correlación del calendario Mexica." In *Calendars in Mesoamerica and Peru: Native American Computations of Time*. Edited by Anthony F. Aveni and Gordon Brotherston. Oxford: B.A.R. International Series 174, 1983, pp. 145–164.

———. "Templo Mayor as Ritual Space." In *The Great Temple of Tenochtitlan: Center and Periphery in the Aztec World*. Edited by Johanna Broda, Davíd Carrasco, and Eduardo Matos Moctezuma. Berkeley: University of California Press, 1987, pp. 61–123.

———. "Geography, Climate and the Observation of Nature in Pre-Hispanic Mesoamerica." In *The Imagination of Matter: Religion and Ecology in Mesoamerican Traditions*. Edited by Davíd Carrasco. Oxford: B.A.R. International Series 515, 1989, pp. 139–153.

———. "The Sacred Landscapes of Aztec Calendar Festivals: Myth, Nature, and Society." In *To Change Place: Aztec Ceremonial Landscapes*. Edited by Davíd Carrasco. Niwot: University Press of Colorado, 1991, pp. 74–120.

Brotherston, Gordon. *Image of the New World: The American Continent Portrayed in Native Texts*. London: Thames and Hudson, 1978.

Brown, Peter. *The Cult of Saints: Its Rise and Function in Latin Christianity*. Chicago: University of Chicago Press, 1981.

———. *The Body and Society: Men, Women, and Sexual Renunciation in Early Christianity*. New York: Columbia University Press, 1988.

Brundage, Burr C. *The Fifth Sun: Aztec Gods, Aztec World*. Austin: University of Texas Press, 1975.

Bucher, Bernadette. *Icon and Conquest: A Structural Analysis of the Illustrations of de Bry's Great Voyages*. Translated by Basia Miller Gulati. Chicago: University of Chicago Press, 1981.

Bucher O.F.M., Raymond. "Francis of Assisi." *The Encyclopedia of Religion*, vol. 5. Edited by Mircea Eliade. New York: Macmillan Publishing Co., 1986, p. 409.

Burkert, Walter. *Homo Necans: The Anthropology of Ancient Greek Sacrificial Ritual and Myth*. Translated by Peter Bing. Berkeley: University of California Press, 1983.

Burkhart, Louise M. "Doctrinal Aspects of Sahagún's *Colloquios*." In *The Work of Bernardino de Sahagún: Pioneer Ethnographer of Sixteenth-Century Aztec Mexico*. Edited by J. Jorge Klor de Alva, Henry B. Nicholson, and Eloise Quiñones Keber. Austin: University of Texas Press, 1988, pp. 65–82.

———. *The Slippery Earth: Nahua Christian Moral Dialogue in Sixteenth Century Mexico*. Tucson: University of Arizona Press, 1989.

———. "Aztecs in Limbo: The Harrowing of Hell in Nahua-Christian Literature." Paper presented at the 47th International Congress of Americanists. Tulane University, New Orleans, 11 July 1991.

Burridge, Kenelm. *Mambu: A Study of Melanesian Cargo Movements and Their Social and Ideological Background*. New York: Harper Torchbooks, 1960.

Cabrera Castro, Rubén, Saburo Sugiyama, and George Cowgill. "The Templo de Quetzalcoatl Project at Teotihuacan, a Preliminary Report." *Ancient Mesoamerica* 2 (1991): 77–92.

Calnek, Edward. "Settlement Pattern and Chinampa Agriculture at Tenochtitlan." *American Antiquity* 37, no. 1 (1972): 104–115.

———. "The Localization of the Sixteenth Century Map Called the Maguey Plan." *American Antiquity* 38, no. 2 (1973): 190–195.

———. "Organización de los sistemas de abastecimiento urban de alimentos: El caso de Tenochtitlan." In *Las ciudades de América Latina y sus áreas de influencia a través de la historia*. Edited by Jorge E. Hardoy and Richard P. Schaedel. Buenos Aires: Ediciones SIAP, 1975, pp. 41–60.

Campbell, R. Joe. *A Morphological Dictionary of Classical Nahuatl: A Morpheme Index to the Vocabulario en Lengua Mexicana y Castellana of Fray Alonso de Molina*. Madison, WI: The Hispanic Seminary of Medieval Studies, 1985.

Canby, Thomas. "The Anasazi: Riddles in the Ruins." *National Geographic* 162, no. 5 (1982): 562–592.

Caro Baroja, Julio. *The World of the Witches*. Translated by O.N.V. Glendinning. Chicago: University of Chicago Press. 1965.

Carrasco, Davíd. "Templo Mayor: The Aztec Vision of Place." *Religion* 11 (1981): 257–297.

———. *Quetzalcoatl and the Irony of Empire: Myths and Prophecies in the Aztec Tradition*. Chicago: University of Chicago Press, 1982.

———. "Myth, Cosmic Terror, and the Templo Mayor." In *The Great Temple of Tenochtitlan: Center and Periphery in the Aztec World*. Edited by Johanna Broda, Davíd Carrasco, and Eduardo Matos Moctezuma. Berkeley: University of California Press, 1987, pp. 124–62.

———. "Toward the Splendid City: The Study of Mesoamerican Religions." *Religious Studies Review* 14, no. 4 (1988): 289–302.

———, ed. *The Imagination of Matter: Religion and Ecology in Mesoamerican Traditions*. Oxford: B.A.R. International Series no. 515, 1989.

———. *Religions of Mesoamerica: Cosmovision and Ceremonial Centers*. San Francisco: Harper & Row, Publishers, 1990.

———, ed. *To Change Place: Aztec Ceremonial Landscapes*. Niwot: University Press of Colorado, 1991.

———. "Cosmic Jaws: We Eat the Gods and the Gods Eat Us." *Journal of the American Academy of Religion* LXIII, no. 3 (fall 1995): 429–463.

Carrasco, Davíd, Philip Arnold, Lawrence Desmond, and Rebecca Herr, eds. *Conversations with Anthony Aveni: Archaeoastronomy and the History of Religions*. Boulder, CO: Mesoamerican Archive and Research Project Working Papers, no. 1, 1985.

Carrasco, Davíd, Lindsay Jones, and Scott Sessions, eds. *Mesoamerica's Classic Heritage: Teotihuacán to the Aztecs*. Niwot: University Press of Colorado, 1999.

Castelló Yturbide, Teresa, ed. *Presencia de la comida prehispanica*. Mexico City: Fomento Cultural Banamex, A.C., 1987.

Castillo-Cárdenas, Gonzalo. *Liberation Theology from Below: The Life and Thought of Manuel Quintín Lame*. Maryknoll, NY: Orbis Books, 1987.

Cervantes, Fernando. *The Devil in the New World: The Impact of Diabolism in New Spain*. New Haven, CT: Yale University Press, 1994.

Chartier, Roger. *The Order of Books: Readers, Authors, and Libraries in Europe Between the Fourteenth and Eighteenth Centuries*. Translated by Lydia G. Cochrane. Stanford, CA: Stanford University Press, 1994.

Chaunu, Huguette, and Pierre Chaunu. *Seville et l'Atlantique de 1504 à 1650*. 8 vols.. Paris: A. Colin, 1955–1959.

Chiappelli, Fredi, ed. *First Images of America: The Impact of the New World on the Old*. 2 vols.. Berkeley: University of California Press, 1976.

Christian Jr., William A. *Apparitions in Late Medieval and Renaissance Spain*. Princeton, NJ: Princeton University Press, 1981.

———. *Local Religion in Sixteenth-Century Spain*. Princeton, NJ: Princeton University Press, 1981.

Churchill, Ward, and M. Annette Jaimes. "American Indian Studies: A Positive Alternative." *The Bloomsbury Review* (September/October 1988): 27.

Clendinnen, Inga. "The Cost of Courage in Aztec Society." *Past and Present* 107 (1985): 44–89.

———. *Aztecs, an Interpretation*. Cambridge: Cambridge University Press, 1991.

Clifford, James, and George E. Marcus, eds. *Writing Culture: The Poetics and Politics of Ethnography*. Berkeley: University of California Press, 1986.

Codex Fejérváry-Mayer, facsimile. Codices Selecti, vol. 26. Graz, Austria: Akademische Druck-und Verlagsanstalt, 1971.

Codex Magliabechiano, The Book of Life of the Ancient Mexicans, facsimile and commentary. 2 vols. Edited and commentary by Elizabeth Boone. Berkeley: University of California Press, 1983.

Códice Borgia, facsimile. Commentary by Eduard Seler. 3 vols. Mexico City: Fondo de Cultura Económica, 1963.

Códice Chimalpopoca: Anales de Cuauhtitlan y Leyenda de los Soles. Translated by Primo Feliciano Veázquez. Edited by Walter Lehmann. Mexico City: Imprenta Universitaria, 1945.

Códice Matritense de la Real Academia de la Historia, vol. 8. Edited by Francisco del Paso y Troncoso. Madrid: Fototipia de Hauser y Menet, 1907.

Códice Matritense del Real Palacio, vol. 7. Edited by Francisco del Paso y Troncoso. Madrid: Fototipia de Hauser y Menet, 1905.

Coe, Micheal D. "The Chinampas of Mexico." *Scientific American* 211, no. 1 (1964): 90–98.

Comaroff, Jean, and John Comaroff. *Of Revelation and Revolution: Christianity, Colonialism, and Consciousness in South Africa*, vol. 1. Chicago: University of Chicago Press, 1991.

Couliano, Ioan P. *Eros and Magic in the Renaissance*. Translated by Margaret Cook. Chicago: University of Chicago Press, 1987.

Covarrubias, Miguel. *Indian Art of Mexico and Central America*. New York: Knopf, 1957.

Crosby, Alfred W. *Ecological Imperialism: The Biological Expansion of Europe, 900–1900*. Cambridge: Cambridge University Press, 1986.

Daniel, E. Randolph. *The Franciscan Concept of Mission in the High Middle Ages.* Lexington: University Press of Kentucky, 1975.

Darch, J. P. "Drained Fields in the Americas: An Introduction." In *Drained Field Agriculture in Central and South America.* Edited by J. P. Darch. Oxford: B.A.R. International Series 189, 1983, pp. 1–10.

de Bry, Theodor. *Discovery of the New World; (1594–95).* Facsimile of engravings. Text by Gerolamo Benzoni. Amsterdam: van Hoeve, 1979.

——. *Conquistadors, Aztecs and Incas; (1596).* Facsimile of engravings. Amsterdam: van Hoeve, 1980.

——. *Discovering the New World: Based on the Works of Theodore de Bry.* Edited by Michael Alexander. New York: Harper & Row, 1976.

de Certeau, Michel. *The Practice of Everyday Life.* Translated by Steven Rendall. Berkeley: University of California Press, 1984.

——. *Heterologies: Discourse on the Other.* Translated by Brian Massumi. Theory and History of Literature, vol. 17. Minneapolis: University of Minnesota Press, 1986.

Deloria Jr., Vine. *Custer Died for Your Sins.* New York: Avon Books, 1970.

——. "A Simple Question of Humanity: The Moral Dimensions of the Reburial Issue." *Native American Rights Fund Legal Review* 14, no. 4 (1989): 1–12.

——. "Sacred Lands and Religious Freedom." *Native American Rights Fund Legal Review* 16, no. 2 (1991): 1–6.

——. *God Is Red: A Native View of Religion, a Classic Work Updated.* Second edition. Golden, CO: Fulcrum Publishing, 1994.

Denevan, William M. "Aboriginal Drained Field Cultivation." *Science* 169 (1970): 647–654.

——. "Hydraulic Agriculture in the American Tropics: Forms, Measures, and Recent Research." In *Maya Subsistence: Studies in the Memory of Dennis E. Puleston.* Edited by Kent V. Flannery. New York: Academic Press, 1982, pp. 181–203.

Detienne, Marcel, and Jean-Pierre Vernant, eds. *The Cuisine of Sacrifice Among the Greeks.* Translated by Paula Wissing. Chicago: University of Chicago Press, 1989.

Diaz del Castillo, Bernal. *The Discovery and Conquest of Mexico; 1517–1521.* Translated by A. P. Maudslay. New York: Farrar, Straus, and Cudahy, 1956.

D'Olwer, Luis Nicolau. *Fray Bernardino de Sahagún; 1499–1590.* Translated by Mauricio Mixco. Salt Lake City: University of Utah Press, 1987.

Doniger O'Flaherty, Wendy. *Other People's Myths: The Cave of Echoes.* New York: Macmillian Publishing Co., 1988.

Douglas, Mary. "Deciphering a Meal." *Daedalus* 101, no. 1 (1972): 61–81.

Durán, Fray Diego. *Book of the Gods and Rites and the Ancient Calendar.* Edited and translated by Fernando Horcasitas and Doris Heyden. Norman: University of Oklahoma Press, 1971.

Durkheim, Emile. *The Elementary Forms of the Religious Life.* Translated by Joseph W. Swain. New York: The Free Press, 1965.

References

Duverger, Christian. *L'Èsprit du jeu chez les Aztèques*. Paris: Mouton Èditeur, 1978.

———. *La flor letal: Economia del sacrificio Azteca*. Translated by Juan José Utrilla. Mexico City: Fondo de Cultura Económica, 1983.

Ebersole, Gary L. *Ritual Poetry and the Politics of Death in Early Japan*. Princeton, NJ: Princeton University Press, 1989.

Edgerton Jr., Samuel T. *The Renaissance Rediscovery of Linear Perspective*. New York: Basic Books, Inc., 1975.

Edmonson, Munro S. "Introduction." In *Sixteenth Century Mexico: The Work of Sahagún*. Edited by Munro S. Edmonson. Albuquerque: School of American Research and University of New Mexico Press, 1974, pp. 1–15.

Eliade, Mircea. *Myth of the Eternal Return, or, Cosmos and History*. Translated by Willard R. Trask. Princeton, NJ: Bollingen Series, Princeton University Press, 1954.

———. *Patterns in Comparative Religion*. Translated by Rosemary Sheed. New York: Meridian Books, 1958.

———. *The Forge and the Crucible*, 2nd edition. Translated by Stephen Corrin. Chicago: University of Chicago Press, 1978.

———. "*Homo Faber* and *Homo Religiosus*." In *The History of Religions: Retrospect and Prospect*. Edited by Joseph M. Kitagawa. New York: Macmillan Publishing Co., 1985, pp. 1–12.

Esser O.F.M., Kajetan. *Origins of the Franciscan Order*. Translated by Aedan Daly O.F.M. and Dr. Irina Lynch. Chicago: Franciscan Herald Press, 1970.

Evans-Pritchard, E. E. *The Nuer: A Description of the Modes of Livelihood and Political Institutions of a Nilotic People*. Oxford: Oxford University Press, 1940.

———. *Nuer Religion*. Oxford: Oxford University Press, 1956.

Fabian, Johannes. *Time and the Other: How Anthropology Makes Its Object*. New York: Columbia University Press, 1983.

Farrington, Ian S. "The Wet, the Dry and the Steep: Archaeological Imperatives and the Study of Agricultural Intensification." In *Prehistoric Intensive Agriculture in the Tropics*. Edited by Ian S. Farrington. Oxford: B.A.R. International Series 232, 1985, pp. 1–10.

Flannery, Kent V. "Archaeological Systems Theory and Early Mesoamerica." In *Anthropological Archaeology in the Americas*. Edited by Betty J. Meggers. Washington, DC: The Anthropological Society of Washington, 1968, pp. 67–87.

Fogleman, Ronald R. *Empiricism and Repetition: A Philosophical Examination of Alterity, Colonial Discourse, and Ethnography in the Study of Religion*. Ph.D. dissertation, Syracuse University, 1995.

Foucault, Michel. *The Order of Things: An Archaeology of the Human Sciences*. New York: Random House, Inc., 1970.

Frazer, Sir James George. *The Golden Bough: A Study in Magic and Religion*, vol. 1. Abridged edition. New York: Collier Books, 1950.

Freud, Sigmund. *Totem and Taboo: Resemblances Between the Psychic Lives of Savages and Neurotics*. New York: Vintage Books, 1946.

Furst, Jill Leslie McKeever. *The Natural History of the Soul in Ancient Mexico*.

New Haven, CT: Yale University Press, 1995.

Furst, Peter T. "Jaguar Baby or Toad Mother: A New Look at an Old Problem in Olmec Iconography." In *The Olmec and Their Neighbors: Essays in Memory of Matthew W. Stirling.* Edited by Elizabeth P. Benson. Washington, DC: Dumbarton Oaks, 1981, pp. 149–162.

———. "Human Biology and the Origin of the 260-Day Sacred Almanac: The Contribution of Leonhard Schultze Jena (1872–1955)." In *Symbol and Meaning Beyond the Closed Community: Essays in Mesoamerican Ideas.* Edited by Gary H. Gossen. Albany: State University of New York Press, 1986, pp. 69–76.

Gadamer, Hans-Georg. *Truth and Method,* 2nd edition. Translated and revised by Joel Weinsheimer and Donald G. Marshall. New York: Continuum, 1989.

Galinier, Jacques. *Pueblos de la Sierra Madre: Etnografía de la comunidad Otomí.* Mexico City: Instituto Nacional Indigenista, número 17, 1983.

Gampel, Benjamin R. *The Last Jews on Iberian Soil: Navarrese Jewry; 1479/1498.* Berkeley: University of California Press, 1989.

Garibay, Angel María. *Historia de la literatura Náhuatl.* 2 vols. Mexico City: Editorial Porrúa, 1953–54.

———. *Teogonía e historia de los Mexicanos: Tres opúsculos del siglo XVI.* Mexico City: Editorial Porrúa, 1965.

Geertz, Clifford. *Works and Lives: The Anthropologist as Author.* Stanford, CA: Stanford University Press, 1988.

Gibson, Charles. *The Aztecs Under Spanish Rule: A History of the Indians of the Valley of Mexico; 1519–1810.* Stanford, CA: Stanford University Press, 1964.

Gill, Sam D. *Native American Religions: An Introduction.* Belmont, CA: Wadsworth Publishing Co., 1982.

Gingerich, Willard. "Tlaloc, His Song." *Latin American Indian Literatures* 1 (1977): 79–88.

Ginzburg, Carlo. *The Cheeze and the Worms: The Cosmos of a Sixteenth-Century Miller.* Translated by John and Anne Tedeschi. New York: Peguin Books, 1982.

———. *The Night Battles: Witchcraft and Agrarian Cults in the Sixteenth and Seventeenth Centuries.* Translated by John and Anne Tedeschi. Baltimore: Johns Hopkins University Press, 1983.

Girard, René. *Violence and the Sacred.* Translated by Patrick Gregory. Baltimore: Johns Hopkins University Press, 1977.

Glaser, Lynn. *America on Paper: The First Hundred Years.* Philadelphia: Associated Antiquaries, 1989.

Goldman, Irving. *The Mouth of Heaven: An Introduction to Kwakiutl Religious Thought.* New York: John Wiley and Sons, 1975.

Gómez-Pompa, Arturo, Hector Luis Morales, Epifanio Jiménez Ávila, and Julio Jiménez Ávila. "Experiences in Traditional Hydraulic Agriculture." In *Maya Subsistence: Studies in Memory of Dennis E. Puleston.* Edited by Kent V. Flannery. New York: Academic Press, 1982, pp. 327–342.

Gonzalez Aparicio, Luis. *Plano reconstructivo de la region de Tenochtitlan.* Book and map. Mexico City: Instituto Nacional de Antropología e Historia, 1973.

González Torres, Yolotl. *El sacrificio humano entre los Mexicas*. Mexico City: Instituto Nacional de Antropología e Historia and Fondo de Cultura Económica, 1985.

Gossen, Gary H., ed. *Symbol and Meaning Beyond the Closed Community: Essays in Mesoamerican Ideas*. Studies on Culture and Society, vol. 1. Austin: University of Texas Press, 1986.

Gould, Stephen Jay. *The Mismeasure of Man*. New York: W.W. Norton & Co., 1981.

Grafton, Anthony. *New Worlds, Ancient Texts: The Power of Tradition and the Shock of Discovery*. Cambridge, MA, and London: Harvard University Press and The Belknap Press, 1992.

Graulich, Michel. *Quetzalcoatl y el espejismo de Tollan*. Antwerp: Instituut voor Amerikanistiek v.z.w., 1988.

Green, Deirdre. *Gold in the Crucible: Teresa of Avila and the Western Mystical Tradition*. Longmead, Shaftsbury, Dorset, England: Element Books Ltd, 1989.

Grodzins Gold, Ann. *Fruitful Journeys: The Ways of Rajasthani Pilgrims*. Berkeley: University of California Press, 1987.

Gruzinski, Serge. *The Conquest of Mexico: The Incorporation of Indian Societies into the Western World, 16th–18th Centuries*. Translated by Eileen Corrigan. Cambridge: Polity Press, 1993.

Gueusquin, Marie-France. "Tlaloc 'celui qui fait germer' et sis subordonnés les tlaloque." Dissertation for E.P.H.E. Paris: Institut d'Ethnologie, Museé de l'Homme, microfiche, 1971.

Hanke, Lewis. *Aristotle and the American Indians*. Bloomington: Indiana University Press, 1959.

Hanks, William F. *Referential Practice: Language and Lived Space Among the Maya*. Chicago: University of Chicago Press, 1990.

Helitzer, F. "The Princeton Galaxy." *Intellectual Digest* 3, no. 10 (1973): 25–32.

Hellmuth, Nicholas M. "Echoes of a Lost Colony." *Natural History* 3 (1992): 18–25.

Heyden, Doris. "An Interpretation of the Cave Underneath the Pyramid of the Sun in Teotihuacan, Mexico." *American Antiquity* 40, no. 2 (1975): 131–147.

―――. "The Skin and Hair of Tlaltecuhtli." In *The Imagination of Matter: Religion and Ecology in Mesoamerican Traditions*. Edited by Davíd Carrasco. Oxford: B.A.R. International Series 515, 1989, pp. 112–124.

―――, translator. *The History of the Indies of New Spain by Fray Diego Durán*. Norman: University of Oklahoma Press, 1994.

―――. "Guajolote, guajolote, en realidad quién eres?" In *Códices y Documentos sobre México, Primer Simposio*. Edited by Constanza Vega. Mexico City: Colección Científica, INAH, 1995, pp. 173–192.

Hodder, Ian. *Reading the Past: Current Approaches to Interpretation in Archaeology*. Cambridge: Cambridge University Press, 1986.

Hubert, Henri, and Marcel Mauss. *Sacrifice: Its Nature and Function*. Translated by W. D. Halls. Chicago: University of Chicago Press, 1967.

Huizinga, Johan. *Homo Ludens: A Study of the Play-Element in Culture*. Boston: Beacon Press, 1950.

Hymes, Dell. *"In Vain I Tried to Tell You": Essays in Native American Ethnopoetics*. Studies in Native American Literature I. Philadelphia: University of Pennsylvania Press, 1981.

Iwaniszewski, Stanislaw. "La arqueología de alta montaña en México y su estado actual." *Estudios de cultura Náhuatl* 18 (1986): 249–273.

Iwaniszewski, Stanislaw, and Iván Sprajc. "Field Reconnaissance and Mapping of the Archaeological Site at Mt. Tlaloc." Unpublished manuscript, December 1987.

Jackson, Michael. *Barawa and the Ways Birds Fly in the Sky: An Ethnographic Novel*. Washington, DC: Smithsonian Institution Press, 1986.

Jay, Nancy. *Throughout Your Generations Forever: Sacrifice, Religion, and Paternity*. Chicago: University of Chicago Press, 1992.

Jones, Lindsay. *Twin City Tales: A Hermeneutical Reassessment of Tula and Chichén Itzá*. Niwot: University Press of Colorado, 1995.

Josserand, J. Kathryn, and Karen Dakin, eds. *Smoke and Mist: Mesoamerican Studies in Memory of Thelma D. Sullivan*. Oxford: B.A.R. International Studies, 402(i), 1988.

Karttunen, Frances. *An Analytical Dictionary of Nahuatl*. Austin: University of Texas Press, 1983.

Katz, Friedrich. *The Ancient American Civilizations*. Translated by K. M. Lois Simpson. New York: Preager Publishing, 1972.

Keber, John. "Sahagún and Hermeneutics: A Christian Ethnographer's Understanding of Aztec Culture." In *The Work of Bernardino de Sahagún: Pioneer Ethnographer of Sixteenth-Century Aztec Mexico*. Edited by J. Jorge Klor de Alva, Henry B. Nicholson, and Eloise Quiñones Keber. Austin: University of Texas Press, 1988, pp. 53–63.

Kitagawa, Joseph M., ed. *The History of Religions: Retrospect and Prospect*. New York: Macmillian Publishing Co., 1985.

Klein, Cecelia F. "Who Was Tlaloc?" *Journal of Latin American Lore* 6, no. 2 (1980): 155–204.

Klor de Alva, J. Jorge. "Sahagún and the Birth of Modern Ethnography: Representing, Confessing, and Inscribing the Native Other." In *The Work of Bernardino de Sahagún: Pioneer Ethnographer of Sixteenth-Century Aztec Mexico*. Edited by J. Jorge Klor de Alva, Henry B. Nicholson, and Eloise Quiñones Keber. Austin: University of Texas Press, 1988, pp. 31–52.

———. "European Spirit and Mesoamerican Matter: Sahagún and the 'Crisis of Representation' in Sixteenth-Century Ethnography." In *The Imagination of Matter: Religion and Ecology in Mesoamerican Traditions*. Edited by Davíd Carrasco. Oxford: B.A.R. International Series 515, 1989, pp. 17–29.

———. "Religious Rationalization and the Conversions of the Nahuas: Social Organization and Colonial Epistemology." In *To Change Place: Aztec Ceremonial Landscapes*. Edited by Davíd Carrasco. Niwot: University Press of Colorado, 1991, pp. 233–245.

Knab, Tim. *Words Great and Small: Sierra Nahuatl Narrative Discourse in Everyday Life.* Unpublished manuscript, 1983.

———. "Geografía del inframundo." *Estudios de cultura Nahuatl* 21 (1991): 31–57.

Kroeber, Karl, ed. *Traditional American Indian Literatures: Texts and Interpretations.* Lincoln: University of Nebraska Press, 1981.

Lapsanski, Duane V. *Evangelical Perfection: An Historical Examination of the Concept in the Early Franciscan Sources.* New York: Franciscan Institute Publications, St. Bonaventure University, 1977.

las Casas, Bartolomé de, abstractor. *The Diario of Christopher Columbus's First Voyage to America, 1492–1493.* Transcribed and translated by Oliver Dunn and James E. Kelly Jr. Norman: University of Oklahoma Press, 1989.

———. *The Devastation of the Indies, A Brief Account.* Translated by Herma Briffault. Introduction by Bill M. Donovan. Baltimore: The Johns Hopkins University Press, 1992.

———. *The Only Way.* Translated by Helen Rand Parish and Francis P. Sullivan. Mahwah, NJ: Paulist Press, 1992.

Le Flem, Joseph Pérez, Jean-Marc Pelorson, José M.ª López Piñero, and Janine Fayard. *Historia de España.* vol. V, *La frustración de un imperio (1476–1714).* Series edited by Manuel Tuñón de Lara. Barcelona: Editorial Labor S.A., 1984.

León Portilla, Miguel. *Aztec Thought and Culture.* Translated by Jack Emory Davis. Norman: University of Oklahoma Press, 1963.

Le Roy Ladurie, Emmanuel. *The Territory of the Historian.* Translated by Ben and Siân Reynolds. Chicago: University of Chicago Press, 1979.

———. *Carnival in Romans.* Translated by Mary Feeney. New York: George Braziller, Inc., 1979.

Lévi-Strauss, Claude. *Structural Anthropology.* Translated by Claire Jacobson and Brooke Grundfest Schoepf. New York: Basic Books, 1963.

———. *The Savage Mind.* Chicago: University of Chicago Press, 1966.

———. *The Raw and the Cooked: Introduction to the Science of Mythology,* vol. 1. Translated by J. and D. Weightman. London: Jonathan Cape, 1970.

———. *The Naked Man: Introduction to the Science of Mythology,* vol. 4. Translated by J. and D. Weightman. London: Jonathan Cape, 1981.

Lincoln, Bruce. *Myth, Cosmos, and Society: Indo-European Themes of Creation and Destruction.* Cambridge, MA: Harvard University Press, 1986.

———. *Emerging from the Chrysalis: Rituals of Women's Initiation,* 2nd edition. New York: Oxford University Press, 1991.

Little, Lester K. *Religious Poverty and the Profit Economy of Medieval Europe.* Ithaca, NY: Cornell University Press, 1978.

Long, Charles H. "New Space, New Time: Disjunctions and Context for New World Religions." *Criterion* 24, no. 1 (1985): 2–7.

———. *Significations: Signs, Symbols, and Images in the Interpretation of Religion.* Philadelphia: Fortress Press, 1986.

López Austin, Alfredo. "The Research Method of Fray Bernardino de Sahagún:

The Questionnaires." In *Sixteenth-Century Mexico: The Work of Sahagún*. School of American Research. Edited by Munro S. Edmonson. Albuquerque: University of New Mexico Press, 1974, pp. 111–173.

———. *The Human Body and Ideology: Concepts of the Ancient Nahuas*. 2 vols. Translated by Thelma Ortiz de Montellano and Bernard Ortiz de Montellano. Salt Lake City: University of Utah Press, 1988.

———. *Tamoanchan y Tlalocan*. Mexico City: Fondo de Cultura Económica, 1994.

López Austin, Alfredo, Leonardo López Luján, and Saburo Sugiyama. "The Temple of Quetzalcoatl at Teotihuacan, Its Possible Ideological Significance." *Ancient Mesoamerica* 2 (1991): 93–105.

López Luján, Leonardo. *The Offerings of the Templo Mayor of Tenochtitlan*. Translated by Bernard R. Ortiz de Montellano and Thelma Ortiz de Montellano. Niwot: University Press of Colorado, 1994.

Lorenzo, José Luis. *Las zonas arquelógicas de los volcanoes Iztaccíhuatl y Popocatépetl*. Mexico City: Instituto Nacional de Antropología e Historia, 1957.

Lyons, Oren, and John C. Mohawk, eds. *Exiled in the Land of the Free: Democracy, Indian Nations, and the U.S. Constitution*. Santa Fe, NM: Clear Light Publishers, 1992.

Malinowski, Bronislaw. *The Language of Magic and Gardening*. Volume 2 of *Coral Gardens and Their Magic*. Bloomington: Indiana University Press, 1965.

Matos Moctezuma, Eduardo. "The Great Temple of Tenochtitlan." *Scientific American* 251, no. 2 (1984): 80–89.

———. "The Templo Mayor of Tenochtitlan: Economics and Ideology." In *Ritual Human Sacrifice in Mesoamerica*. Edited by Elizabeth Boone. Washington, DC: Dumbarton Oaks, 1984, pp. 133–164.

———. "The Templo Mayor of Tenochtitlan, History and Interpretation." In *The Great Temple of Tenochtitlan: Center and Periphery in the Aztec World*. Edited by Johanna Broda, Davíd Carrasco, and Eduardo Matos Moctezuma. Berkeley: University of California Press, 1987, pp. 15–60.

———. *Life and Death in the Templo Mayor*. Translated by Bernard R. Ortiz de Montellano and Thelma Ortiz de Montellano. Niwot: University Press of Colorado, 1995.

Mauss, Marcel. *The Gift: Forms and Functions of Exchange in Archaic Societies*. Translated by Ian Cunnison. New York: W.W. Norton & Co., 1967.

McGinn, Bernard, ed. *Apocalyptic Spirituality: Treatises and Letters of Lactantius, Adso of Montier-en-der, Joachim of Fiore, the Franciscan Spirituals, Savonarola*. New York: Paulist Press, 1979.

———. *The Calabrian Abbot: Joachim of Fiore in the History of Western Thought*. New York: Macmillan Publishing Co., 1985.

Merleau-Ponty, M. *Phenomenology of Perception*. London: Routledge and Kegan Paul, 1962.

Millon, Rene. *Urbanization at Teotihuacan, Mexico: The Teotihuacan Map*. Austin: University of Texas Press, 1973.

Mitchell, Timothy. *Passional Culture: Emotion, Religion, and Society in Southern*

Spain. Philadelphia: University of Pennsylvania Press, 1990.

Moffitt Watts, Pauline. "Prophecy and Discovery: On the Spiritual Origins of Christopher Columbus's 'Enterprise of the Indies.'" *The American Historical Review* 90 (1985): 73–102.

Mohawk, John. "Discovering Columbus: The Way Here." *Northeast Indian Quarterly* 7, no. 3 (1990): 37–46.

Moholy-Nagy, Hattula. "A Tlaloc Stela from Tikal." *Espedition* 4, no. 2 (1962): 27.

Molina, Alonso de. *Vocabulario en lengua Castellana y Mexicana, y Mexicana y Castellana.* Mexico City: Editorial Porrúa, 1977.

Moore, R. I. *The Origins of European Dissent.* Oxford: Basil Blackwell, Ltd., 1985.

Motolinía, Fray Toribio (de Benavente). *Memoriales o libro de las cosas de Nueva España y de los naturales de ella.* Edited by Edmundo O'Gorman. Mexico City: Universidad Nacional Autónoma de México, 1971.

Munn, Nancy D. "Transformation of Subjects into Objects in Walbiri and Pitjantajara Myth." In *Australian Aboriginal Studies.* Edited by Ronald M. Berndt. Nedlands: University of Western Australia Press, 1970, pp. 141–163.

———. *The Fame of Gawa: A Symbolic Study of Value Transformation in a Massim (Papua New Guinea) Society.* Cambridge: Cambridge University Press, 1986.

Mus, Paul. *India Seen from the East: Indian and Indigenous Cults in Champa.* Translated by I. W. Mabbett. Monash Paper on Southeast Asia, no. 3. Monash University, Australia: Centre of Southeast Asian Studies, 1975.

Nagao, Debra. *Mexica Buried Offerings: A Historical and Contextual Analysis.* Oxford: B.A.R. International Series 235, 1985.

———. "The Planting of Sustenance: Symbolism of the Two-Horned God in Offerings from the Templo Mayor." *RES Anthropology and Aesthetics* 10 (1985): 5–27.

Nandy, Ashis. *The Intimate Enemy: Loss and Recovery of Self Under Colonialism.* Delhi: Oxford University Press, 1983.

Nicholson, Henry B. "Religion in Pre-Hispanic Central Mexico." In *Handbook of Middle American Indians: Guide to the Ethnohistorical Sources,* vol. 11. Edited by R. Wauchope. Austin: University of Texas Press, 1971, pp. 395–445.

———. "Recent Sahaguntine Studies: A Review." In *The Work of Bernardino de Sahagún: Pioneer Ethnographer of Sixteenth-Century Aztec Mexico.* Edited by J. Jorge Klor de Alva, Henry B. Nicholson, and Eloise Quiñones Keber. Austin: University of Texas Press, 1988, pp. 13–30.

Nolan, Mary Lee, and Sidney Nolan. *Christian Pilgrimage in Modern Western Europe.* Chapel Hill: University of North Carolina Press, 1989.

Nutini, Hugo G. *Todos Santos in Rural Tlaxcala: A Syncretic, Expressive, and Symbolic Analysis of the Cult of the Dead.* Princeton, NJ: Princeton University Press, 1988.

Obeyesekere, Ganath. *The Apotheosis of Captain Cook: European Mythmaking in the Pacific.* Princeton, NJ: Princeton University Press, 1992.

O'Callaghan, Joseph F. *A History of Medieval Spain.* Ithaca, NY: Cornell University Press, 1975.

O'Gorman, Edmundo. *The Invention of America: An Inquiry into the Historical Nature of the New World and the Meaning of Its History.* Bloomington: Indiana University Press, 1961.

O'Mack, Scott. "Yacateuctli and Ehecatl-Quetzalcoatl: Earth-Divers of Central Mexico." *Enthnohistory* 38, no. 1 (winter 1991): 1–33.

Ortiz de Montellano, Bernard R. "Las hierbas de Tláloc." *Estudios de cultura Náhuatl* 14 (1980): 287–314.

———. "The Body, Ethics and Cosmos: Aztec Physiology." In *Imagination of Matter: Religion and Ecology in Mesoamerican Traditions.* Edited by Davíd Carrasco. Oxford: B.A.R. International Series 515, 1989, pp. 191–209.

———. *Aztec Medicine, Health, and Nutrition.* New Brunswick, NJ: Rutgers University Press, 1990.

Otto, Rudolph. *The Idea of the Holy: An Inquiry into the Non-Rational Factor in the Idea of the Divine and Its Relation to the Rational.* Translated by John W. Harvey. Oxford: Oxford University Press, 1923.

Padden, R. C. *The Hummingbird and the Hawk: Conquest and Sovereignty in the Valley of Mexico; 1503–1541.* New York: Harper & Row, 1967.

Pagden, Anthony. *The Fall of Natural Man: The American Indian and the Origins of Comparative Ethnology.* Cambridge: Cambridge University Press, 1982.

Parsons, Jeffrey R. *Prehistoric Settlement Patterns in the Texcoco Region, Mexico.* Memoirs of the Museum of Anthropology, no. 3. Ann Arbor: University of Michigan, 1971.

———. "Chinampa Agriculture and the Aztec Urbanization in the Valley of Mexico." In *Prehistoric Intensive Agriculture in the Tropics.* Edited by Ian S. Farrington. Oxford: B.A.R. International Series 232, 1985, pp. 49–96.

Parsons, Jeffrey, Elizabeth Brumfiel, Mary Parsons, and David Wilson. *Prehistoric Settlement Patterns in the Southern Valley of Mexico, the Chalco-Xochimilco Region.* Memoirs of the Museum of Anthropology, no. 14. Ann Arbor: University of Michigan, 1982.

Parsons, Jeffrey, Keith Kintigh, and Susan Gregg. *Archaeological Settlement Pattern Data from the Chalco, Xochimilco, Ixtapalapa, Texcoco, and Zumpango Regions, Mexico.* Museum of Anthropology Technical Reports, no. 14. Research Reprints in Archaeology Contributions 9. Ann Arbor: University of Michigan, 1983.

Parsons, Jeffrey, et al. "Political Implications of Pre-Hispanic Chinampa Agriculture in the Valley of Mexico." Paper presented at the 45th International Congress of Americanists. Bogotá, Colombia, 1–6 July 1985.

Pazstory, Esther. *The Iconography of the Teotihuacan Tlaloc.* Studies in Pre-Columbian Art and Archaeology, vol. 15. Washington, DC:. Dumbarton Oaks, 1974.

———. *The Murals of Tepantitla, Teotihuacan.* New York: Garland Publishing, Inc., 1976.

———. "The Aztec Tlaloc: God of Antiquity." In *Smoke and Mist, Mesoamerican*

Studies in Memory of Thelma D. Sullivan. Edited by J. Kathryn Josserand and Karen Dakin. Oxford: B.A.R. International Series 402(i), 1988, pp. 289–327.

Perrin, Michel. *The Way of the Dead Indians: Guajiro Myths and Symbols*. Translated by Michael Fineberg and Michel Perrin. Austin: University of Texas Press, 1987.

Phelan, John Leddy. *The Millennial Kingdom of the Franciscans in the New World: A Study of the Writings of Geronimo de Mendieta; (1525–1604)*. University of California Publications in History, vol. 42. Berkeley: University of California Press, 1956.

Pomar, Juan Bautista. *Relaciones de Texcoco y de los señores de la Nueva España*. Mexico City: S. Chavez Hayhoe, 1941.

Primeros Memoriales. Edited by Francisco del Paso y Troncoso. Vol. 6. Madrid: Fototipia de Hauser y Menet, 1905.

Puleston, Dennis E. "Experiments in Prehistoric Raised Field Agriculture: Learning from the Past." *Journal of Belize Affairs* 5 (1977): 36–43.

Quiñones Keber, Eloise. "The Sahaguntine Corpus: A Bibliographic Index of Extant Documents." In *The Work of Bernardino de Sahagún: Pioneer Ethnographer of Sixteenth-Century Aztec Mexico*. Edited by J. Jorge Klor de Alva, Henry B. Nicholson, and Eloise Quiñones Keber. Austin: University of Texas Press, 1988, pp. 341–345.

Rappaport, Joanne. *The Politics of Memory: Native Historical Interpretation in the Colombian Andes*. Cambridge: Cambridge University Press, 1990.

Read, Kay Almere. *Time and Sacrifice in the Aztec Cosmos*. Bloomington: Indiana University Press, 1998.

Reynolds, Frank E., and Mani B. Reynolds, translators. *Three Worlds According to King Ruang: A Thai Buddhist Cosmology*. Berkeley: University of California Press, Berkeley Buddhist Studies Series, no. 4, 1982.

Richard, Robert. *The Spiritual Conquest of Mexico*. Translated by Lesley Byrd Simpson. Berkeley: University of California Press, 1966.

Ricoeur, Paul. *Interpretation Theory: Discourse and the Surplus of Meaning*. Fort Worth: Texas Christian University Press, 1976.

Robertson, Donald. *Mexican Manuscript Painting of the Early Colonial Period: The Metropolitan Schools*. New Haven, CT: Yale University Press, 1959.

———. "The Sixteenth Century Mexican Encyclopedia of Fray Bernardino de Sahagún." *Cuadernos de historia mundial* 9, no. 3 (1966): 617–628.

Robertson Smith, W. *Lectures on the Religion of the Semites: The Fundamental Institutions*. New York: Meridan Books, 1957.

Sahagún, Fray Bernardino de. "Relación breve de las fiestas de los dioses." Translated by Angel María Garibay. *Tlalocan* 2, no. 4 (1948): 289–321.

———. *Florentine Codex: General History of the Things of New Spain*. 12 books, 13 parts. Edited and translated by Arthur J. O. Anderson and Charles E. Dibble. Monographs of the School of American Research, no. 14. Salt Lake City: University of Utah Press, 1951–1982.

———. *Historia de las indias de Nueva España*. 2 vols. Edited by Angel María Garibay. Mexico City: Editorial Porrúa, 1967.

———. *El Códice Florentino de Fray Bernardino de Sahagún*, facsimile. 3 vols.

Mexico City: Secretaría de Gobernación, 1979.

Sahlins, Marshall. "Culture as Protein and Profit: Review of *Cannibals and Kings* by Marvin Harris." *The New York Review of Books* (23 November 1978): 45–52.

———. *Islands of History*. Chicago: University of Chicago Press, 1985.

Sanders, William T., and Michael H. Logan. "The Model." In *The Valley of Mexico: Studies in Pre-Hispanic Ecology and Society*. Edited by Eric R. Wolf. School of American Research. Albuquerque: University of New Mexico Press, 1976, pp. 31–58.

Sanders, William T., Jeffrey R. Parsons, and Robert S. Santley. *The Basin of Mexico: Biological Processes in the Evolution of a Civilization*. Book and maps. New York: Academic Press, 1979.

Sandstrom, Alan R. *Corn Is Our Blood: Culture and Ethnic Identity in a Contemporary Aztec Indian Village*. Norman: University of Oklahoma Press, 1991.

Sandstrom, Alan R., and Pamela Effrein Sandstrom. *Traditional Papermaking and Paper Cult Figures of Mexico*. Norman: University of Oklahoma Press, 1986.

Saussure, Ferdinand de. *Course in General Linguistics*. Chicago: University of Chicago Press, 1966.

Schele, Linda, and Mary Ellen Miller. *The Blood of Kings: Dynasty and Ritual in Maya Art*. New York: George Braziller, Inc., 1986.

Schele, Linda, and David Freidel. *A Forest of Kings: The Untold Story of the Ancient Maya*. New York: William Morrow and Co., Inc., 1990.

Schivelbusch, Wolfgang. *Tastes of Paradise: A Social History of Spices, Stimulants, and Intoxicants*. Translated by David Jacobson. New York: Vintage Books, 1993.

Schwaller, John Frederick. "A Catalogue of Pre-1840 Nahuatl Works Held by the Lilly Library." *Indiana University Bookman* 11 (1973): 69–88.

Seler, Eduard. *Einige Kapitel aus dem Geschichtwerk des Fray Bernardino de Sahagún aus dem Aztekischen übersetzt*. Edited by Caecilie Seler-Sachs, Walter Lehmann, and Walter Krickeberg. Stuttgart: Strecher and Schroeder, 1927.

———. *Gesammelte Abhandlungen zur Amerikanschen Sprach-und Alterhumskunde*. 5 vols. Graz, Austria: Akademische Druck-und Verlangsanstalt, 1960–1961.

Siméon, Rémi. *Diccionario de la lengua Nahuatl o Mexicana*. Mexico City: Siglo Veintiuno editores, 1977.

Smith, Brian K. *Reflections on Resemblance, Ritual, and Religion*. New York: Oxford University Press, 1989.

———. "Gods and Men in Vedic Ritualism: Toward a Hierarchy of Resemblance." *History of Religions* 24, no. 4 (1985): 291–307.

Smith, Jonathan Z. *Map Is Not Territory: Studies in the History of Religions*. Leiden, Netherlands: E.J. Brill, 1978.

———. *Imagining Religion: From Babylon to Jonestown*. Chicago: University of Chicago Press, 1982.

———. *To Take Place: Toward Theory in Ritual*. Chicago: University of Chicago

Press, 1987.

Soustelle, Jacques. *La pensee cosmologique des anciens mexicains, représentation du monde et de l'espace.* Paris: Hermann & Cie, 1940.

Stannard, David E. *American Holocaust: The Conquest of the New World.* New York: Oxford University Press, 1992.

Steward, Julian H. *Theory of Culture Change.* Urbana: University of Illinois Press, 1955.

Stoller, Paul, and Cheryl Olkes. *In Sorcery's Shadow: A Memoir of Apprenticeship Among the Songhay of Niger.* Chicago: University of Chicago Press, 1987.

Sugiyama, Saburo. "Worldview Materialized in Teotihuacan, Mexico." *Latin American Antiquity* 4, no. 2 (1993): 103–129.

Sullivan, Lawrence E. "Astral Myths Rise Again: Interpreting Religious Astronomy." *Criterion* 22 (1983): 12–17.

———. "Sound and Senses: Toward a Hermeneutics of Performance." *History of Religions* 26, no. 1 (1986): 1–33.

———. *Icanchu's Drum: An Orientation to Meaning in South American Religions.* New York: Macmillan Publishing Co., 1988.

———, ed. *Healing and Restoring.* New York: Macmillan Publishing Co., 1989.

———, ed. *Native American Religions: North America.* Religion, History, and Culture selections from *The Encyclopedia of Religion.* Edited by Mircea Eliade. New York: Macmillan Publishing Co., 1989.

———. "Body Works: Knowledge of the Body in the Study of Religion." *History of Religions* 30, no. 1 (1990): 86–99.

———. " 'Seeking an End to the Primary Text' or 'Putting an End to the Text as Primary.' " In *Beyond the Classics? Essays in Religious Studies and Liberal Education.* Edited by Frank E. Reynolds and Sheryl L. Burkhalter. Atlanta: Scholars Press, 1990.

———. "Memory Distortion and Anamnesis: A View from the Human Sciences." In *Memory Distortion: How Minds, Brains, and Societies Reconstruct the Past.* Edited by Daniel L. Schacter. Cambridge, MA: Harvard University Press, 1995.

Sullivan, Thelma. "Tlaloc: A New Etymological Interpretation of the God's Name and What It Reveals of His Essence and Nature." In *Proceedings of the 40th International Congress of Americanists,* vol. 2. Genoa: Tilgher, 1974, pp. 213–219.

———. "The Rhetorical Orations, or Huehuetlatolli, collected by Sahagún." In *Sixteenth Century Mexico: The Work of Sahagún.* Edited by Munro S. Edmonson. School of American Research. Albuquerque: University of New Mexico Press, 1974, pp. 79–109.

Tambiah, Stanley J. *Buddhism and the Spirit Cults in North-East Thailand.* Cambridge: Cambridge University Press, 1970.

Tedlock, Barbara. *Time and the Highland Maya.* Albuquerque: University of New Mexico Press, 1982.

Thanksgiving Address, Greetings to the Natural World; Ohén:ton Karihwatêhkwen,

Words Before All Else. Six Nations Indian Museum and The Tracking Project, 1993.

Tilley, Christopher, ed. *Interpretive Archaeology*. Oxford: Berg Publishers, 1993.

———. *A Phenomenology of Landscape: Places, Paths and Monuments*. Oxford: Berg Publishers, 1994.

Todorov, Tzvetan. *The Conquest of America*. Translated by Richard Howard. New York: Harper Torchbooks, 1984.

Torquemada, Fray Juan de. *Monarquía indiana*. 4 vols. Mexico City: Editorial Porrúa, 1969.

Tovar, Juan de. *The Tovar Calendar: An Illustrated Mexican Manuscript ca. 1585*. Edited and commentary by George Kubler and Charles Gibson. Memoirs of the Connecticut Academy of Arts and Sciences, Volume XI. New Haven, CT: Yale University Press, 1951.

Townsend, Richard. *State and Cosmos in the Art of Tenochtitlan*. Studies in Pre-Columbian Art and Archaeology, no. 20. Washington, DC: Dumbarton Oaks, 1979.

———. "Pyramid and Sacred Mountain." In *Ethnoastronomy and Archaeo-Astronomy in the American Tropics*. Edited by Anthony F. Aveni and Gary Urton. New York: *Annals of the New York Academy of Sciences* 385, 1982, pp. 37–62.

———. "The Mt. Tlaloc Project." In *To Change Place: Aztec Ceremonial Landscapes*. Edited by Davíd Carrasco. Niwot: University Press of Colorado, 1991, pp. 26–30.

———. *The Aztecs*. London: Thames and Hudson, 1992.

Tracy, David. *Plurality and Ambiguity: Hermeneutics, Religion, Hope*. New York: Harper & Row, 1987.

———. *Dialogue with the Other: The Inter-Religious Dialogue*. Louvain Theological & Pastoral Monographs. Louvain and Grand Rapids, MI: Peeters Press and William B. Eerdmans Publishing Co., 1990.

Traditional Teachings. Cornwall Island, Ontario: North American Indian Travelling College, 1984.

Tylor, Sir Edward Burnett. *Primitive Culture*. Volume II, *Religion in Primitive Culture*. New York: Harper Torchbooks, 1958.

Urton, Gary. *At the Crossroads of the Earth and Sky: An Andean Cosmology*. Austin: University of Texas Press, 1981.

Valdeón, Julio, José M.ª Salrach, and Javier Zabalo. *Historia de España*. Volume IV, *Feudalismo y consolidación de los pueblos Hispánicos (siglos XI–XV)*. Series edited by Manuel Tuñón de Lara. Barcelona: Editorial Labor S.A., 1983.

Valeri, Valerio. *Kingship and Sacrifice: Ritual and Society in Ancient Hawaii*. Translated by Paula Wissing. Chicago: University of Chicago Press, 1985.

van der Leeuw, Gerardus. *Religion in Essence and Manifestation*. Translated by J. E. Turner. Edited by Hans H. Penner. Princeton, NJ: Princeton University Press, 1986.

van der Loo, Peter. *Codices costumbres continuidad: Un estudio de la religión*

References

Mesoamericana. Leiden, Netherlands: Indiaanse Studies 2, Archeologisch Centrum R.U., 1987.

van Esterik, Penny. "Interpreting a Cosmology: Guardian Spirits in Thai Buddhism." *Anthropos* 77 (1982): 1–15.

———. "Feeding Their Faith: Recipe Knowledge Among Thai Buddhist Women." *Food and Foodways* 1 (1986): 197–215.

van Sertima, Ivan. *They Came Before Columbus.* New York: Random House, Inc., 1976.

van Zantwijk, Rudolph. *The Aztec Arrangement: The Social History of Pre-Spanish Mexico.* Norman: University of Oklahoma Press, 1985.

Vasey, D. E. "Nitrogen Fixation and Flow in Experimental Island Bed Gardens: Implications for Archaeology." In *Prehistoric Agriculture in the Tropics.* Edited by Ian S. Farrington. Oxford: B.A.R. International Series 232, 1985, pp. 233–246.

Wheatley, Paul. "City as Symbol." Inaugural lecture delivered at the University College, London, 20 November 1967, unpublished manuscript.

Wicke, Charles, and Fernando Horcasitas. "Archaeological Investigations of Monte Tlaloc, Mexico." *Mesoamerican Notes* 5 (1957): 83–96.

Wilbert, Johannes. "Eschatology in a Participatory Universe and Destinies of the Soul Among Warao Indians of Venezuela." In *Death and Afterlife in Pre-Columbian America.* Edited by Elizabeth P. Benson. Washington, DC: Dumbarton Oaks, 1975, pp. 163–189.

Wolf, Eric, ed. *The Valley of Mexico: Studies in Pre-Hispanic Ecology and Society.* School of American Research. Albuquerque: University of New Mexico Press, 1976.

Yuasa Yasuo. *The Body: Toward an Eastern Mind-Body Theory.* Edited by Thomas P. Kasulis. Translated by Nagatomo Shigenori and Thomas P. Kasulis. Albany: State University of New York Press, 1987.

Zepp Jr., Ira G. *The New Religious Image of Urban America: The Shopping Mall as Ceremonial Center.* 2nd edition. Introduction by Davíd Carrasco. Niwot: University Press of Colorado, 1997.

Zimmerman, Francis. *The Jungle of the Aroma of Meats: An Ecological Theme in Hindu Medicine.* Comparative Studies of Health Systems and Medical Care. Berkeley: University of California Press, 1987.

Zuidema, R. Thomas. *The Ceque System of Cuzco: The Social Organization of the Capital of the Inca.* International Archives of Ethnography. Supplement to volume 50. Leiden, Netherlands: E.J. Brill, 1964.

———. "The Inca Calendar." In *Native American Astronomy.* Edited by Anthony F. Aveni. Austin: University of Texas Press, 1977, pp. 219–259.

Maps Consulted

Mexico City: Instituto Nacional de Estadística, Geografía e Informática.
Zumpango de Ocampo (E14 A19). Carta topográfica, 1: 50,000 (1987).
Cuautitlan (E14 A29). Carta topográfica, 1: 50,000 (1986).
Ciudad de México (E14 A39). Carta topográfica, 1: 50,000 (1986).
Milpa Alta (E14 A49). Carta geológica, 1: 50,000 (1984).
Texcoco (E14 B21). Carta topográfica, 1: 50.000 (1985).
Chalco (E14 B31). Carta topográfica, 1: 50,000 (1984).
Amecameca (E14 B41). Carta topográfica, 1: 50,000 (1986).

Index

A

Acacalomeh, 97
Action, landscape referents for, 131
Acxoyacalco, 46
Agricultural revolution, impact of,
 188
Ahuachquemitl, 100, 152, 153
Ahuitzotl, 58
Aire malo, dead and, 75n95
Albert of Cologne, 184
Alphabetic writing, introduction of,
 200
Altepetl, 45, 48, 51, 147; tlaloque and,
 48
Amacuexpalli, 102
Amahualli, 146
Amaranth, 111, 117, 118, 161; ash,
 107; fish, 107, 110
Amatl, 121n14, 156, 174n61
Amecameca Valley, 134
American holocaust, xv, 219
Ancestors, 188; as natural resources,
 246
Anderson, Arthur J. O., 95, 126n60;
 on human sacrificial offering, 81;
 translations by, 78, 120nn6, 7
Andrews, Richard: on Tlaloc, 35
Ánima, 59, 75n94
Animal beings, 154–59
Animistic centers, 21n8, 56–57;
 landscape and, 60
Aompayotl, 60
Aquinas, Thomas, 185
Archaeology (Flavius Josephus), 184
Aristotle, 184, 185
Arnold, Dean, E.: cybernetic model of,
 15

Atemoztli (Descending Water) (XVI),
 64, 78, 105, 113 (fig.), 114 (fig.),
 140, 141, 142, 163; ceremonial
 sites for, 141 (map); decorations
 of, 159; described, 112–19; food/
 reciprocity and, 162; human-
 mountain figures and, 147;
 humans/landscape and, 117;
 instruments in, 150; landscape
 and, 139, 143, 149; tepictoton and,
 164; tlaloque during, 158; water
 and, 144
Atl cahualo (water left; drought) (I),
 64, 79 (fig.), 80 (fig.), 87, 90, 97,
 104, 107, 117, 130–31, 134–37,
 142; blood and, 147, 158; conch
 shells and, 150; described, 78–79,
 81–86; map of, 132; names for,
 156; rituals at, 161; sacrifice
 during, 131, 143, 147, 149, 159,
 160; Sahagún on, 140; water and,
 144, 147. See also Quahuitl ehua
Atoyatl, 145, 172n40
Atzapillin, 102, 154; gathering of, 155
Augustinians, 185, 230n12
Autosacrifices, 122n41, 139, 151, 156
Aveni, Anthony, 45, 60, 74n89, 92,
 122n32; etymological interpretation by, 75n98; on pecked circles,
 41, 42, 67n31; on spatial/temporal
 realities, 61–62; on Tenochtitlan
 axis, 135
Axoquen, 98, 124n46
Ayacachtli, 115, 150
Ayauhcalco, 109, 111, 116
Ayauhcalli, 85, 97, 100
Ayauhquemitl, 100, 152, 153
Ayochicahuaztli, 96, 97, 102, 150
Ayotl, 150, 173n48

Index

Index

Ihiyotl, 58, 59, 60
Ilamateuctli, 48, 175n71
Illnesses. *See* Diseases
Imagination, xv, 12; magical, 118; material referents and, 18; religion and, 4
Indigenous people, 18, 46, 217; as commodities, 238; Europeans and, 218; remains of, 246, 248, 251n16; status of, 237; writing by, 240
Intercardinal directions, 61
Interpretation, 11, 227, 241; consequences of, 245; material life and, 224, 245; methodology of, 63; primacy and, 198–205; religion and, 233; violent character of, 234
Interpreters: active/creative, 204; objective/authoritative, 204
Iwaniszewski, Stanislaw, 122n32
Ix group, 56
Izcalli (XVIII), 78, 117
Iztaccihuatl volcano, 115, 134, 140, 142, 149
Iztactepetl, 115

J

Joachim of Fiore, 208n25

K

Karttunen, Frances: on Tlaloc, 35, 65n2
Kinship, 26n36, 174n57
Klor de Alva, J. Jorge, 194, 240

L

Lake Chalco, 134, 148
Lake Texcoco, 133, 140, 148, 171nn36, 37; harvesting reeds at, 93
La Malinche, 83, 133
Land: access to, 8; consumerism and, 242; fertility of, 14; landscape and, 16, 17; materialism and, 242; occupation of, 1, 4, 17, 54, 130; Otherness of, 17, 248; as point of reference, 241, 242; religion and, xiv, xv, 1, 241; status of, 246–47; understandings of, 3, 16

Landscape, 7, 129, 141, 179, 224, 239; as abstraction, 203; animistic centers and, 60; appeal to, 227; blood and, 91; celestial phenomena at, 136; colonial strategies of, 242; divinatory knowledge in, 202; food and, 111, 163; humans and, 12, 111, 117, 150; land and, 16, 17; living, xiii, xv, 244; materiality and, 19; occupation of, 7, 242, 243; orientation to, 245, 247, 248; practitioners and, 118; pre-Columbian, 198, 203; symbolic representations of, 90; Tlaloc and, 138, 159; understanding of, 2–3, 198, 217; water and, 122n35. *See also* Eating landscape
Language: activity of, 14; as embodiment, 15; ritual use of, 14
Las Casas, Bartolomé de, 184, 185–86, 218, 236; Black Legend and, 237
León-Portilla, 36, 73n83
Lévi-Strauss, Claude, 243; criticism of, 26n36; mythic language and, 25n36
Leyenda de los Soles, 38, 82, 231n16; on Nanahuatl, 47
Life: Aztec thought on, 39; blood and, 55
Lightning, *tlaloque* and, 108
Linares, Edelmira, 70n60, 174n55
Lincoln, Bruce, 24n26; *homo faber* and, 27n39
Little, Lester K., 190; on St. Francis, 188
Liver, condition of, 59–60
Long, Charles H., 226; on materiality, 19; on religion, 4, 21n3, 245
López Austin, Alfredo: on bodily design/temporal origination, 73n79; on cowlicks, 82; on hidden invisible beings, 119n1; on human sacrificial offering, 81; on Mesoamerican world structure, 54; on Nahua/body, 55; on Quetzalcoatl Temple, 44; on Sahagún, 181, 182; on *tonalli*, 57, 82; on transmitted energies, 55; on trees/human bodies, 158
López Luján, Leonardo, 49, 51, 52–53; on Quetzalcoatl Temple, 44

T